IDENTITY AND MYSTERY IN
THEMES OF CHRISTIAN FAITH

There is much to be done in the area of Wittgenstein and theological method. Hallett's clearly written argument advances both the theological use of Wittgenstein and the philosophical discussion of theology. The best sort of cross-disciplinary work.
　　　—John K. Downey, Professor of Religious Studies, Gonzaga University, USA

This book will be well received and celebrated by people in Wittgenstein studies who are interested in theology.
　　　—Professor David Stagaman, Loyola University Chicago, USA

Identity and Mystery in Themes of Christian Faith presents the first sustained study of the identities that run through the heart of Christian faith and theology: the identity of Jesus with God, of each of the three divine persons with God, of the Eucharist with the body and blood of Christ, of present teaching with traditional teaching and of traditional teaching with revelation, of the present church with the church of the Apostles, of the risen Christ with the crucified Christ, and of the blessed with the deceased. Resisting essentialism and stressing Wittgensteinian analogy, Hallett makes due room for mystery. By locating rather than explaining the mystery he throws new light on each of the identities studied.

Identity and Mystery in Themes of Christian Faith

Late-Wittgensteinian Perspectives

GARTH L. HALLETT
Saint Louis University, USA

ASHGATE

Published by
Ashgate Publishing Limited
Gower House
Croft Road
Aldershot
Hampshire GU11 3HR
England

Ashgate Publishing Company
Suite 420
101 Cherry Street
Burlington, VT 05401-4405
USA

Ashgate website: http://www.ashgate.com

British Library Cataloguing in Publication Data
Hallett, Garth
  Identity and mystery in themes of Christian faith : late-
  Wittgensteinian perspectives
  1. Wittgenstein, Ludwig, 1889–1951 2. God – Attributes
  3. Identity (Philosophical concept) 4. Mysteries, Religious
  I. Title
  231.4

Library of Congress Cataloging-in-Publication Data
Hallett, Garth.
    Identity and mystery in themes of Christian faith : late-Wittgensteinian perspectives / Garth L. Hallett.
        p. cm.
    Includes bibliographical references (p.) and index.
    ISBN 0-7546-5034-0 (alk. paper)
    1. Philosophical theology. 2. Identity (Philosophical concept) 3. Wittgenstein, Ludwig, 1889–1951. I. Title.

    BT55.H35 2004
    230—dc22

                                                                                2004005862

ISBN 0 7546 5034 0

Printed and bound by Athenaeum Press, Ltd.,
Gateshead, Tyne & Wear.

Contents

Preface

From the beginning, successive streams of non-Christian thought have flowed into Christian tradition, sometimes muddying its waters, but also feeding it and strengthening its current. I think, for example, of the fusion of Aristotelian philosophy with Christian faith in Aquinas, or of evolutionary science with Christian faith in Teilhard de Chardin. So too, I sensed early in my writing career, Wittgenstein's later philosophy might make its own distinctive contribution. "Christian thought may then be swelled by still another tributary," I suggested, "and continue to mirror in its growth the process by which the Christian community grows, through the accretion of ever new peoples, inhabiting continents unknown to the apostles."[1] From this conviction a number of studies have followed over the years, including now the present one.

I speak of Wittgenstein's later thought, not his earlier, because of major deficiencies in his *Tractatus Logico-Philosophicus*, subsequently targeted by his *Philosophical Investigations*. Two defects are most pertinent here. Wittgenstein's youthful classic was representative of much philosophy and theology, first in its essentialism and second in its related disregard for its own and others' use of words. Thus (to cite key Tractarian examples), names all had a single essence, as did propositions, and as did languages, regardless of how anyone did or might legitimately employ the terms "name," "proposition," and "language" or their German near-equivalents. Unfortunately, both these traits continue strong in our day, despite Wittgenstein's later critique. They are evident, for instance, in philosophical and theological treatments of identity, the theme here chosen for inquiry because it runs, so significantly, through so many central Christian beliefs. Counteracting this essentialistic influence as I do here, doctrine by doctrine, makes more room for mystery than is often allowed in theory or in theological practice. Hence my choice of title.

Wittgenstein, essentialism, identity, word use, mystery—these may appear abstruse matters, remote from the concerns of all but a few theologians, despite the centrality of the themes considered. Yet my experience suggests the contrary. I recall, for example, a discussion long ago with a class of sophomore boys concerning Christ's Eucharistic presence, and the reaction of one of them: "But you don't mean, Mr. Hallett, that there is more than one kind of presence!?" How natural such essentialism is. Indeed, how readily and unquestioningly (Chapter 5 suggests) it led medieval theologians to suppose that there is only one kind of identity, that of a single thing with itself, and to conclude that if Jesus said "This is my body" and "This is my blood," no bread and wine remained. Finding this doctrine of "transubstantiation" hard to accept, a family friend of mine left the

---

[1] Hallett, *Darkness and Light*, 167.

Catholic fold, as have others. Pluckier believers, on the other hand, may share the attitude of the college coed with whom I once spoke, who supposed that her Catholic, Christian faith required her to accept contradictions—with regard, say, to the Trinity or the Incarnation. That is what essentialism, so widespread among Christians and others, and specifically essentialism with regard to identity, suggests; and she, like others, was ready to do her best. Little wonder, then, that non-Christians, too, have had difficulty with Christian beliefs. I recall, for instance, the Muslim gentleman to whom I gave instructions on the Catholic faith before he took a Catholic bride, and the assurance with which he spotted contradiction in the attempt to combine monotheism with the belief that Jesus is God or that each of three divine persons is God. Christians have no monopoly on the essentialistic notion of identity that prompted his objections. Thus, as Chapter 4 notes, where Christians see mystery, many Muslims see idolatry or denial of the sole Lord and God of all, and polarization results.

I could go on in this fashion, yet some might still wonder about the real-life significance of such theoretical differences and debates. So let me add a word about my priorities. Inquirers such as Galileo, Darwin, Einstein, Hubble, Watson, and Crick did not go in search of "real-life significance": that came automatically. They desired primarily to penetrate reality—to understand life, its history, the galaxies, the universe. Similarly, Christians seek deeper understanding of God, Christ, Redemption, Trinity, Eucharist, Revelation, Church, Resurrection, and other transcendent realities within the Christian world view. Such understanding cannot then fail to have implications for Christian life and worship. I shall here mention a few notable implications; but on the whole, being directly engaged with sufficiently complex questions, I shall not widen my perspective to include speculation about the existential ramifications—varied, broad, complex, and often problematic—of understanding the major Christian mysteries one way or another.

This work owes much to those who kindly offered comments on the whole (Ronald Modras and James Voiss) or on parts (Joseph Bracken, John Cooper, Thomas Lennon, Gerald O'Collins, Kenneth Steinhauser, Francis Sullivan, and Christina Van Dyke), to the helpful suggestions of publishers' readers, and to the stylistic editing of Victoria Carlson-Casaregola. Warm thanks to them all.

List of Abbreviations

CCL   *Corpus Christianorum.* Series Latina (Turnholt: Brepols, 1954–).

CSEL   *Corpus scriptorum ecclesiasticorum latinorum* (Vienna: Apud C. Geroldi filium, 1866–).

DS   *Enchiridion symbolorum definitonum et declarationum de rebus fidei et morum.* 34th edn. Ed. Henry Denzinger and Adolf Schönmetzer (Barcelona: Herder, 1957).

DTC   *Dictionnaire de théologie catholique.* (Paris: Letouzey & Ané, 1899-1950).

PG   *Patrologiae cursus completus, series graeca* (Paris: Migne, 1857-66).

PL   *Patrologiae cursus completus, series latina* (Paris: Migne: 1844-90).

Chapter 1

Perspectives and Paradigms

In 1913, young Ludwig Wittgenstein, struggling with the complexities of logic, wrote Bertrand Russell: "Identity is the very Devil and *immensely important; very much more so than I thought. It hangs—like everything else—directly together with the most fundamental questions.*"[1] The like might be said of Christian theology. There, too, identity is deeply perplexing. There, too, its importance has not been fully appreciated. Yet it connects with the most central Christian beliefs— Incarnation, Redemption, Trinity, Eucharist, Revelation, Church, Resurrection, Eternal Life. "Jesus *is* God," says popular Christian belief. "Jesus *is* the Word, the Second Person of the Holy Trinity," says theology, more precisely. And each divine Person, tradition has maintained, is God: the Father is God, the Son is God, and the Holy Spirit is God. Other identities connect with these traditional ones and with one another; for example: Eucharistic identities ("This is my body, this is my blood"); doctrinal identities ("same doctrine, same sense, same meaning"); eccle-sial identities (with the Church of Christ, with the church the Apostles founded); and personal identities (of the risen Christ with the crucified Christ, of the blessed with the deceased). It is evident, furthermore, that not only do these identities connect with the central beliefs; the beliefs are stated as identities, and the identities run through their heart. In each instance, one senses, to understand the identity would be to understand the mystery believed.

From these examples readers may surmise how the term "identity" is here being used—not for individuality ("She has a sense of her own identity"), nor for a characteristic or set of characteristics ("When she met the President, she did not realize his identity"), but, as my dictionary puts it, for "the quality or condition of being the same as something else." *Sameness* is this study's concern, the path to be pursued from theme to theme, doctrine to doctrine. But why? Why should faith take this direction in search of understanding? All of the identities, or apparent identities, just cited have previously been studied, sometimes precisely as identities. However, no comprehensive study has been made of them, as here, within this common focus—comparing the identities, connecting them, reviewing previous treatments, and attempting new solutions and approaches, in light of a common theoretical background appropriately developed and applied.

This may help to explain why so many treatments of the individual identities, as identities, seem unsatisfactory in one way or another. The major deficiency that I

---

[1] Wittgenstein, *Notebooks 1914-1916*, 122 (Wittgenstein's emphasis).

have come to recognize is a pervasive essentialism, of the kind Wittgenstein at first exemplified and later critiqued. As noted in an earlier work,[2] "essentialism" can mean many things, as can its root term "essence." In one sense, "an essence is the 'quiddity' of a thing . . . An essence is any character of a thing whereby that thing is what it is."[3] It is the fuzziness of a peach, the splendor of a sunset, the keenness of a person's wit. With such essences there can be little quarrel. Similarly innocuous are the frequent formulations which assume that all members of a class of things (games, books, humans, propositions) have *something* in common—however various, irregular, or ill-defined (for example, a shared "family resemblance")—that makes them all members of that class. More problematic, but still not my concern, is the essentialism that interests modal logicians, namely, "the view that some attributes belong to an object by necessity whereas others belong to it contingently."[4] Although these attributes are sometimes termed "essential," they do not qualify as "essences" unless, singly or collectively, they constitute sufficient as well as necessary conditions of membership in a class. Essences, in this traditional sense, are core properties or clusters of properties present, necessarily, in all and only those things which bear the common name. Knowledge is one thing; language is one thing; beauty, meaning, humanity, life, law, justice—each is a single, invariant reality, present in the most varied instances, or in a separate realm of forms.

Identity, too, is often so conceived, as a single, invariant reality. This viewpoint, long implicit in discussions such as some we shall examine, became explicit in modern times. Thus, from Descartes to Kant, Avrum Stroll observes, "almost all the writers . . . took the term 'identity' to mean that an object 'is the same with itself' (Hume). These formulations were expressed by the logical principle, regarded as one of the basic laws of reasoning, $[(x)x=x]$." To be sure, as Rudolf Carnap later noted, "Identity, in common usage and also in the usage of science, is not always taken in the strictest sense. Language often treats objects which are not identical in the strict, logical sense as identical."[5] The populace speak loosely, he might say, but serious thinkers take more care with their words. Thus today, as in the past, much discussion proceeds "as though somewhere there exists in itself an exceptional sense of the word 'identical,' in which things are really identical."[6]

---

[2] Hallett, *Essentialism*, 2.

[3] Russell, *The Problems of Philosophy*, 94.

[4] Ibid., 91.

[5] Carnap, *Logical Structure*, 251.

[6] Waismann, "Über den Begriff der Identität," 59. "There are not different *kinds* of identity," Harold Noonan insists, "to be differently analysed. There is just the *one* relation of identity, and there is nothing in any way puzzling about it. As David Lewis puts the point: 'Identity is an utterly unproblematic notion. Everything is identical to itself. Nothing is identical to anything else. There is never any problem about what makes something identical to itself; nothing can fail to be. And there is never any problem about what makes two things identical; two things never can be identical'" ("Substance, Identity and Time," 81, and *Personal Identity*, 105, quoting—none too accurately—Lewis, *On the Plurality of Worlds*, 192-93).

Distinctions are drawn, it is true, between conceptual identity and real identity, personal identity and physical identity, identity at a time and identity over time, and so forth. Yet this multiplicity, many would insist, does not entail that there is no single absolute relation of identity or that the expression "the same" is equivocal, assuming different senses in different contexts.[7] No, whatever *a* and *b* may be, if they really are identical, their identity is that of a thing with itself, and whatever is truly predicable of one must be truly predicable of the other.[8] Identity entails indiscernibility.

For reasons that will emerge, I shall not enter into debate about what identity "really is," but, in view of the restrictive usage in some quarters and the expansive usage in others, I shall simply clarify my own use of terms. Throughout this study, it will be important to keep in mind that, as already in this chapter, when I speak of "identity statements" and the "identities" which they express, I shall intend not only statements such as "Tully is Cicero" or "Bush is the President" and the strict identities which they express but also statements of the kind already cited—e.g., "Jesus is God" or "This is my body"—and whatever relations they express. These latter statements conceivably might state strict identities and many people have supposed that they either do or should. It is this tendency that concerns me more than any restrictions placed on the terms "identity," "same," and the like.

The tendency occasions concern because none of the major themes of faith just noted has escaped the influence of essentialism in general or of this form—identity-essentialism—in particular. Though largely unnoticed, this influence has been profound and, I shall argue, correspondingly unfortunate. To understand why the influence has not been more noticed and more effectually countered, it will help to consider the doctrine that might have proved a more effective antidote had it been suitably developed and applied—namely, the doctrine of analogy. In the present preparatory chapter I shall undertake such development, specifically with regard to identity, and note where it leads. To counteract the influence of essentialism, as I repeatedly shall, is to make due room for mystery. Yet the mystery can at least be intelligibly stated. Between the Scylla of strict, essentialistic identity, which occasions so many problems, and the Charybdis of religious obscurantism, which invokes mystery to skirt the problems, a way can be found.

---

[7] Dummett, "Frege," 229.

[8] Cf. Morris, *Understanding Identity Statements*, 138 ("a conceptually unrevised Leibniz's Law is the touchstone of warranted assertion, and thereby of truth, in matters of identity"); Oderberg, "Reply to Sprigge," 131; Scruton, *Modern Philosophy*, 147; Savellos, "How To Be," 241: "Leibniz's Law is explicative of our normal notion of identity. So if sortal identity is *identity* nonetheless, it must adhere to the Leibnizian principle." The grip of this current dogma is revealed in the remark of a reader: "This is just a matter of standard first-order quantifier-logic, which has become standard because it catches so well an understanding with which one can credit any competent speaker of a natural language." One might as well argue that the inclusive, truth-table sense of "or" catches an understanding with which one can credit any competent speaker of a natural language. So it does, but the word has another common sense and does not appear in just any natural language, but in English.

Analogy and Identity

Faced with the transcendence of God, on the one hand, and the doctrines of Christian faith, on the other, Aquinas insisted that terms such as "good" and "wise" are not predicated univocally of God and of humans, but analogously. God's goodness and wisdom far transcend those of creatures, yet the resemblance between the created and divine analogs suffices to legitimate application of the same terms to God as to creatures. "Thus God is called wise," Aquinas explains, "not simply because he begets wisdom but because, insofar as we are wise, we imitate to some extent the divine source of our wisdom."[9]

Concerning this doctrine, long in vogue, several points can be noted. First, the doctrine centers on descriptive adjectives ("good," "wise," "great," "powerful") and verbs ("know," "love," "live," "will"), not on expressions of identity ("identical with," "same as," "is"). Second, the favored terms figure in predications of properties or actions (e.g., "God is loving" or "God loves"), not in statements of identity (e.g., "Jesus is God" or "I am the way, the truth, and the life"). Third, the predications are warranted by "some kind of likeness,"[10] guaranteed, in Aquinas's view, by the fact that an effect must somehow resemble its cause. Fourth, to be adequate, this appeal to resemblance clearly needs further development. If God created trees, is God leafy? If God created stones, is God a stone? What kind or degree of similarity suffices for valid analogical predication?

Though God made stones, Aquinas explains, God is not rightly called a stone, since the word "stone" indicates a determinate mode of being that distinguishes stones from God. More abstract terms, however, such as "being" and "goodness," do not specify any particular mode or degree of perfection, so can rightly be predicated of God.[11] Such terms can be stretched, whereas terms like "stone" cannot—or at least not as far as God. But if not that far, how far? And if the other terms can be applied to God in virtue of some kind or degree of likeness, and not just because they indicate no limitation, what kind or degree of likeness is that? Can anything more definite be said to justify some predications rather than others?

Aquinas's account, appealing to similarity, overlooks the competing claims of alternative expressions. Crimson may closely resemble scarlet and might be called scarlet were it not for the competing claim of the rival term "crimson." Trees may closely resemble bushes and might be called bushes were it not for the competing claim of the rival term "tree." And so it is quite generally. The requisite similarity cannot be stated absolutely, as close, distant, or in-between, but it must be stated relative to the language at large and what terms occupy what parts of the semantic landscape. Where concepts cluster thickly, as for colors, similarity must be close. Where no concepts come close, as for God, similarity may be looser. In either case,

---

[9] Aquinas, *Summa contra gentiles* 1.31. Aquinas denies the symmetry of the relation. A man does not resemble his picture, but the picture resembles the man (e.g., *De Veritate* 2.11.ad 1; 4.4.ad 2).

[10] Aquinas, *Summa theologica* 1.13.2.c.

[11] Aquinas, *Summa contra gentiles* 1.31; *Summa theologica* 1.13.3.ad 1.

it might be suggested, a statement's use of terms should resemble more nearly the established uses of terms than would the substitution of any rival, incompatible expression.[12]

In illustration of this cryptic suggestion, consider a diverting but instructive example. When, at the tender age of two, a niece of mine first saw the Gulf of Mexico, she exclaimed "Big bathtub!" Bathtubs she knew, and sinks, buckets, and the like, but neither oceans nor lakes nor ponds nor swimming pools. So of the terms she was acquainted with, "bathtub" came closest. She realized, of course, that this expanse of water and its receptacle differed notably from the familiar ones at home; the ones she now gazed on were enormous. Still, given the limited verbal means at her disposal, her choice of words was apt. The only trouble was that, unknown to her, English possesses a whole series of terms in successful competition with "bathtub." "Pool" and "pond" come closer to what she saw, "lake" still closer, "ocean" and "bay" closer still, and "gulf" closest of all. Hence, despite the increasing similarity between their referents and the Gulf of Mexico, "bathtub," "pool," "pond," "lake," "ocean," and "bay" do not qualify as true or apt descriptions of that body of water, whereas "gulf" does. Only "gulf" satisfies the suggested requirement.

Now, how should this requirement be taken: as a test of truth or just of aptness? Clearly, "It's the Gulf of Mexico" qualifies as true, whereas "It's a bathtub" does not. However, suppose "bathtub" really were the closest term available: would an utterance which stretched the term that far, from bathtub to gulf, be a *true* utterance or merely a *descriptively apt* utterance? In this imagined situation, the former accolade is more doubtful than the latter: if "bathtub" were the closest term available, then, clearly, that would be the one to employ. It would give a better idea of the body in question than would "kettle," "cup," or any other rival expression. Some theological utterances may stretch terms this far or farther, while others may not. However, since most such utterances to be considered here probably do, I shall adopt the less controversial alternative and treat the proposed criterion as a test of descriptive aptness and not necessarily of truth.

This distinction and this concession should occasion no alarm, given their parallel with the traditional "three ways." There, the *via affirmativa* asserts divine properties, the *via negativa* denies them, and the *via eminentiae* reasserts them, "eminently." So here, when statements extend expressions far beyond their accustomed range (*via affirmativa*), the statements' truth may be questioned (*via negativa*), but their descriptive aptness may validate them, nonetheless (*via eminentiae*). We may assert, meaningfully and legitimately, that God is good, wise, powerful, and so forth.

How, though, should we understand this linguistic test, of relative similarity—as a *necessary* condition of descriptive aptness or, like traditional models of analogy, as a *sufficient* condition? The preceding illustration suggests at least the general validity of the first understanding, and so do choices such as those just cited. Taken

---

[12] For fuller, different development of this line of thought, see Hallett, *Language and Truth*, and *A Middle Way to God*, 14-15.

as a necessary condition, the criterion would, for example, rule out calling God "silly" or "weak," since the rival terms "wise" and "powerful" conform more nearly with the established uses of words. Typically, the criterion excludes what should be excluded. However, not always. A challenge lies implicit in Wittgenstein's critique of similarity as the sole basis of verbal stretching.[13] Do we call thoughts "deep" because they resemble deep wells or answers "sharp" because they resemble needles or notes "high" because they resemble mountains? And is it only now, when they are standard, that such turns of phrase may be used to make apt assertions? Taken as a necessary condition, the proposed criterion appears too stringent. Besides, a necessary condition of descriptive aptness looks less relevant for this study than does a sufficient condition. So let us consider that alternative: for descriptive aptness, does it *suffice* that a statement's use of terms resemble more closely the established uses of terms than would the substitution of any rival, incompatible expression?

Suppose I draw two concentric circles and join them by a wavy line. That line resembles a circle more than it does a square, triangle, or octagon; "circle" comes closest. But it does not come close enough for descriptive aptness. Were I to report simply that I drew a circle, those who heard me would suppose I had drawn a different sort of figure, one with all its points more nearly equidistant from a central point. It would therefore be preferable to say I drew a "wavy circle." That description would be perfectly apt, indicating both the general similarity to ordinary circles and the dissimilarity. Hearers would get a good idea what sort of figure I had drawn. To capture the difference thus exemplified, we might modify our criterion to read: For descriptive aptness, it suffices that a statement's use of terms resemble more closely the established uses of terms than would the substitution of any rival, incompatible expression and that, when necessary, the statement add an appropriate modifier.

Often, no such modifier is needed. Consider, for example, the extension of the term "chess" to the game played by computers. No people, no hands, no pieces, no board, no squares, no moving of pieces, no rules for moving or removing pieces how notably computer chess differs from human! Yet "chess"—not "checkers," "poker," or any other rival expression—is clearly the right term to employ for this new activity. It comes closer than any rival term; the criterion of relative similarity is satisfied. Similarly, we feel few qualms about saying, for example, that Deep Blue beat Kasparov in chess. We need not note the difference from ordinary chess; reference to the computer Deep Blue already signals that. So, too, in theological discourse, we may either refer to "divine knowledge" or "divine will" to signal the difference from human knowing or willing, or we may say simply "*God* knows our desires" or "*God* wills our salvation" and let the subject term signal the difference.

Examples could probably be imagined which would challenge the accuracy of even this refined criterion of descriptive aptness, as they might that of any modified version, no matter how carefully crafted. I might add, for example, that the word "statement" here refers to written or spoken utterances or speech acts, not

---

[13] Wittgenstein, *The Blue and Brown Books*, 130.

to mere sentences or their meanings; that the word-uses in question are those established at the time of the utterance; that word-uses may be established by stipulation as well as by usage; that "word-use" embraces semantics as well as grammar (words alone do not account for the truth of most true statements). I might try to specify just when a modifier is needed, what qualifies as an appropriate modifier, what counts as a rival, incompatible expression, what type of utterance is intended by the term "statement," and so forth. Nonetheless, experience suggests that contrary or at least dubious cases, challenging the norm, might still be conceived. A precise universal formula, stating sufficient conditions of apt predication, may not be feasible. However, neither does it seem needful. The possibility of problematic fringe cases casts no doubt on the sample sayings I have cited, nor does it call in question the general validity of the criterion as formulated. (Let us call it the Criterion of Relative Similarity, or CRS for short.) As an antidote to essentialism, its chief purpose here, the criterion can serve as it stands. As "I drew a wavy circle on the board," "Deep Blue beat Kasparov in chess," and "God knows our desires" can satisfy this reasonable standard, so too may statements such as those cited at the start—"Jesus is God," "This is my body," "The one who rose is the one who died," and so forth—even if they do not state strict identities.

In their everyday employment, statements of this form ("*a* is *b*," where "*a*" and "*b*" are nouns, pronouns, or noun phrases) are not all of a piece. The "is" in "God is love," for example, does not signal the same relation as does the "is" in "Cicero is Tully," "This is my wife" (gesturing to the person at my side), "This is my brother" (pointing to a picture), "Olivier is Hamlet" (in the movie), "Klaus is the man on the left," "The evening star is the morning star," "Ignorance is bliss," "War is war," or "Life is a bowl of cherries." Neither do these latter utterances all express the same relation as each other.[14]

Such is current usage. In an inquiry like this one into themes of Christian faith, it is important to recognize that, if anything, still greater freedom of expression has characterized scriptural, patristic, and theological sayings. Witness the varied responses to Jesus' query, "Who do people say that the Son of Man is?" Witness the rich variety of Johannine "I am" sayings and kindred utterances such as Jn 6:63 ("The words that I have spoken to you are spirit and life"). Witness the New Testament's Eucharistic variants: "This my body" (Mk 14:22; Mt 26:26); "This is my blood" (Mk 14: 22, 24; Mt 26: 28); "This cup that is poured out for you is the new covenant in my blood" (Lk 22: 20; cf. 1 Cor 11:25); "The cup of blessing that we bless, is it not a sharing in the blood of Christ? The bread that we break, is it not a sharing in the body of Christ?" (1 Cor 10:16). Witness, too, Ignatius of Antioch's Eucharistic sayings—e.g., "I want only God's bread, which is the flesh of Jesus Christ, formed of the seed of David, and for drink I crave his blood which is love that cannot perish"[15]—or his Christological variations: "Jesus Christ, our

---

[14] Other languages add further variety, e.g.: "L'État, c'est moi," (Louis XIV); "La France, c'est moi" (Charles de Gaulle, 1940).

[15] Ignatius of Antioch, Letter to the Romans (Roman breviary for Oct. 17).

hope";[16] "Christ Jesus, our common hope";[17] "may you possess an unhesitating spirit, for this is Jesus Christ";[18] "Jesus Christ, our inseparable life, is the will of the Father."[19] Or compare Paul's "living is Christ and dying is gain" (Phil 1:21), "The rock was Christ" (1 Cor 10:4), "The Spirit is life because of righteousness" (Rom 8:10); "You are the body of Christ" (1 Cor 12:27); "I am not ashamed of the gospel; it is the power of God for salvation" (Rom 1:16).

Similar freedom has characterized theological utterance down to our day. One can still read, for example: "Our salvation is Jesus himself. As formerly Origen did not hesitate to say that Jesus is the Gospel, that he is the Kingdom in person, so today a Karl Rahner speaks of 'the *salvific* event which Jesus Christ himself *is*."[20] For Walter Kasper, "Jesus is nothing but the incarnate love of the Father and the incarnate response of obedience."[21] For Emile Mersch, Jesus is God's "decree that is realized and, we may say, incarnated."[22] In Christ, "the alliance between God and men becomes the very person of the Man-God."[23] "The redemption is not an abstract concept or theory. It is a Person who is intensely alive."[24] Indeed, "The Church is Christ,"[25] "Christianity is Christ,"[26] "Christ is . . . everything,"[27] "He is all, all in all; for He is God."[28] In such subject-predicate pairings as these, the linking verb hardly signals some single, invariant relationship.

Given this fluidity, it is difficult to distinguish standard usage from creative usage and creative usage from license. Clearly, however, a great variety of utterances, and not some single privileged set, constitute the "established uses of words" in reference to which "*a* is *b*" statements (or their analogs in other persons, tenses, or tongues) typically pass or fail the CRS test of assertability. The like holds for variants which, for example, substitute "is identical with" for "is" (e.g., "Jesus' *I* is identical with that Wisdom or Logos of God, which is identical with

---

[16] Ignatius of Antioch, Letter to the Magnesians 11.1 (*The Apostolic Fathers*, vol. 1, 209).

[17] Ignatius of Antioch, Letter to the Philadelphians 11.2 (*The Apostolic Fathers*, vol. 1, 251); Letter to the Ephesians 21.2 (*The Apostolic Fathers*, vol. 1, 197).

[18] Ignatius of Antioch, Letter to the Magnesians, 15.1 (*The Apostolic Fathers*, vol. 1, 211).

[19] Ignatius of Antioch, Letter to the Ephesians, 3.2 (*The Apostolic Fathers*, vol. 1, 177).

[20] Rahner, *Foundations of Christian Faith*, 293 (Rahner's emphasis). Bernard Sesboüé notes that St. Paul "did not hesitate to say that Jesus in person has become for us 'justice, sanctification, and redemption' (1 Co, 1, 30)" (*Jésus-Christ l'unique médiateur*, 12).

[21] Kasper, *Jesus the Christ*, 233.

[22] Mersch, *The Theology of the Mystical Body*, 320.

[23] Mersch, *The Whole Christ*, 36.

[24] Mersch, *The Theology of the Mystical Body*, 319.

[25] Mersch, *The Whole Christ*, 578.

[26] Demarest, *The Cross and Salvation*, 167.

[27] Mersch, *The Theology of the Mystical Body*, 320.

[28] Mersch, *The Whole Christ*, 127.

God's own salvific and creative intention through which the world was created"[29]). It may not matter, therefore, whether we classify a given utterance (e.g., "God is love") as an "identity statement." Regardless of how we classify it, familiarity with varied usage roundabout would be more helpful for assessing its assertability than would a narrow theory of identity, based on some single type of example or—still worse—on some never-achieved ideal. ("Identity is a precise conception," wrote Russell, "and no word, in ordinary speech, stands for anything precise."[30])

True, I might attempt to draw a sharp demarcation of my own, and inform my readers more precisely than I already have just what I mean by "identity statements." This might convey a gratifying sense of clarity, but it might also prove counterproductive, by obscuring the heterogeneous complexity of the reality being sliced. Besides, in the present inquiry it would serve no useful purpose. As preparation for the consideration of theological identity statements, two points seem essential: that possibilities not be confined to existing usage and that this usage not be narrowly conceived. CRS makes the first point, and my sample bundle of "*a* is *b*" utterances makes the second.

Theorists are, of course, free to define identity as they please in the abstract realms of logic and theory construction, but it is evident what conflicts an essentialistic mindset, unquestioned and unquestioning, has occasioned in theology. Faced with the apparent contradiction in an "*a* is *b*" assertion linking strongly disparate terms, all parties—Christian theologians, non-Christian critics, and Christian faithful—have typically focused on the terms of the relation and not on the relation. To the query "How can *a* possibly be *b*?" theologians have responded by carefully defining, distinguishing, and comparing *a* and *b*, critics have replied by applying "Leibniz's law" (the indiscernibility of identicals) and challenging the theologians' solutions, and the faithful have responded by either accepting the apparent contradiction (such, they may believe, are the requirements of faith) or losing their faith (such may appear the requirements of reason) or leaving the whole matter to the experts and simply living with mystery. Too seldom do any of these parties question the underlying assumption which generates the apparent incoherence, namely the assumption that the doctrine in question states an identity and that the identity must be strict. It is this assumption that diverts attention from the stated relationship to its terms. Repeatedly, a simpler solution would be to question this underlying, essentialistic assumption. The apparent contradiction may signal a variation in the copula and not in the subject or the predicate.

To this query, centered on the copula, the answer may be: "I don't know the nature of the stated relationship, and have no way of knowing it. It looks like some sort of identity, but I can't conceive what kind it is." Given CRS, such a reply need not negate the meaningfulness or aptness of the problematic statement, especially in the realms of theology and metaphysics. Indeed, even non-metaphysical examples teach openness to undreamed-of possibilities.

---

[29] Skarsaune, *Incarnation*, 133.

[30] Russell, *The Analysis of Mind*, 180.

In recent psychology, the study of fugues, psychogenic amnesias, multiple personalities, and other dissociative states has posed intriguing problems for personal identity. Consider the well-known case of Christine Beauchamp, of whom Morton Prince wrote:

> In addition to the real, original or normal self, the self that was born and which she was intended by nature to be, she may be any one of three different persons. I say three different, because, although making use of the same body, each, nevertheless, has a distinctly different character; a difference manifested by different trains of thought, by different views, beliefs, ideals, and temperament, and by different acquisitions, tastes, habits, experiences, and memories. Each varies in these respects from the other two, and from the original Miss Beauchamp.[31]

In this complex web, some of the members had knowledge of others and some did not, some had knowledge of others' thoughts as well as of their actions while others did not, some spoke French and some did not, some recalled Christine's life after 1893 and some did not, some were at odds with this or that member of the dissociated family and others were not, and so forth. Now, in some sense, Christine was her "original or normal self." In some sense, she was each of her other selves. In some sense, her various selves were identical with each other. But in no two pairings was the relationship the same. And in no instance was the relationship the same as for the familiar paradigms of identity—e.g., "Cicero is Cicero" or "Cicero is Tully"—that tend to cramp our thinking essentialistically.

Identity and Mystery

This sample, like the preceding, exemplifies a methodological preference, here and hereafter, for illuminating paradigms rather than precise analytic formulations. CRS is inimical to the popular style of theorizing that states sufficient and/or necessary conditions without regard for how people customarily employ the term in question (e.g., "same" or "identical") and without stipulating an alternative sense of the term in place of the familiar one. Too often, veiled redefinitions pose as statements of metaphysical fact. ("The essential thing about metaphysics," commented Wittgenstein: "it obliterates the distinction between factual and conceptual investigations."[32]) The alternative procedure which I have been following—neither essentialistic argumentation nor conceptual reconstruction—is the one Wittgenstein proposed and practiced. Paraphrasing a programmatic passage in his *Blue Book*,[33] I might say: If we want to study the problems of identity in Christian theology, we may with great advantage look at simpler, more primitive examples in which the same fundamental issues arise as in more complex cases,

---

[31] Prince, *The Dissociation of a Personality*, 1. More recently, see Wilkes, *Real People*, 112-27, on the same case.

[32] Wittgenstein, *Zettel*, §458.

[33] Wittgenstein, *The Blue and Brown Books*, 17.

but without the confusing background of theological debate and speculation. When we examine such simple examples, the mental mist which seems to enshroud our ordinary theological discussions dissipates. We see questions and distinctions which are clear-cut and transparent. On the other hand, we recognize that these examples are not separated by a break from the more complicated ones. The same questions and distinctions apply in the latter as in the former.

The preceding example, stimulating our sluggish imaginations, should make us slow to dismiss as empty the suggestion that a given identity statement may be exemplified in some manner which satisfies CRS yet which we cannot conceive. Addressing this fundamental issue, without the confusing background of theological debate and speculation, it takes this first step toward the recognition of mystery. Another sample can carry us farther in the same direction; for the Christine example, with its ample analysis, could foster a deep illusion. It might suggest that the more detailed the analysis offered, the clearer a doctrine becomes, whereas, paradoxical though it may sound, the reverse often holds true.

A scriptural paradigm can illustrate this point, plus others, in the manner Wittgenstein proposed. In Matthew 16:13-14 we read: "Now when Jesus came into the district of Caesarea Philippi, he asked his disciples, 'Who do people say that the Son of Man is?' And they said, 'Some say John the Baptist, but others Elijah, and still others Jeremiah or one of the prophets.'" Each of these identifications appears puzzling. We may wonder, for example, how Jesus could be the long-departed prophet Elijah. He might be Elijah *redevivus*, back from heaven; but then he could not be Jesus of Nazareth, born some thirty years before. He might come "in the spirit and power of Elijah" (Lk 1:17); but that would be feeble backing for "Jesus *is* Elijah." To skirt these difficulties, we could have recourse to our principle: Jesus might indeed "be" Elijah, in a manner we do not know or understand but which, nonetheless, would satisfy the conditions set by CRS. This, however, could appear an evasion, a shirking of one's speculative duty. *How* might these two men be identical?

A common expedient in such a tight spot is to assume real identity (everybody knows what that means) and work on the terms of the relation. This might be done in either of two familiar ways: either by endowing familiar expressions with new, unfamiliar meanings, or by substituting new, metaphysical expressions for familiar ones. Thus we might suggest that Jesus and Elijah are not the same person in any ordinary sense of "person" but rather in a transcendent, metaphysical sense of the term. Or, introducing technical terminology, it might be suggested that these two "personae" or "modes" or "hypostases" form a single person, in the ordinary sense of "person." The metaphysical sense (in the first suggestion) or the metaphysical expression (in the second) would ward off patent contradiction while permitting "real," Leibnizian identity between subject and predicate, Jesus and Elijah. For neither the metaphysical sense nor the metaphysical expression, we may suppose, has been carefully, clearly defined by those who make use of it.[34]

---

[34] To allay possible misgivings at this point, let me note in advance that I do not believe that incarnational doctrine developed in the manner here described. See Chapter 2.

Despite this terminological fuzziness, such a reading may appear, and may in a sense be, more definite than the mere assertion, "In some way or other, unknown to us, the statement satisfies CRS." Take the proposal that Jesus and Elijah are two "hypostases" forming a single "persona." To distinguish between a hypostasis and a persona, we define a hypostasis as "an individual qua substance" and a persona as "an individual qua person." Greater definiteness might land us in contradiction and greater indefiniteness might wash out all meaning; so we strike this compromise. The Elijah *redevivus* reading (with only one substance) is now excluded, and so is the spiritual kinship reading (with two persons). Thus the meaning of "Jesus is Elijah" has, in a sense, been made more definite: these possibilities are excluded. However, in both of the excluded readings we had a good idea what relationship was intended (strict identity in one case, spiritual kinship in the other), whereas now the nature of the union has become entirely mysterious, thanks to the greater definiteness; and all the added terms—"hypostasis," "persona," "substance," "person"—are fuzzier than the original ones, "Jesus" and "Elijah." Such, one senses, has often been the result in theological inquiry. Attempts at greater definiteness have led away from greater clarity and into greater obscurity.

Not only may the distinction between greater definiteness and greater clarity easily go unnoticed, but our speculative limitations may also be obscured in another way. Consider the reasons for our slight efforts to resolve the unclarity surrounding the saying "Jesus is Elijah." One obvious reason is the claim's apparent unimportance. However, in further explanation it is also evident that we shall never be able to discover who, if anyone, made the reported identification of Jesus with Elijah and that we could not interview them even if we knew their identities. The chances of their having provided a written explanation of their meaning, or of such a written account still existing, waiting to be found, are virtually nil. And even if we did not exclude that possibility, we would have no idea where to look for such a written record. Thus, there is no mystery about the mysteriousness of this mystery. Not only do we have no prospect of clarifying the uncertain meaning, but we see—concretely and in detail—why we have none. With regard to the transcendent mysteries of Christian faith, we possess no comparable understanding—clear, concrete, detailed—of their mysteriousness, and we therefore run the risk of embarking on inquiries or attempting explications which stand no better chance of succeeding than would random digging in the hills of Galilee in search of a papyrus record spelling out the meaning of the claim "Jesus of Nazareth is Elijah." Paradoxically, the very transcendence of such mysteries may veil their full mysteriousness.

I have now cited two likely reasons for excessive confidence in theological speculation concerning the mysteries of faith. One is the failure to distinguish between definiteness and clarity. A second is the difficulty of recognizing how transcendent the mysteries of faith really are, precisely because they are transcendent. This second reason links with a third, which has extensively affected theological inquiry. It might be termed the "words suffice" syndrome, for it consists in the implicit or explicit assumption that any verbal formulation which avoids evident contradiction or incoherence should be given the benefit of the doubt as expressing a genuine possibility.[35] After all, even in the most complex speculations on the most abstruse matters, do not the words all have meanings and are not the sentences all grammatical?

Richard Swinburne has expressed and defended the attitude I here have in mind. Discussing various forms of afterlife, he writes: "The fact that there seems (and to so many people) to be no contradiction hidden in these stories is good reason for supposing that there is no contradiction hidden in them—until a contradiction is revealed. If this were not a good reason for believing there to be no contradiction, we would have no good reason for believing any sentence at all to be free of hidden contradiction."[36] Swinburne's all-or-nothing argument resembles this one: "The fact that people see no snakes in high grass is a good reason for supposing that there are none there—until one is spotted. If we started to suspect their presence in high grass, we would have to suspect their presence everywhere—on the patio, on the path, and on the well-manicured lawn." Presented with such an argument, we would distinguish between seeing no snakes in the grass and seeing that there are no snakes in the grass; and we would then note that whereas we can see that there are no snakes on the patio and the lawn, we do not see that there are none in the high grass. Philosophical and theological discourse is high grass. Theological inquiry about Trinitarian processions, the self-emptying of the Word, Jesus' real presence in the Eucharist, and the like, is very high grass indeed. There, many a contradiction may lurk without our spotting it, or our even being able to detect it if we tried.

To illustrate my general point, consider the statement, "One day someone will trisect an angle using only ruler and compass." Many people, seeing no contradiction in this prediction, have striven to be the first to verify it. Now, however, it has been shown, a priori and not just empirically, that no such thing is possible. Outside mathematics the like may hold, for example, regarding the harnessing of nuclear fusion. Despite the meaningfulness of the proposal and its lack of evident contradiction, it may not state a genuine possibility. A fortiori, the like may hold regarding more transcendent mysteries. Indeed, it would be surprising if speculative thinkers, ignorant though they are of the transcendent realities they discuss,

---

[35] A nice illustration, of the explicit sort: "It is not to be denied, that another mode is possible to God, viz. that God could effect that the Body of Christ should be in the Sacrament, the substance of bread remaining. For all hold that God can do whatever does not imply a contradiction. But, that the Body of Christ should be in this Sacrament, without conversion of the substance of the bread into Itself, no more implies a contradiction, than that it should be in the Sacrament, the conversion having taken place. As then one is possible, so is the other" (Durandus, in Pusey, *The Doctrine of the Real Presence*, 12).

[36] Swinburne, in Shoemaker and Swinburne, *Personal Identity*, 25. Cf. Nagel, *The View from Nowhere*, 97-98 ("Unless it has been shown positively that there cannot be such things—that the idea involves some kind of contradiction [like the idea of things that are not self-identical]—we are entitled to assume that it makes sense even if we can say nothing more about the members of the class, and have never seen one"). Cf. Suárez, *De incarnatione*, 40 ("since God is omnipotent, so long as something is not proved repugnant from that very omnipotence of God, it is likely that it can be done by God").

were to state nothing but genuine possibilities when they slap terms together. One should *expect* some snakes in grass that high. What wonderful shelter it makes![37]

The weakness of Swinburne's argument suggests strong commitment to a style of speculative inquiry which, though favored by many, I view as showing insufficient regard for mystery. When faith seeks understanding, this may mean several things: first, seeking to clarify a mystery; second, seeking to locate the mystery—that is, to identify just where, why, and to what extent a doctrine escapes our comprehension; and, third, seeking to understand when the former is not possible but only the latter. Not surprisingly, emphasis has fallen on the first type of pursuit rather than the second or the third, for we naturally prefer to mitigate mystery and not merely to locate it. Here, the emphasis will be different, for the reasons indicated: 1) Theological discourse has need of analogy, and the kind it needs is CRS. But this criterion, countering essentialistic narrowness, opens undreamed-of possibilities. It extends far beyond our ability to specify precisely how a theological utterance's use of terms resembles more closely the established use of terms than would the substitution of any rival expression. 2) Given such transcendence, attempts at greater definiteness may easily beget greater obscurity, without our noting the difference. 3) The farther the transcendent lies beyond our ken, the less clearly it may signal its transcendence. 4) CRS permits us to enunciate not only undreamed-of possibilities but also undreamed-of impossibilities, and it furnishes no means to differentiate between the two. Cumulatively, these points do not indicate the futility of theological reflection, even on the most transcendent mysteries of Christian faith, but they do suggest why the present inquiry will seek to locate mystery more than to clarify it. I shall not, for instance, add my reply to those in Mt 16:14-15 and say who Jesus is. I shall not attempt to explain the hypostatic union, the Trinitarian processions, Christ's Eucharistic presence, the nature of his resurrection, or the manner of the life to come. Rather than explicate mystery, I shall typically undertake the lesser but still daunting task of discerning where mystery lies and where it lies thickest.

Our scriptural paradigm can illustrate the chief alternative locations: first, mysterious relation versus mysterious terms of the relation; second, mysterious *what* (the relation's nature) versus mysterious *how* (the relation's possibility). Thus, if the relation between Jesus and Elijah is one of strict identity, mystery centers on the terms rather than the relation and on the how rather than the what: how is it possible that these men, apparently two, are really only one? Is the man they call "Jesus of Nazareth" really a Nazarene born several decades earlier, or a Tishbite born many centuries earlier? How can contradiction be avoided? If, instead, the relation is not one of strict identity and the men are indeed two, mystery shifts from the terms to the relation and from the how to the what: if not strict identity, what is the nature of the relation expressed by saying, "Jesus is

---

[37] For further development of this theme, see, e.g.: Inwagen, *God, Knowledge, and Mystery*, 12-14; Baillie, "Identity, Survival, and Sortal Concepts," 185-86; Hallett, *A Middle Way to God*, 95-96. See also Chapter 8 here, where I discuss Charles Taliaferro's distinction between weak and strong conceivability and the use he makes of the latter.

Elijah"? Similarly (to anticipate the next chapter), if the relation expressed by "Jesus is God" (or "Jesus is God the Son") is strict identity, mystery centers on the terms rather than the relation and on the how rather than the what: how is it possible for God and a human being to be strictly, self-identically the same? On this supposition, modifications may be necessary either with regard to God or with regard to the human being in order to avoid outright contradiction. If, instead, God is fully God and Jesus is fully human and the relationship between them is not one of strict identity, mystery shifts from the terms to the relation and from the how to the what: if not strict identity, what is the nature of the relation expressed by saying, "Jesus is God" (or "Jesus is God the Son")?

Given this focus of inquiry, on mystery and its location, I should say a word about my use of the term "mystery"; for the free-and-easy way I have applied the term till now is sure to occasion misgivings, if not outright objections, in some quarters. Karl Rahner's manner of thinking is representative. "What are we to think of mystery?" he asks. "Can it be regarded as a defective type of another and better knowledge which is still to come?"[38] So are there genuine mysteries in history, chemistry, and elsewhere, as well as in theology,[39] and are they multiple?[40] No, replies Rahner; such a conception misses "the actual phenomenon of 'mystery.'"[41] In the "authentic and primordial" sense of the term, he maintains, there is but a single mystery—the mystery of God—and that mystery is triune. "The absolute self-communication of God to the world, as the mystery which has drawn nigh, is Father as the absolutely primordial and underivative; it is Son, as the principle which itself acts and necessarily must act in history in view of this free self-communication; it is Holy Spirit, as that which is given, and accepted by us."[42]

From the preceding pages, readers can already sense how differently from Rahner I approach theological issues, including this one. I do not believe in an "essence" of mystery,[43] or in any "strict," "true," "perfect," "authentic," "primordial" sense of the term.[44] Accordingly, I detect no shallowness or theoretical infelicity in my dictionary's first entry for the word "mystery": "Something

---

[38] Rahner, "The Concept of Mystery," 42.

[39] Ibid., 44-45.

[40] Ibid., 41.

[41] Ibid., 45. Compare the words of the theological commission that presented the first chapter of *Lumen Gentium* to the Second Vatican Council: "The word 'mystery' does not mean merely something unknowable or obscure, but, as is now generally recognized, it signifies a reality which is divine, transcendent and salvific, and which is also revealed and manifested in some visible way" (*Acta synodalia Concilii Vaticani II*, quoted by Sullivan, *The Church We Believe In*, 8). This, too, treats terms' meanings as though they were competing theories. As a matter of semantics, the word "mystery" often does have the former meaning and not the latter. And the latter meaning is not a higher, privileged sense of the term; it is just more suitable on some occasions, as is the former on others.

[42] Rahner, "The Concept of Mystery," 70.

[43] Ibid., 48.

[44] Ibid., 42, 53, 60.

not fully understood or eluding the understanding."[45] I am particularly ready to employ the term in this sense when, as in the present inquiry, understanding not only eludes us momentarily but doubtless will continue to do so, despite our best efforts. Locating mystery will not eliminate it.

---

[45] Neither do I believe that, consistently and normatively, "By mystery theologians mean the incomprehensibility of God as God," and that the dictionary sense of the word therefore has no place in theological discourse (LaCugna, "Philosophers and Theologians on the Trinity," 175).

Chapter 2

Incarnation and Identity

"Christology seems to fall fairly clearly into two divisions," wrote C. J. F. Williams some decades ago. "The first is concerned with the truth of the two propositions: 'Christ is God' and 'Christ is a man.' The second is concerned with the mutual compatibility of these propositions."[1] Whereas the first concern takes us to Scripture, the second, in Williams's view, takes us to logic. For at first glance it seems impossible that the assertions "Christ is God" and "Christ is a man" should both be true; and this impossibility appears to be logical. "It is no use therefore," writes Williams, "in discussing the Incarnation to appeal, as St Augustine did, to the Divine Omnipotence; . . . for it is not part of the Christian faith that God can do the logically impossible."[2] When, however, we do turn to logic,

> We cannot discover what it means to say that God the son is identical with Jesus of Nazareth simply by examining the concept of identity. Examining this concept will, however, drive us to go on to examine what criteria of identity are appropriate for a being who is a man and what for a being who is God. Criteria of identity will be understood together with criteria for impossibility of identity. It is therefore the same examination which will determine whether we are to trust the *prima facie* appearance of inconsistency between the two propositions "Christ is a man" and "Christ is God." The way to clarify all these problems is to look at what it is to be a man, at what it is to be God.[3]

Such was Williams's "programme for Christology."

Many have taken the same approach and, like Williams, have closely examined the terms of the relation—what it is to be a man, what it is to be God—rather than the relationship that binds them.[4] Yet suppose it were suggested, "In order to

---

[1] C. Williams, "A Programme for Christology," 513.

[2] Ibid., 515.

[3] Ibid., 523.

[4] A chapter of C. S. Evans's, entitled "Is the Incarnation Logically Possible?," illustrates this approach. "We neither know God nor ourselves as we need," he writes. "Yet to know that 'the god-man' is a logical contradiction, we would have to have a fair degree of clarity about both concepts, just as we need to be relatively clear about what is a square and what is a circle in order to recognize their logical incompatibility" (*The Historical Christ*, 123). No comparable need arises with regard to the nature of the identity linking God and man, for: "If we accept the metaphysical principle of the indiscernibility of identicals (roughly, that *a* and *b* must have identical properties if they are identical), then we

determine whether we are to trust the *prima facie* appearance of inconsistency in the proposition 'Jesus is Elijah,' we must look at what it is to be Jesus and what it is to be Elijah." This line of inquiry would not take us very far, for in "Jesus is Elijah" the copula is more ambiguous than either of the terms it connects. The like holds, I suggest, for "Jesus is God."

Granted, Alister McGrath's contrary emphasis contains some truth. "It is quite astonishing," he writes, "how the question, 'Is Christ divine?' is discussed as if we had an excellent idea about what God was like, while Christ himself remained something of an enigma. But exactly the opposite is so obviously the case! Christ confronts us through the gospel narratives and through experience, whereas we have no clear vision of God. As John's gospel reminds us: 'No one has ever seen God; the only Son, who is in the bosom of the Father, has made him known' (John 1:18)."[5] This reminder, though salutary, sheds little light on Williams's question. Metaphysics, going beyond what the Son has made known, may have sharpened the contrast between the human and the divine ("How could the immutable, impassible God become incarnate and suffer in Christ?"[6]), but it did not beget the notion of divine transcendence. And no one has supposed that the God with whom Jesus has been identified is some other than the Christian God. I therefore repeat my suggestion that the most serious ambiguity in "Jesus is God" lies in the copula, rather than in the terms it connects.

Jon Sobrino, amplifying McGrath's suggestion, stresses both terms of the relationship, the human as well as the divine. In Sobrino's judgment, for creedal statements such as those of Nicaea and Chalcedon

> the most basic difficulty is that the formulas give the impression that one knows at the very outset who God is and what it means to be a human being. Thus the only remaining problem lies in the assertion that these two dimensions, already known from the very start, are united in the person of Christ. But the problem that Christology poses to us is quite the opposite. For it tells us that it is on the basis of Christ that we know who God is and what it means to be a human being.[7]

Thus, "To be a human being is not simply to possess the essence of a rational animal; it is to be like Jesus."[8] Abstracting from multiple difficulties here, we may accept Sobrino's suggestion and adopt a Christian view of humans as well as of God. A Hobbesian or Freudian viewpoint, for example, might cause unnecessary problems. However, this move to a Christian conception leaves the Christological

---

cannot affirm that Jesus as God has some property or properties that Jesus as a human lacks" (ibid., 122). Cf. Swinburne, *The Christian God*, 192-97.

[5] McGrath, *Understanding Jesus*, 109-10, echoing Temple, "The Divinity of Christ," 213-15. Cf. Haight, *Jesus, Symbol of God*, 291.

[6] LaCugna, *God For Us*, 300.

[7] Sobrino, *Christology at the Crossroads*, 329 (pages 333-34 implicitly negate this one-sided emphasis).

[8] Ibid., 329-30.

problem basically where it has always been, for that problem has not arisen from non-Christian notions of either term of the relation. Conceptions of both God and human nature may vary, even for Christians, and some of them may narrow the gap between the human and the divine, but none comes near to closing it. Paraphrasing Williams, I therefore propose, again: "The way to clarify all these problems of consistency is to look at what it is for Jesus to *be* God."

What blocks this shift of focus and explains the typical contrary fixation? Williams drops a clue when he asserts without discussion: "No relationship is adequate to unite the Son of Mary with the Son of the Father except the relationship of numerical identity."[9] The likely sense of such stress on "numerical identity," and its implications for Christological inquiry, rise more clearly to the surface in Richard Sturch's paper "Can One Say 'Jesus Is God'?" To this query many have replied, "Yes, one can and should." Yet few Christian theologians, Sturch notes, would accept such a formulation without qualification. They are not just being finicky. The statement "Jesus is God" does not appear in Scripture, nor in any of the church's historic creeds, nor even in the confession of the Council of Chalcedon. And for this silence Sturch sees good reasons:

> There are, irritatingly, certain difficulties in claiming either that the "is" in "Jesus is God" is one of identity or that it is one of predication. If it is one of identity, the statement should be reversible. The detective at the end of the whodunit may say either "Sykes is the guilty party" or "the guilty party is Sykes"; for the two assertions of identity have the same meaning, and if one is true the other must be also. But even someone willing to say "Jesus is God" might well balk at saying "God is Jesus." "God is *in* Jesus," yes; but "God is Jesus" by itself suggests that there is no more to God over and above the man Jesus, which is not true.[10]

In Sturch's view, similar difficulties attend a favored reformulation of popular belief. We cannot escape by invoking the doctrine of the Trinity and saying that, although Jesus is not strictly speaking God, he *is* one person of the Blessed Trinity, he is the Son. "For this once again makes the 'is' one of identity, and so reversible; and this cannot be done. There is more to the person of God the Son, over and above the human Jesus—and more to the human Jesus than just the person of God the Son."[11]

Implicitly, in both stages of his critique Sturch relies on a single, strict notion of identity. For him an "is" of identity has but one sense, and that sense requires reversibility, for it also requires indiscernibility. Whatever holds of one term of an identity must hold also of the other; there cannot be "more" to one term than to the other. Thus "God is love," for example, would not qualify as stating a genuine identity, since it cannot truly be said, in reverse, that love is God. There is more to

[9] C. Williams, "A Programme for Christology," 523.

[10] Sturch, "Can One Say," 328. See Sturch, *The Word and the Christ*, 23.

[11] Sturch, "Can One Say," 329.

love than God, and more to God than love. So the statement "God is love" must be classified some other way. There is only one kind of identity.

As operative in Sturch's reasoning, this strict-identity supposition (hereafter SIS) may be compared to the default setting in a computer. If no contrary command is entered, the computer automatically formats copy a given way (single spacing, one-inch margins, Times Roman font, or the like). SIS functions similarly in the thinking of many thinkers. Automatic, unnoticed, unquestioned, and unchallenged as it often is, the setting typically remains unexplained and unjustified. The task of the present chapter will be to note, document, and challenge this way of thinking and to do so specifically with regard to the doctrine of the Incarnation, where it has exercised such pervasive and often decisive influence. Not only does SIS divert attention away from the "is" in Christological identities such as "Jesus is God" and "Jesus is God the Son," as something clear and needing no scrutiny; not only does it thereby divert attention away from the place where an answer might be found for the apparent incoherence of such statements; but SIS is itself the chief source of that appearance.

The Strict-Identity Supposition

"From the day of Pentecost," declares Joseph Rickaby, "the issue was plain. Jesus Christ crucified, risen, and ascended into heaven, either is God or He is not."[12] Yes or no, black or white, nothing in between. Doubtless Rickaby would not speak the same way about Jesus' messiahship. He would not say: "The issue was plain from the start. Jesus either was or was not the Messiah." For the term "Messiah," as Scripture itself makes clear, could be variously understood. But for Rickaby, as for many others, the term "is" poses no similar problems.[13] Its sense, many assume, is plain and unequivocal from case to case. When it states an identity, that can mean only one thing; and what that one thing is can be surmised from remarks like Sturch's: strict identity, strict indiscernibility.

This assumption often reveals itself in what might be termed "calculus reasoning."[14] To exemplify the genre and sense the reason for the label, consider

---

[12] Rickaby, *The Divinity of Christ*, 34.

[13] For Daniel Helminiak, the question whether Jesus is God "calls for an answer of either 'Yes' or 'No.' There can be no third alternative. Even Arius knew this. He tried to place the Son somewhere between God and creation, outside of time yet not co-eternal with the Father. Nonetheless, he was forced to profess that the Son was, therefore, a creature and not God" (*The Same Jesus*, 107). In the same revealing vein, Bernard Sesboüé writes: "Here it is necessary to repeat the conviction of the early Fathers of the Church: either Jesus is the Son of God in the strongest sense or he is only a creature. In such a domain there is no middle ground" (*Jésus-Christ dans la tradition*, 40). "God" and "creature" may form a sharp dichotomy, but what about the copula?

[14] Hallett, *Essentialism*, Chapter 3. "'Invariant-unit reasoning' might be a fitting label for such thinking, but 'calculus-reasoning' is more suggestive. For it is characteristic

Venerable Bede's demonstration that John the Baptist died for Christ: "Does not Christ say: *I am the truth*? Therefore, because John shed his blood for the truth, he surely died for Christ."[15] Such reasoning should give us pause, and probably does. It is as though Bede were operating a verbal calculus in which all the items—including the terms "am" and "truth"—had a single, undeviating sense or application from sentence to sentence and context to context. For Bede's reasoning to work, the copula in "I am the truth" would have to state a strict identity; yet it is not evident how it might plausibly do so. In Christological debate, similar reasoning abounds. For example, evident similarity links Bede's mode of thinking with Novatian's: "If Christ is God, and Christ died, then God died."[16] Such logic has elicited few qualms in many.[17] And yet, to cite Chapter 1's example, suppose it were said that Jesus was Elijah, and suppose that the meaning of the assertion were the one suggested by Luke 1:17, that Jesus came in the spirit and power of Elijah. Would it follow, for example, that if Jesus died on the cross, then Elijah, too, was crucified? No, what Novatian's argument needs and apparently assumes is strict identity: all traits must be shared, if Jesus *is* God.[18]

In Hilary, notoriously, all traits receive like treatment and SIS reveals its pervasive power. Hilary's first premise is the same as Novatian's: "The man Christ Jesus the only-begotten God, by flesh and the Word both Son of Man and Son of God, assumed the true man according to the likeness of our manhood without departing from being God."[19] From this explicit premise, together with an implicit SIS reading of "being God," Hilary concludes (in R. P. C. Hanson's partial summation):

> Christ could not have been afraid; he could not have been "sorrowful unto death." He could not have seriously asked that the cup should pass from him. The utterance "My God, my God why hast thou forsaken me?" could not have meant any consciousness

---

of various calculi—propositional, predicate, mathematical, and others—to employ invariant units (the *p*'s and *q*'s of propositional logic, the phi's and psi's of predicate logic, and so forth), and to value their invariance as permitting valid reasoning without regard for context. Within such calculi, calculus-reasoning is appropriate; for there the units are invariant. It becomes inappropriate when the units are the concepts of any natural language" (ibid., 48).

[15] St. Bede, *Hom.* 23 (CCL 122, 354; translation from the Roman Breviary for August 29).

[16] Novatian, *De Trinitate* 22, 25 (Tapia, *The Theology of Christ*, 85).

[17] "The argument was a sheer logical exercise, an analysis of propositions" (Helminiak, *The Same Jesus*, 130). "Although it seems illogical to attribute birth to God, who according to most theological definitions has no beginning and cannot experience any process of becoming, if Jesus is fully God, then when Jesus is born, logic requires us to say that God is born and to be willing to call Mary, his mother, the 'God-bearing one'" (H. Brown, *Heresies*, 172). Logic so requires, with one little addition: SIS.

[18] In the words of C. J. F. Williams (quoted by Morris at the start of *The Logic of God Incarnate*), "No relationship is adequate to unite the Son of Mary with the Son of God except the relationship of numerical identity."

[19] Hilary, *De Trin.* 10.23 (CCL 62A, 477).

of the absence of God's presence. The cross represented no weakness and no disgrace. In short "although suffering was inflicted on the body, yet it did not introduce the quality of pain into the body.". . ."Sorrowful unto death" meant sorrowful in such a way that death would terminate the sorrow. Jesus was omniscient because he was God. He was sad not for himself but for his apostles. The bloody sweat was no sign of weakness. He did not need any comfort. And so Hilary continues to the end of the tenth book . . .[20]

The same two premises, explicit and implicit, that begot these conclusions led some seventeenth-century writers to infer that Jesus must have been *the* supreme mathematician, doctor, orator, philosopher, and so on. If Jesus was God, then he knew what God knew; there could be no difference between them. And any human who knew that much about everything would be supreme in every field.[21]

Those familiar with theological literature will have met reasoning of this abundant variety. They will also have encountered passages which, with respect to "Jesus is God" or "Jesus is God the Son," ask *how* such a thing is possible but do not pause to inquire *what* relationship is indicated by the connective "is." Momentous consequences follow.

> The question, then, [writes John Hick] is whether it makes coherent sense to hold that Jesus Christ had both all essential divine and all essential human attributes, so as to be both fully God and fully man. On the face of it, this does not make sense. For how could anyone have both divine omniscience and human ignorance, divine omnipotence and human weakness, divine goodness and human temptability, divine omni-presence and a finite human body?[22]

If Jesus *is* both God and man, then surely (many suppose) Jesus possesses all these apparently contradictory properties. For the copula seems clear enough and rigidly defines the relationship. Any flexibility must reside in one or the other term of the relation. Given these limited options, some find insufficient flexibility in the terms joined and conclude that the doctrine is incoherent, while others modify the terms of the relation so as to resolve, or at least mitigate, the apparent incoherence. The prevalence of these alternative solutions powerfully suggests the pervasive influence of SIS.[23]

Consider first some denials. For Don Cupitt, to declare that the eternal God and a historical man—"two beings of quite different ontological status"—are identical is

---

[20] R. Hanson, *Search*, 499-500.

[21] R. Brown, *Jesus God and Man*, 44-45.

[22] Hick, *Disputed Questions*, 66.

[23] That is, their prevalence *as* solutions does. Many have lost interest in the formulations which give rise to problems of identity (Henry, *Identity*, 89-94). Yet the present discussion is not completely irrelevant to contemporary concerns. Henry comments: "Whatever complaints there may be that Chalcedon did not fully or adequately grasp the riches of Christology, the fact remains that most evangelically orthodox, like traditional Catholic, theologians have shown little desire to undo the Chalcedon Definition" (ibid., 95).

simply unintelligible.[24] For John Hick, as for Spinoza, such an assertion is comparable to "This circle is a square."[25] For John Knox, it is "impossible, by definition, that God should become a man."[26] In Anthony Hanson's view, such a belief states "an impossible antinomy."[27] Jesus' divinity is impossible, writes Georges Morel, "since the concept of the incarnation of God contradicts the essence of man and of God."[28] Less categorically, Maurice Wiles judges that *"Prima facie* at least there is a case of self-contradiction involved."[29] And substituting "Jesus is God the Son" for "Jesus is God" does not resolve the difficulty. As Thomas Morris notes, the latter formulation, like the former, is "commonly rejected as false because it is believed to stand in violation of the indiscernibility principle governing identity statements. Because of what God and men are, the charge goes, we can know that, as a man, Jesus had properties any divine being lacks, and that, conversely, any divine being has properties that Jesus lacked."[30] Abandon the supposition of strict identity and no contradiction would appear. But, for reasons we shall examine, either explicitly or implicitly that option has often been excluded.

Theologians have long struggled with the resulting impasse. Thus the history of heresy in the early Church, it has been suggested, "may almost be read as several attempts to avoid the charge of self-contradiction."[31] Ebionism, adoptionism, and Arianism diminish or deny Christ's Godhead. Docetism, Apollinarianism, mono-

---

[24] Cupitt, "The Finality of Christ," 625.

[25] Hick, "Jesus and the World Religions," 178. Cf. Hick, "Incarnation and Atonement," 83. C. S. Evans notes: "Hick does not provide any argument for the accusation, and he has in fact recently retreated from the claim that the doctrine of the incarnation is logically incoherent, in favour of the weaker charge that no one has successfully stated a coherent version of the doctrine that is also religiously satisfying" (*The Historical Christ*, 121, citing Hick, *The Metaphor of God Incarnate*, 3-4).

[26] Knox, *Humanity*, 67.

[27] A. Hanson, *Grace and Truth*, 76.

[28] Morel, *Questions d'homme*, 125.

[29] Wiles and McCabe, "The Incarnation," 543. See C. Williams, "A Programme for Christology," 515, 522.

[30] Morris, *The Logic of God Incarnate*, 21.

[31] Herbert, *Paradox and Identity in Theology*, 87. Cf. Temple, "The Divinity of Christ," 229-30, and C. Williams, "A Programme for Christology," 515 ("All these theories then can be seen as attempts to avoid the apparent inconsistency of asserting of one and the same Christ that he is at once truly God and truly, completely, without any compromise, a man"). An alternative perspective is equally though less evidently relevant: "When either one or the other, either the deity or the humanity, is considered in isolation and its implications systematically developed, a one-sided presentation results, eventually leading to a position the orthodox reject as heresy" (H. Brown, *Heresies*, 160). For example: "Apollinaris argued that Christ himself, in order to be wholly God, had to be immutable (*atreptos*) and thus could not have a human soul, for if so he would have been mutable" (ibid., 163). The underlying logic of such "implications"—the tacit, unacknowledged premise causing or permitting one pole to undermine the other—is SIS.

physitism, and monothelitism diminish or deny Christ's humanity. Many recent efforts take the same two general directions. On one side: "By general consent it is agreed that, if the Incarnation is in truth the invasion of the Triune God into human life, some form of divine self-limitation is involved in this historic process."[32] "If we take seriously the human conditions of the life of Jesus and His personal identity and continuity with the Eternal Word, 'then a Kenotic Christology appears to be indispensable.'"[33] The Son of God "had to shed himself of all aspects of divinity not compatible with human life."[34] On the other side, Morris has argued that most problems with Leibniz's laws can be solved once we recognize that there is no compelling reason to suppose that all the ways in which human beings are in fact limited—say with respect to knowledge, power, and goodness—pertain to the very nature of humanity.[35] Most people, for example, do not exist before their birth; but that may be just a shared trait of human beings, not an essential, necessary property.[36] This antithetical solution of Morris's, diminishing Jesus' humanity rather than his divinity, has led one reviewer to comment: "If the only constituents of the human nature Christ takes on are those properties essential to human beings but not incompatible with any divine properties, what I share with Christ as regards human nature seems rather meager."[37] Thus, back and forth (from minimal divinity to minimal humanity) the pendulum swings, to avoid resting squarely in apparent contradiction.

Such is the power of SIS. Most theologians who have conducted the debate in this fashion have not attended to the default setting in their thinking, nor have they offered arguments for maintaining it. Insofar as reasons are given nowadays, they tend to take the following (Anglophone) form. The word "is" may function variously—to state existence, to describe, or to identify. But the "is" of identity, if "literal," is strictly Leibnizian (that is, governed by indiscernibility); otherwise it is "figurative," "metaphorical," "non-literal." Since the orthodox, Chalcedonian identity is not merely figurative or metaphorical, it must be Leibnizian. That, therefore, is the only kind of identity we need seriously consider in discussing the

---

[32] Taylor, *The Person of Christ*, 258.

[33] Ibid., 269, quoting Creed, "Recent Tendencies," 136. Cf. Anderson, *The Mystery of the Incarnation*, 146: "if the eternal Logos/Son was really incarnate in the man Christ Jesus . . . this must necessarily have involved a very real 'humiliation' or limitation of some sort."

[34] Smedes, *The Incarnation*, 2 (on Gore). Concerning this doctrine of kenosis, Bonhoeffer comments: "A comparison with the Chalcedonian Definition shows that once again an attempt was being made to soften and balance opposites, which were both contradictory and exclusive" (*Christ the Center*, 97).

[35] Senor, "God," 359.

[36] Morris, *The Logic of God Incarnate*, 89.

[37] Stump, Review, 220. "Such logic," writes another reviewer, "leaves one wondering what kind of humanity Jesus really had, and how much resemblance he bears to the rest of the human race . . . " (Weinandy, Review, 370).

doctrine of the Incarnation. Such, roughly, is the thinking often encountered in both critics[38] and defendants[39] of the doctrine. Morris is most explicit:

> The core claim of the traditional Christian doctrine of the Incarnation, the fundamental and most distinctive tenet of the Christian faith as defined at the Council of Chalcedon (A.D. 451), is the claim that the person who was and is Jesus of Nazareth is one and the same individual as God the Son, the Second Person of the divine Trinity—a literal statement of absolute, numerical identity. As an identity statement, it, like any other such statement, stands under the requirement of indiscernibility. It is not true unless Jesus had all and only the properties of some divine being, in particular the individual referred to in Christian theology as God the Son.[40]

A response to this apologia for the SIS setting in Christology might challenge the underlying sharp dichotomy between "literal" and "non-literal" identity. Expressions of identity—"is," "same," and the like, in this and other languages, at this and other times—vary as much as do other expressions; and CRS (the Criterion of Relative Similarity) applies to them as much as it does to others. But CRS draws no sharp borders between "literal" and "non-literal" uses of terms, nor between "identity" and "nonidentity." Thus SIS reflects an arbitrary fixation or terminological restriction, not any fact of logic or semantics. No a priori ground warrants or requires that all identity be equated with "absolute, numerical identity."

Well and good, in general. Yet if, specifically with regard to the Incarnation, the most authoritative sources of Christian belief do require that strict supposition, then it would seem that Morris and other defendants are right to continue their search for a solution of the resulting dilemma, and critics may be right in rejecting all their efforts. The really crucial question, therefore, demanding full consideration, is whether either the New Testament or the Council of Chalcedon, which Morris invokes, does indeed so define this central Christian belief. Does SIS, at least in this instance, have authoritative backing?

New Testament Soundings

"There is much truth," writes Raymond Brown, "to Athanasius' contention that the Nicene definition that Jesus was God and not a creature 'collects the sense of Scripture.'"[41] On the other hand, there is also much truth in Maurice Wiles's contention that "[t]he outstanding characteristic of the witness of Scripture in the

---

[38] Cf., e.g., Cupitt, "Jesus and the Meaning of 'God,'" 36; Hick, *Disputed Questions*, 76.

[39] E.g., Macquarrie, *Jesus Christ in Modern Thought*, 117. Cf. Badham, "Meaning," 90-91.

[40] Morris, *The Logic of God Incarnate*, 17-18.

[41] R. Brown, "Does the New Testament," 546.

matter is its ambiguity."[42] Many pertinent passages do not suggest Jesus' divinity or equality with the Father, much less strict identity with God or God the Son. Hence, for possible evidence of strict identity, we cannot consult the overall impression conveyed by the New Testament but must instead consider individual texts.

The fourth gospel appears our likeliest source. If strict identity is not to be found there, either in the prologue or in Thomas's closing confession (Jn 20:28), it is not likely to be found anywhere in the New Testament.[43] And since the pro-logue, as long understood, is most explicit—"The Word was God" (Jn 1:1) and "The Word was made flesh" (Jn 1:14)—let us start with it.[44] No verse mentions Jesus by name, yet the implication is clear: the Word which was God and which was made flesh became incarnate in Jesus. Accordingly, there are two identities to be considered: first the Word's identity with God, then Jesus' identity with the Word.

Concerning the former identity, stated in verse one, John Macquarrie observes:

> We have two statements, which on the surface appear contradictory: "The Word was with (*pros*) God, and the Word was God." When we say "The Word was with God," that seems to imply that God and the Word are two distinct, though closely related, entities. When we say "The Word was God," that seems to imply that God and the Word are one, or are identical. By this subtle use of language, John is in effect saying that the Word, as coming forth or proceeding from the Father, is distinct; yet, when he immediately adds, "The Word was God," he seems to be virtually identifying God and Word. But is this not entirely true to the "apt and beautiful" metaphor he is using? When I speak a word, that word acquires a kind of separateness or independence, it has been "uttered" or externalized, it can be heard and appropriated by others, it can even be written down. It has "proceeded" from the speaker, to use a traditional theological term. Yet in another way that word is still an extension or part of the speaker, it is my word in which I have expressed myself. In this sense a word is, to use another traditional term of theology, "of the same being" (*homoousios*) as the one who speaks it.[45]

---

[42] Wiles, *The Making of Christian Doctrine*, 162.

[43] Cf. Cullmann, *The Christology of the New Testament*, 308; M. Harris, *Jesus as God*, 271; Macquarrie, *Jesus Christ in Modern Thought*, 47. Concerning Heb 1:8-9, R. Brown comments: "Of course, we have no way of knowing what the 'O God' of the psalm meant to the author of Hebrews when he applied it to Jesus" ("Does the New Testament," 563). A broader, alternative focus to the one I shall adopt is that suggested by Schnackenburg, *Jesus in the Gospels*, 310-11: "Jesus' divine sonship, in addition to his Messiahship and closely connected with it, is the main bearing column of the early Christian confession of Christ." Schnackenburg straightway comments, pertinently: "Now, *Son of God* is an analogous mode of expression adopted from the human realm, which cannot claim freedom from ambiguity." However, this much is clear: the analogy does not suggest, much less imply, strict identity between Father and Son.

[44] The majority of scholars prefer "The Word was God" to "The Word was divine." See Carson, *The Gospel according to John*, 117.

[45] Macquarrie, *Jesus Christ in Modern Thought*, 108-09. To the same effect, see ibid., 44; Boismard, *St. John's Prologue*, 8-9; Brodie, *The Gospel according to John*, 136-

Exegetical digging does not resolve this surface antinomy between distinctness and identity, and point in the direction of identity alone, still less does it point in the direction of strict identity. Thus C. H. Dodd, in general agreement with most recent scholarship, has written:

> The opening sentences . . . of the Prologue are clearly intelligible only when we admit that λόγος, though it carries with it the associations of the Old Testament Word of the Lord, has also a meaning similar to that which it bears in Stoicism as modified by Philo, and parallel to the idea of Wisdom in other Jewish writers. It is the rational principle in the universe, its meaning, plan or purpose, conceived as a divine hypostasis in which the eternal God is revealed and active.[46]

This principle, meaning, plan, or purpose, this hypostasis in which God is revealed and active, is not strictly identical with God. Things can be said of God which cannot be said of it, and things can be said of it which cannot be said of God. Some passages, it is true, suggest more strongly than others an identity of Wisdom or God's Word with God. Brown notes, for example: "If like Prov 8:22, Sir 24:9 speaks of the creation of Wisdom, the more Hellenistically patterned Wis 7:25-26 describes Wisdom as an aura of the might of God, a pure effusion of the glory of the Almighty (compare John 1:14), the effulgence of eternal light."[47] However, even texts such as this one, more favorable to identity of some sort, hardly establish strict identity; and no specific background passage, however suggestive it may be,[48] connects so securely with John's prologue that the sense of Jn 1:1 can be derived from it alone.

Some readers may need no convincing that Jn 1:1 does not teach strict, Leibnizian identity of the Word with God. Still, the point seems worth making. For the other New Testament utterance that might appear most clearly, explicitly to indicate Jesus' divine identity is Thomas's confession, "My Lord and my God" (Jn

---

37; Cullmann, *The Christology of the New Testament*, 266-67; Goergen, *The Jesus of Christian History*, 21.

[46] Dodd, *The Interpretation of the Fourth Gospel*, 280. Cf. Kysar, *The Fourth Evangelist*, 108, citing Brown, Moeller, Braun, and Feuillet. James Dunn, adopting a broader perspective, comments germanely: "This union of Logos christology and Son of God christology, with its possibility of combining the metaphors and imagery appropriate to the personified Wisdom and the idea Logos of pre-Christian Judaism with the more intimate personal language appropriate to talk of Father and Son, became the matrix from which developed the christologies of subsequent centuries—a dynamic combination, but one always in danger of slackening the tension of personal-impersonal and of falling back into either a less personal monotheism or a polytheism of two or more Gods" (*Christology in the Making*, 245). SIS ignores this tension.

[47] R. Brown, *Introduction*, 210.

[48] Boismard cites Is 55:10 as the text "which was perhaps the chief mainspring of St. John's thought" in the prologue, and comments: "This text of Isaias, in which the Word of God really appears as a Person distinct from God, is St. John to the letter" (*St. John's Prologue*, 100).

20:28). And if that confession is read in the light of Jn 1:1, and Jn 1:1 states no strict identity, then neither does the confession state a strict identity. Likewise, if the confession is read in the light of John's gospel as a whole, it need state no strict identity. For, as Jn 1:1 suggests both distinctness and identity, so does the whole fourth gospel. Thus J. M. Creed points out: "The adoring exclamation of St Thomas 'my Lord and my God' (Joh. xx. 28) is still not quite the same as an address to Christ as being without qualification God, and it must be balanced by the words of the risen Christ himself to Mary Magdalene (*v*.17): 'Go unto my brethren and say to them, I ascend unto my Father and your Father, and my God and your God.'"[49] To these words in Jn 20:17 Brown adds Jn 14:28 ("the Father is greater than I") and Jn 17:3 ("that they may know you, the only true God"), "which, prima facie, would not favor equating Jesus with God or putting him on the same level as the Father."[50]

What, then, of Jn 1:14, which speaks, not of God (as in Thomas's confession), but of the Word? If the Word "became flesh" in Jesus, does that imply or suggest that Jesus was strictly identical with the Word? Did the Word "become flesh" in the way a person becomes an artist or a doctor, or rather in the way an actor becomes a character in a play, or perhaps in the way a mental word "takes flesh" and becomes a spoken word—physical, audible, accessible to all, hence not strictly identical with the word from which it proceeded? How is the Greek term *egeneto* to be understood? John does not say. Hymns, such as the one John's prologue apparently incorporates, do not usually draw fine distinctions. And the prologue itself should not be read as a treatise in metaphysics. "This conjunction of divine and human, Logos and flesh, God and a man, is nowhere defined or analysed by St John; it is simply part of his witness that this Jesus is the God-man through faith in whom men may have eternal life."[51] Thus Pheme Perkins can summarize:

> John has not explained the "how" of Jesus' extraordinary relationship with the Father. He has simply and unmistakably set out the terms in which the relationship should be discussed. Jesus is one with the Father and is the son sent by him. He is "only begotten God" (1:18) and "Word become flesh" (1:14). He is divine and also a real human person, who died and was buried like others. Much of the debate about christology in the following centuries attempts to articulate in conceptual terms the vision of Jesus which John has presented in symbolic ones.[52]

When, however, subsequent debate supposes strict identity between Jesus and God or Jesus and God the Son, it goes beyond John; for that is not among the parameters which he "simply and unmistakably" set out.

---

[49] Creed, *The Divinity of Jesus Christ*, 123.

[50] R. Brown, *Introduction*, 193. On the resultant "Johannine paradox" of distinction-within-unity, see Pollard, *Johannine Christology*, 17-18.

[51] Pollard, *Johannine Christology*, 19.

[52] Fuller and Perkins, *Who Is This Christ?*, 105. See Schnackenburg, *Jesus in the Gospels*, 292; Dunn, *Christology in the Making*, 58.

The assumption of strict identity also goes beyond other likely ascriptions of divinity to Jesus in the New Testament. Concluding a review of such passages, Brown remarks: "As far as I can see, none of the eight instances we have discussed attempts to define Jesus metaphysically. The acclamation of Jesus as God is a response of prayer and worship to the God revealed in Jesus."[53] How, then, we may ask, did the acclamation arise? If we trace this worshipful response back to its source, may we there discern more clearly the reality expressed in such sayings as Jn 1:1 and Jn 20:28?

Murray Harris suggests that "if John 20:28 has a claim to historical reliability, it is natural to associate the origin of the christological use of θεός with the resurrection appearances of Christ."[54]

> As later with Paul, a personal appearance of the risen Christ caused a drastic change of attitude that led to the recognition of the divinity of Jesus. In John 2:22 the evangelist notes that the resurrection transformed the disciples' spiritual perception. For Paul, Jesus "was designated Son of God in power . . . through his resurrection from the dead" (Rom. 1:4); for Thomas and John, he was shown to be "God" by his resurrection from the dead.[55]

Without relying on the historical accuracy of John 20:24-29, many others have attached similar significance to Jesus' resurrection.[56] According to Norman Anderson, Jesus' rising from the dead "was almost certainly the basic reason why the disciples began to confess that 'Jesus is Lord,' to apply to him references to Yahweh in the Old Testament, and to have no hesitation in worshipping him and addressing him in prayer."[57] Karl-Josef Kuschel agrees:

> One basic insight here is decisive for systematic theology: it was only after Easter, on the basis of the conviction that God himself had not left the righteous man from Nazareth in death, that the followers of Jesus will have become really deeply "aware" of who Jesus essentially always was: not yet one more prophet, man of God, son of God, teacher of the law and wisdom, but *the* emissary, *the* word, *the* wisdom, *the* Son of God.[58]

But Jesus' being God himself, or God the Son, in indiscernible identity—was that revealed by Jesus' resurrection? Was that part of the disciples' original awareness?

---

[53] R. Brown, *Introduction*, 195.

[54] M. Harris, *Jesus as God*, 278.

[55] Ibid., 279.

[56] E.g., R. Brown, *Introduction*, 105, 109, 113, 115; Dunn, *Christology in the Making*, 36; Longenecker, *Christology*, 149; Marchi, *La cristologia in Italia*, 319-20; McDermott, *Word Become Flesh*, 159, 175; McGrath, *Understanding Jesus*, 16, 92; Moingt, "Christology," 66; Pannenberg, *Jesus—God and Man*, 321-22.

[57] Anderson, *The Mystery of the Incarnation*, 70.

[58] Kuschel, *Born Before All Time?*, 492.

The answer depends on how the disciples interpreted the paschal experience;[59] and the dominant New Testament perspective is the one that runs through Acts 13:

> "We bring you the good news that what God promised to our ancestors he has fulfilled for us, their children, by raising Jesus; as also it is written in the second psalm,
>> 'You are my Son; today I have begotten you.'
> As to his raising him from the dead, no more to return to corruption, he has spoken in this way,
>> 'I will give you the holy promises made to David.'
> Therefore he has also said in another psalm,
>> 'You will not let your Holy One experience corruption'" (32-34).

God raised Jesus from the dead; Jesus did not raise himself. And the one who did the raising was not identical with the one raised. This perspective, repeated nineteen times in the New Testament,[60] alters partially in John 2:19-21 and 10:17-18: Jesus himself will rebuild the temple of his body; Jesus himself will lay down his life and take it up again. However, even in these verses, neither identity with the Father is suggested ("For this reason the Father loves me, because I lay down my life in order to take it up again") nor is equality with the Father ("I have received this command from my Father"). Here as elsewhere, John's portrayal of Jesus balances the human and the divine.

Influenced by John, subsequent discussion swung from side to side. Thus, apropos of John 10:30 ("The Father and I are one"), Brown comments:

> On one extreme, the Monarchians (Sabellians) interpreted it to mean "one person," although the "one" is neuter, not masculine. On the other extreme, the Arians interpreted this text, which was often used against them, in terms of moral unity of will. The Protestant commentator Bengel, following Augustine, sums up the orthodox position: "Through the word 'are' Sabellius is refuted; through the word 'one' so is Arius."[61]

This balancing resembles that in Jn 1:1. There, "with" contrasts with "is," suggesting both distinctness and identity. Here, "are" contrasts with "one," suggesting a similar bipolarity. Neither here in John 10:30, nor elsewhere in the fourth gospel, nor elsewhere in the New Testament, do we find any clear indication of strict incarnational identity, equating Jesus indiscernibly with God or God the Son.

---

[59] Cf. Badham, "Meaning," 89: "I would be prepared to acknowledge that if one already had an exalted concept of the person of Christ, then belief in his resurrection might well serve as the coping stone holding together the edifice of personal faith in him. But taken on its own, it simply cannot carry the weight placed upon it by so many contemporary Christian scholars."

[60] R. Brown, *The Gospel According to John,* vol. 1, 116.

[61] Ibid., 403.

At this stage of inquiry, the image that suggests itself is that of an asteroid plunging into the sea and sending out waves, concentrically, to distant shores. The waves locate the point of impact and, by their height, reveal its power; but they do not reveal the asteroid's shape. So it is here. Already in John, Paul, and Hebrews—indeed still earlier[62]—the Christological waves run high, and by their height reveal the power of Jesus' impact.[63] But they do not reveal his precise nature, status, or relationship to God. Thus Charles Moule writes: "The evidence, as I read it, suggests that Jesus was, *from the beginning*, such a one as appropriately to be described in the ways in which, sooner or later, he did come to be described in the New Testament period—for instance, as 'Lord' and even, in some sense, as 'God.'"[64] Yes, "in some sense." But nothing in Scripture permits the inference: "Jesus is strictly identical with God," or, "Jesus is strictly identical with God the Son."

To some readers, the preceding sampling may appear to have belabored the obvious. However, I have also encountered the contrary impression, which suggests a possible misunderstanding. I have not argued that a strict-identity reading is incompatible with Scripture (that would, indeed, require fuller demonstration), but that Scripture by no means demands such a reading. Claims for the "orthodoxy" of a strict construal must therefore turn elsewhere for backing. And indeed, Morris did not cite the New Testament as evidence for strict identity; he cited Chalcedon. So let us turn to Chalcedon.

Chalcedonian Orthodoxy

The Council's confession of faith reads as follows:

> In agreement, therefore, with the holy fathers, we all unanimously teach that we should confess that our Lord Jesus Christ is one and the same Son, the same perfect in Godhead and the same perfect in manhood, truly God and truly man, the same of a rational soul and body, consubstantial with the Father in Godhead, and the same consubstantial with us in manhood, like us in all things except sin; begotten from the

---

[62] Macquarrie, *Jesus Christ in Modern Thought*, 45.

[63] Cf. France, "The Worship of Jesus," 24-25; Taylor, *Names of Jesus*, 164-65; Moule, "Comment," 149-50, and *The Origin of Christology*, 6-7: "When one asks, Who could Jesus have been, to affect his disciples and their successors in the ways in which he did? the 'evolutionary' type of answer, plausible though it may seem at first, seems less than adequate. More adequate is an answer which finds, from the beginning, a Person of such magnitude that, so far from pious imagination's embroidering and enlarging him, the perennial problem was, rather, how to reach any insight that would come near to fathoming him, or any description that was not pitifully inadequate. Successive attempts at word-painting are (as I read the evidence) not evolving away from the original. They are all only incomplete representations of the mighty Figure that has been there all the time."

[64] Moule, *The Origin of Christology*, 4.

Father before the ages as regards his Godhead, and in the last days, the same, because of us and because of our salvation begotten from the Virgin Mary, the *Theotokos* [God-bearer], as regards his manhood; one and the same Christ, Son, Lord, only-begotten, made known in two natures without confusion, without change, without division, without separation, the difference of the natures being by no means removed because of the union, but the property of each nature being preserved and coalescing in one *prosopon* [person] and one *hypostasis* [subsistence], not parted or divided into two *prosopa*, but one and the same Son only-begotten, divine Word, the Lord Jesus Christ, as the prophets of old and Jesus Christ himself have taught us about him and the creed of our fathers has handed down.[65]

The Council says that Jesus is "truly God and truly man"; it does not say that he "truly is" God or "truly is" God the Son. It primarily targets the fullness of the divinity and the fullness of the humanity, not the fullness or strictness of the identity (it does not insist, for example, on indiscernibility or on the reversibility of the relationship). Here, as in Matthew and Mark, interest still centers on the "who" more than on the "am" in "Who do you say I am?"—that is, more on the term of the relationship than on the relationship and *its* nature. Furthermore, as scholars have noted, with respect to identity the formula's emphasis is more critical and eliminative than constructive. "Its terms are not calculated to picture the way in which Jesus is put together."[66]

True, the Council speaks of a single *prosopon* and a single *hypostasis*, but that takes us no farther, ontologically, than it would as an explanation of "Jesus is Elijah." Consider the former Greek term. Though its sense is elusive, doubtless Jesus and Elijah both qualify as *prosopa* (roughly, individual selves in social relation[67]). And if Jesus is Elijah, then Jesus and Elijah may in some sense be the same *prosopon*—spatio-temporally, spiritually, functionally, metaphysically, or however. But what, in this instance, *is* the criterion of identity? What *is* the nature of the union? There would lie the mystery—for Jesus and Elijah.

Fortunately, we possess much fuller clues to go by for Chalcedon than for the gospel saying. We can turn, for example, to Leo's *Tome* or to Flavian's profession of faith, from which the formula "one prosopon and one hypostasis" was lifted. Or we can turn to Cyril, as Morris does in his argument for incarnational indiscernibility. "The only purpose of denying indiscernibility," he writes,

> would be to allow that there are some properties Jesus had but God the Son lacked, and vice versa. It is hard to see how in the end such a view could avoid the condemnation of Cyril, bishop of Alexandria (412-444), who attacked the Nestorians for allowing such distinctions between Jesus and God the Son, saying: "If anyone distributes between two characters or persons the expressions used about Christ in the

---

[65] J. Kelly, *Early Christian Doctrines*, 339-40 (bracketed words added as in Inwagen, *God, Knowledge, and Mystery*, 262).

[66] Norris, *The Christological Controversy*, 30-31. Cf. Relton, *A Study in Christology*, 36-38.

[67] D. Brown, "Trinitarian Personhood and Individuality," 51-56.

Gospels, etc. . . . applying some to the man, conceived of separately, apart from the Word . . . others exclusively to the Word . . . let him be anathema." And of course it was the view of Cyril which became recognized as orthodoxy at Chalcedon.[68]

To assess this argument, let me begin with what John McGuckin terms "Cyril's most recurring image of the union of godhead and humanity in Christ."[69] We humans are constituted, Cyril suggests, by the mysterious union of body and soul. The soul is not the body nor the body the soul; each retains its own nature. Nonetheless, the union between them is so intimate, so close, that a single individual results, of whom we readily predicate both physical and spiritual properties. One and the same person, formed of body and soul, possesses both intelligence and intestines. One and the same individual both cheers and rejoices, sits and meditates. To deny any of these ascriptions, or to restrict them to just the soul or just the body ("conceived of separately"), would be to question the closeness of the union that binds body and soul. This is how it is, Cyril suggests, for the single individual formed by the hypostatic union. Using the name "Jesus" for that one, composite individual, we can say that Jesus is divine. Using the name "God the Son" for that same individual, we can say that God suffered and died. But this mode of speech—this "communication of idioms"—implies no confusion between the human and divine terms of the relation, any more than the corresponding mode of speech implies confusion of body and soul in the single human composite.[70]

In a fuller exchange of idioms, one could say of the human component what-ever one could say of the divine component (e.g., "Jesus the man existed from eternity") and vice versa.[71] However, this would be like saying "The body is wise" or "The soul has a toothache," and clashes with Cyril's comparison. The point of the comparison is to stress the close union of human and divine in Christ, resulting in a single subject of attribution, not two. Nestorius erred, in Cyril's eyes, when he singled out a human subject for certain attributions and a divine subject for others (note Morris's quotation, above). Cyril did not react by singling out a human subject for all attributions, transferred and non-transferred, and a divine subject for all the same attributions. When he insisted that God the Word died on the cross, he did not mean to say that God the Word, as distinct from the man who hung there, also died on the cross. He did not (as Chalcedon put it) proclaim "the marvelous

---

[68] Morris, *The Logic of God Incarnate*, 29. The quotation is from Bettenson, *Documents of the Christian Church*, 46.

[69] McGuckin, *St. Cyril of Alexandria*, 198-201, citing: "Scholia 9; Letter to the Monks, para. 12; 1st Letter to Succensus; Explanation of the Twelve Chapters (Expln. 3) and passim." See also *In Jo.* (e.g., PG 74, 344B and 737D).

[70] For fuller discussion of this analogy, see D. Brown, *The Divine Trinity*, 253-54.

[71] Luther sometimes suggests this more thorough-going communication of idioms. See Congar, "*Lutherana*," 186-90.

doctrine" that the Godhead, or divine nature, of the Only-begotten is passible. He meant to stress the indivisible unity of God and man in Christ.[72]

Accordingly, for Cyril the great Christological challenge is not to resolve contradictions arising from ontological indiscernibility, or even from predicational indiscernibility, but to explain the union that warrants the communication of idioms. Such understanding, he insists, will forever elude us. The hypostatic union is entirely "ineffable," "inconceivable," "incomprehensible."[73] How, possibly, could such disparate relata as God and man be so intimately joined as to constitute a single subject of ascription? At best he can offer analogies—the soul-body analogy, or the classical analogy to which he repeatedly has recourse, of an object suffused by fire without being consumed.[74] The comparison with the live coal of Isaiah's vision seemed particularly apt. As J. N. D. Kelly comments, "When the charcoal was penetrated by the fire, each retained its distinct identity; and in the same way the Word remained very Word while appropriating what was human, and the humanity continued unchanged while having the operation of the Word's nature conferred upon it."[75]

Compare this perspective, now, with Morris's. The central claim of the traditional Christian doctrine of the Incarnation, Morris writes, "is the claim that the person who was and is Jesus of Nazareth is one and the same individual as God the Son, the Second Person of the divine Trinity—a literal statement of absolute, numerical identity."[76] This claim, as stated, admits a Cyrillian interpretation. If "Jesus" designates a composite person (both God and man and not just the human component) and if "God the Son" designates the same composite person (both God and man and not just the divine component), "Jesus is God the Son" states a strict identity, as Morris alleges—as strict as for "Tully is Cicero." "Cicero" and "Tully" are two names for the same individual (composed of body and soul); "Jesus" and "God the Son" are two names for the same individual (composed of God and man). In neither case do the names designate distinct individuals who are somehow identical. Thus, in neither case does any shadow of contradiction arise. Morris, however, sees matters differently. In response to contemporary charges of contradiction and incoherence, he does not resort to this simple distinction of reference. He does not reply, "Strict identity does not hold between Jesus the man

---

[72] McGuckin, *St. Cyril of Alexandria*, 153. Cf. Leo, Sermon 28: "in one and the same Son of God and man, there was Godhead 'without mother' and Manhood 'without father'" (*Select Sermons*, 20). Neither Leo nor Cyril would reverse these attributions and speak of "manhood without mother" or "Godhead without father."

[73] "Cyril . . . rarely speaks of the union without characterizing it as 'incomprehensible' . . . or 'ineffable'" (Liébaert, *La doctrine christologique*, 209).

[74] See McGuckin, *St. Cyril of Alexandria*, 197, citing *Apol. ad Theodosium* (PG 76, 408), *Con. Nest.* (PG 76, 56), *Scholia 9* (PG 75, 1398), and *De recta fide ad reginas* (PG 76, 1364).

[75] J. Kelly, *Early Christian Doctrines*, 321, citing *Ep.* 46 (*ad Succens.* 2) and *quod unus* (PG 77, 241; 75, 1292).

[76] Morris, *The Logic of God Incarnate*, 18 (previously quoted).

and God the Son; it holds between the man-God and the God-man—that is, between the composite referent named 'Jesus' and the composite referent named 'God the Son.'" Instead, Morris meets the challenge "head on,"[77] and seeks to remove the apparent contradiction blocking strict identity between the man Jesus and God the Son. Clearly, if the relation that binds God and man is strict identity, something will have to give on one side or the other. For Morris, as we have seen, it is the human side that gives. The most problematic human traits, he suggests, are not essential to a human being and so can be jettisoned without incurring incoherence. In this view, Jesus is an extremely unusual human being, and that is why he can at the same time be God the Son; whereas for Cyril and Chalcedon, Jesus is "like us in all things except sin."

Cyril has an argument which might cast doubt on this contrast between his perspective and Morris's, since it resembles arguments cited earlier as exemplifying SIS. He writes: "That anyone could doubt the right of the holy Virgin to be called the Mother of God fills me with astonishment. Surely she must be the Mother of God if our Lord Jesus Christ is God, and she gave birth to him?"[78] It might seem that this reasoning, like Novatian's, relies on a strict understanding of the copula in "Jesus is God." If the two terms of the identity are indiscernible, then each shares all the traits of the other. If Jesus has a mother, God has a mother. If Mary is Jesus' mother, Mary is God's mother. Loosen the "is"—allow differences between the terms—and the argument would work no better than would Novatian's. Or so it may seem, and in that case Morris may be right about Cyril and therefore about Chalcedon.

This impression arises from taking the subject and predicate terms in a way Cyril refused to take them. To judge by preceding evidence, for Cyril the state-ment "Our Lord Jesus Christ is God" does not join two distinct individuals—Jesus as man and God as God—and proclaim them identical, then draw an inference concerning Mary's motherhood. The union the sentence states creates a single subject of attribution, named by both subject and predicate, as in "Cicero is Tully." And if Mary is the mother of "Jesus," so understood—if she is the mother of the God-Man, then how could anyone doubt "the right of the holy Virgin to be called the Mother of God"?[79]

---

[77] Ibid., 32.

[78] Cyril of Alexandria, *Ep.* 1 (PG 77, 13B). Compare the Council of Nicaea (Bordoni, *Gesù di Nazaret*, vol. 3, 826); the Act of Union of 433 (ibid., 828); St. Sophronius: "If he whom you are to bear is truly God made flesh, then rightly do we call you God's mother. For you have truly given birth to God" (*Oratio* 2.22; PG 87.3, 3241).

[79] Cf. Leo, Sermon 23 ("For this wondrous child-bearing of the Holy Virgin did bring forth as her offspring one Person, truly human and truly Divine; because both substances did not in any such sense retain their properties, as that there could be in them a difference of persons") and Sermon 28 ("Nestorius dared to call the Blessed Virgin Mary the Mother of a man only, so that no union of the Word and the flesh should be believed to have been effected in her conception and child-bearing. . .") (*Select Sermons*, 6 and 23).

Cyril's alternate argument for Mary's divine maternity casts light on the reasons for his position. "Because the crucified one is truly God," he wrote, "and King by nature, and is also called the Lord of Glory (*1 Cor.2.8*), then how can anyone have scruples about calling the holy virgin the 'Mother of God'?"[80] Here, too, SIS plays no evident role, but Cyril appeals to the New Testament's communication of idioms as a basis for his own. The one they crucified, says Paul, is also the Lord of glory. By itself, the latter expression may not take us as far as Cyril wishes, but other expressions leave less doubt: "Blessed Paul," notes Cyril, "said that he who is of the Jews according to the flesh, that is of the line of Jesse and David, is also the Christ, the Lord of Glory (*1 Cor.2.8*), and is 'God ever blessed and over all' (*Rom.9.5*). In this way Paul declared that it was the very own body of the Word which was fixed to the cross, and therefore he attributed the crucifixion to him."[81] Paul did not in fact speak of the Word, but John did, and for Cyril that sufficed. The New Testament, as a whole, exemplified the communication of idioms which he and other Fathers practiced, and thereby prepared the teaching of Chalcedon: one person (the subject of the varied ascriptions) and two natures (revealed by the varied ascriptions). "The same one," writes Cyril, "is perfect in Godhead and perfect in manhood, and we understand him to be in one prosopon, for there is One Lord Jesus Christ (*1 Cor.8.6*), even though we do indeed take cognisance of the difference of natures out of which we say the ineffable union was formed."[82]

Cyril's perspective not only fits the wording of the Council but also reflects the thinking of the time. Others besides Cyril employed the comparison with the union of body and soul.[83] Others employed the comparison with fire and the object it penetrates.[84] And the viewpoint repeatedly revealed by these and other patristic analogies is the same: distinctness of the components but closeness in their union[85]—such closeness that in the case of the Incarnation, a single subject of attribution results[86]: "one and the same Son only-begotten, divine Word, the Lord

---

[80] Cyril, Letter to the Monks of Egypt, 27 (McGuckin, *St. Cyril of Alexandria*, 261). Cf. Cyril, Scholia on the Incarnation, 34 (ibid., 328-29) and Letter to John of Antioch, 8 (ibid., 346-47).

[81] Cyril, Second Letter to Successus (ibid., 362). Cf. Athanasius's Letter to Epictetus, 10 (ibid., 387).

[82] Cyril, Letter to John of Antioch 8 (ibid., 346-47).

[83] E.g., Gregory of Nyssa, "An Address on Religious Instruction," 288; the "Athanasian Creed" (Schaff, *The Creeds of Christendom*, vol. 2, 69); Vincent of Lerins, "The Commonitory," 141; Augustine, *Ep.* 137, 11.2.8 (PL 33, 745-46).

[84] E.g., Origen, *De princ.* 2.6.6. See J. Kelly, *Early Christian Doctrines*, 155; Norris, *The Christological Controversy*, 16.

[85] The closeness is less pronounced in frequent comparisons with clothes and one who wears them, or a temple and one who occupies it, but more evident in comparisons with the Word immanent in the whole world (e.g., Athanasius, *De Inc.* 41) and with stock and graft (e.g., Rusticus, *Contra Acephalos*, PL 67, 1184B).

[86] Gregory of Nyssa, *Contra Eun.* 5 (PG 45, 705), *Adv. Apoll.* (PG 45, 1277); Origen, *On First Principles* 2.6.3; Augustine, *Ep.* 169.2.8 (PL 33, 745-46); Vigilius

Jesus Christ." For Chalcedonian orthodoxy, that is where the mystery lies—not in the humanity nor in the divinity of Jesus (man is man and God is God), but in the relation that binds them and makes them somehow one.

Implications

If, as I have now contended, a SIS reading of the Incarnation enjoys neither scriptural nor conciliar backing, noteworthy consequences follow—consequences which suggest the reason for arguing at length for a conclusion that may have struck some readers as obvious from the start. First, since the supposition of strict identity creates the appearance of contradiction and this supposition has no basis in the New Testament or in tradition, the much-cited appearance of contradiction in the doctrine of the Incarnation is illusory. Second, since the appearance is illusory, defendants of the doctrine can desist from their often unfortunate attempts to circumvent the apparent contradiction. Third, since non-Christians, understandably, are likely to share the impression of contradiction (in part because Christians themselves have betrayed it), removal of the impression has ecumenical as well as apologetic significance.

In this regard, the words of C. Schoeneveld are revealing:

> It seems that Jews and Christians start from two contradictory and mutually exclusive positions, both of which are claimed to be the true understanding of God. The crucial issue between Judaism and Christianity is here the Christian claim that God became Man. For Israel God cannot be man or become man. For the Church, God can be man and does become flesh. Here is the deep gulf: for Judaism God's holiness and power, so to speak, forbid him to be man; for Christianity God's holiness and power, so to speak, enable him to be man. Two different under-standings of God are here at stake; which understanding of God is the true one? If the Jewish understanding of God is the true one, then Christians are idolaters; if the Christian understanding is the true one, then the Jews were blind and unfaithful and did not pay attention to God's gracious visitation to them.[87]

Tapsensis, *Contra Eut.* 1.9 (PL 62, 100). Of the "mixing" of natures in the Christology of Gregory Nazianzus and Gregory of Nyssa, Marcello Bordoni writes: "Such a conception of unity allowed Gregory [Nazianzen] to fully exploit the principle of the 'communication of properties' (*idioms*), speaking of 'God crucified' and of Mary as 'Mother of God' (*Theotókos*) (Ep. 101, 4)" (*Gesu di Nazaret*, vol. 3, 816). Similarly, of Gregory of Nyssa's body-soul comparison Bordoni writes: "Such unity . . . provides the basis for the 'communication of properties' through which the Virgin could be called 'Mother of God' (*Theotókos*; Ep.3: PG 46, 1024) and suffering and death could be attributed to God" (ibid., 817).

[87] Quoted, without exact reference, in Cohn-Sherbok, "Between Christian and Jew," 91.

Here, typically, attention centers on the terms of the relationship rather than on the relationship itself—that is, on the understanding of the God who Jesus is rather than on the sense in which he "is" that God. Hence there arises Schoeneveld's and others' impression of a "deep gulf," of "two contradictory and mutually exclusive positions."[88] However, neither Nicaea nor Chalcedon nor any other council has defined in what sense Jesus *is* God. Neither has any council explained in what sense "God can *be* man or does *become* flesh." That is left a mystery. Once we recognize the depth of this mystery, the conflict loosens; it is SIS that tightens it.

For full ecumenical benefit, such recognition needs to come on both sides, the Christian as well as the Jewish. The like holds for Christian-Moslem relations, troubled from early on by similar misperception of the central Christian mystery. "Were [Jesus] a god," wrote Ṭabarī in his commentary on the Qur'an, "he could not be contained in the womb of his mother, for the creator of what is in the wombs could not be held within one, for such only contain created beings."[89] Were Jesus really God, Fạhr al-Dīn al-Rāzī similarly urged, he could not be born, grow, eat, sleep, wake up, and the like. "It is well established by the most evident reason that one who begins in time is not eternal *a parte ante*, that one who has need does not have the total independence of one who is rich, that the possible is not the necessary and that the changing does not exist forever."[90] At the very least, Christian belief is riddled with contradictions; at the worst, it is blasphemous idolatry. To address such perceptions, it does not suffice to have recourse to mystery while leaving the impression of contradiction intact. That impression must be removed, by eliminating the assumption that begets it. The hypostatic union is not Leibnizian identity.

---

[88] "Here is where the fundamental disagreement between Christianity and Judaism comes to the fore" (Pawlikowski, *Christ in the Light*, 117, on the thought of Abraham Heschel).

[89] Quoted in Charfi, "Christianity," 130. See ibid., 131.

[90] Quoted (in French) in Jomier, "Unité de Dieu," 157.

Chapter 3

Incarnation and Mystery

The last chapter had a negative outcome: neither Scripture nor Chalcedon backs the assumption of strict God-man identity in Christ. What, now, can be said more positively about Jesus' identity, within the chosen focus of this study? In what sense can we affirm that Jesus *is* God? It has been said that Chalcedon "made crystal clear" the Christian point of view,[1] that it provides "an extremely precise version" of what we encounter in the New Testament,[2] that in the Council's definitive statement "the Church 'lays bare the intrinsic nature and constitutive reason' of the mystery."[3] Yet the Council's formulation does not attempt to explain the mysterious union it so strongly affirms. For some, therein lies its merit[4]: "The very failure of the Definition to solve the insolvable is its best recommendation to our careful consideration."[5] For others, the definition's failure signaled the bankruptcy of Greek patristic theology. "The Fathers had done the best that could be done with the intellectual apparatus at their disposal. Their formula had the right devotional value; it excluded what was known to be fatal to the faith; but it explained nothing."[6] Others question the Council's whole structure of thought—"the pattern of the two natures in Christ"[7]—and recommend "a change of viewpoint that leaves the Chalcedonian problematic behind."[8] Today, "it seems urgent to suggest some further representations that arise clearly out of the contemporary Christian praxis and a critical reflection upon it."[9] Still others take a more positive view of

---

[1] McGrath, *Understanding Jesus*, 104.

[2] Kasper, *Jesus the Christ*, 238. Cf. Helminiak, *The Same Jesus*, 99, 110, 136; Hünermann , *Jesus Christus*, 175: "In its austere architectonic and conceptual precision, the whole formula proves itself a masterpiece."

[3] Galtier, *L'Unité du Christ*, 85. Cf. Sesboüé, *Jésus-Christ dans la tradition*, 25: "The Christian is not a person who relates to Jesus of Nazareth somehow or other; he is one who, at the heart of his faith in Jesus' regard, affirms something very precise in his regard."

[4] Taylor, *The Person of Christ*, 273; Skarsaune, *Incarnation*, 133.

[5] Relton, *A Study in Christology*, 36.

[6] Temple, "The Divinity of Christ," 230. For Temple's second thoughts, see his *Christus Veritas*, 134, and Need, *Human Language*, 4.

[7] Schoonenberg, *The Christ*, 52. Cf. Richard, *What Are They Saying*, 40-41 (on Küng); H. Williams, "Incarnation," 7-9.

[8] Haight, *Jesus, Symbol of God*, 290.

[9] Hellwig, *Jesus the Compassion of God*, 121. "There is every reason to hope," writes Herbert McCabe, "that the modern Church enlightened by a whole range of insights

the Council's limitations and, striking a balance, see it as "more a beginning than an end."[10] Further perspectives beckon, they agree, but even within the parameters set by the Council perhaps persevering inquiry may achieve a deeper understanding of the hypostatic union.[11]

In some quarters, such deepening is seen as not only desirable but mandatory. "A contemporary Christian committed to some version of Chalcedonian orthodoxy is thereby faced with both an apologetic and a positive challenge: she must defend the one person-two natures doctrine against its critics while also offering some particular and constructive model or picture of the Incarnation itself."[12] To be sure, "If the problem as thus defined contained no inconsistencies and seeming contradictions, there would be no need for further investigation. It would be solved!"[13] However, such (it is claimed) is not the case. "Unless *some* element of continuity can be alleged, nobody knows what is being stated, and 'the Word became a man of flesh and blood' is apparently not sense."[14] In reply to such assertions, it can be noted that if the Council's pronouncements satisfy CRS, they make sense. And if, as argued in the last chapter, the assumption of strict identity is groundless, the pronouncements contain no inconsistencies or seeming contradictions. However, all such concerns aside, what are the prospects for faith that simply seeks fuller understanding of the traditional doctrine?

In the last chapter I suggested that much as the shape of an asteroid plunging into the sea cannot be judged from the height of the outgoing waves or their point of origin, so the exact nature of Jesus' relationship to God cannot be discerned from the successive waves of Christological proclamation in the New Testament. But if the New Testament does not indicate the precise nature of the relationship, what are the chances that subsequent theological reflection might detect it? If the asteroid comparison is apt, later waves will be no more revealing than the first ones. But is the comparison apt? How impenetrable is the mystery expressed by the Chalcedonian formula or by the simple profession "Jesus is God"?

Prospects for Understanding

To some extent, contrasting judgments like those just quoted for and against Chalcedon ("extremely precise," "nobody knows what is being stated") reflect Chapter 1's distinction between metaphysical analysis and genuine understand-ing.

---

from Darwin to Heidegger will come up with new and more illuminating ways of presenting the mystery of Jesus" (Wiles and McCabe, "The Incarnation," 547).

[10] O'Collins, *Interpreting Jesus*, 180 (echoing Rahner). See Bordoni, *Gesù di Nazaret*, vol. 3, 844-45.

[11] Kasper, *Jesus the Christ*, 241.

[12] Feenstra and Plantinga, *Trinity, Incarnation and Atonement*, 11.

[13] Relton, *A Study in Christology*, 37-38.

[14] Goulder, "Paradox and Mystification," 54.

Rather than bring greater clarity, added words may only deepen the initial mystery. To illustrate this possibility, I used the saying "Jesus is Elijah," but "Jesus is God" may serve the same illustrative purpose at least as well.

In the New Testament, the saying that comes closest to this simple declaration is Thomas's confession "My Lord and my God!" John's prologue suggests how these words may be understood. The Word is God and Jesus is the Word: there lies the secret of Jesus' divinity; that is how Jesus is God. However, each of these two new identities—of the Word with God and of Jesus with the Word—is as mysterious as the identity explained. Hence, despite the appearance of greater definiteness, the initial mystery is deepened rather than clarified. Two mysteries replace the original one.

Chalcedon reveals the same inverse relationship between analysis and understanding. On the one hand, to the Johannine account it adds greater apparent precision: in Jesus two natures, human and divine, coalesce to form a single *prosopon*, a single *hypostasis*. On the other hand, how the natures coalesce without confusion, in full integrity, and how they form a single *prosopon*, is left mysterious.[15] Indeed, what in this context is meant by the term *"prosopon"* is equally unclear. For example, it is taken for granted that a single *prosopon* cannot consist of multiple *prosopa* (one human and one divine). Yet consider a comparison. In a nontechnical sense, one substance may consist of multiple substances (one human being of many cells, one cell of many molecules, one molecule of many atoms, and so forth). What technical sense of *"prosopon"* precludes similar multiplicity of *prosopa* within a single *prosopon*? It might be simply the sense which so decrees—that is, which by definitional fiat precludes talk of multiplicity and thereby guards against any semblance of disunity. No split must appear! Or, more acceptably, the sense might be fixed by the specific unity expressed. (Compare a sense of "substance" proper to the human composite, which might preclude a multiplicity of substances within the single human being.) Since, however, the nature of the unity expressed by the Council is deeply mysterious, the sense of *"prosopon"* is, in this supposition, equally mysterious, as are the relations the term is used to express.[16] So here, as in John, despite the apparently greater definiteness, the mystery deepens.[17]

---

[15] "St Cyril had preferred *hypostasis* over the rival term *prosōpon* (*persona* in Latin) which some theologians of Antioch favoured. *Prosōpon* appeared to be somewhat vague and even to preserve something of its original meaning of 'mask.' Nevertheless, Chalcedon incorporated both *hypostasis* and *prosōpon* into its final text" (O'Collins, *Interpreting Jesus*, 18). "The Fathers did not indicate a definite philosophical sense of the terms. . . . To future theology was left the task of elaborating concepts in keeping with this new use of the Greek language" (Bordoni, *Gesù di Nazaret*, vol. 3, 835).

[16] Attempts have been made to fix the term's sense at Chalcedon, but they do not agree. Compare, for example, B. Hill, *Jesus the Christ*, 227 ("The notion of person that was used in the definition views personhood metaphysically, as the center of unity") and Bindley, *The Oecumenical Documents*, 102 ("It will, of course, be understood that by *prosopon* is meant not merely the face or appearance of Jesus Christ but everything that He

In most instances a more definite-sounding account does clarify. Consider, for comparison, the statement "Ice is water" and its explication. As one author observes, "If one assumes as background the theory which identifies various ordinary substances with chemically precise compounds and mixtures, then in the appropriate circumstances, the fact that ice is water can be fully explained by the fact that ice is H_2O."[18] Here, the general nature of the identity is understood, and its specific nature is indicated by identities whose nature is likewise understood: ice is H_2O and water is H_2O. Suppose, however, that we understood neither the nature of the original identity, "Ice is water," nor the nature of the explanatory identities, "Ice is H_2O" and "Water is H_2O." Indeed, suppose we did not even know whether water "is" H_2O in the same sense that ice "is" H_2O. In that case, the proffered explanation would only deepen the original mystery. So it is, for example, in John. The nature of the identity expressed by Thomas's confession is unclear; the nature of the explanatory identities in the Prologue is unclear; and it is not evident whether those identities (explicit and implicit) are of the same general kind—that is, whether the Word "is" God in the same sense that Jesus "is" the Word. Thus, a multiple mystery replaces the single mystery.

Let us return, then, to our previous figure. If, as now suggested, the outgoing waves of theological reflection may be still less revealing than those closer to the point of impact, the question arises still more acutely than before: on a matter as mysterious as the Incarnation, what are the prospects that faith, in its search for understanding, might improve on the New Testament? So phrased, the question calls for a second distinction. It is necessary to discriminate between "improving" in the sense of *articulating* the scriptural teaching and "improving" in the sense of *explaining* the teaching. It may be that the first is possible but not the second.

To illustrate the difference, consider the "communication of idioms." Here, what Scripture had practiced, theologians spelled out. Thus, according to Scholastic doctrine:

---

said or did, thereby manifesting both natures in a common exterior"). According to the International Theological Commission, "Terms such as 'nature' and 'person' which the Fathers of the Council use undoubtedly retain the same meaning in today's parlance" (*Select Questions on Christology*, 9); yet in today's parlance the term is extended by some to zygotes and embryos, while for others "A being is a person . . . if it is self-aware and has beliefs and plans and acts on the basis of those beliefs to execute those plans" (Inwagen, *God, Knowledge, and Mystery*, 246). If the Commission is correct, then the Council Fathers, too, were clutching at clouds in their efforts to articulate the mystery of Christ.

[17] Cf. Moingt, *L'homme qui venait de Dieu*, 628: "From definition to definition, there occurs an extension of the discourse of faith, which has the appearance of a cognitive enrichment or even a deepening or growth of the faith; yet this is more appearance than reality, for this extension is primarily dialectical in nature, which is to say it enriches itself only with the logic of the contradictions it rejects."

[18] Ruben, *Explaining Explanation*, 222.

(1) Concrete divine and human attributes of Christ are interchangeable ("God is man"). (2) Abstract attributes of God and man are not interchangeable and abstract attributes cannot be predicated of those which are concrete; it is false to say, "Christ's humanity is the Word made flesh." (3) A proposition which denies Christ an attribute that is his in virtue of either of his natures is false; thus it is false to say, "The Logos did not die." (4) Expressions designating the "becoming" of hypostatic union cannot be predicated of the man Jesus. It is false to say, "man became God." (5) Derivatives or compounds of "God" or "man" must be treated with caution; Nestorius erroneously says, "Christ is a God-bearing man." (6) Expressions used by heretics should only be used with circumspection; for example, the Arian proposition "Christ is a creature," which is susceptible of a correct interpretation.[19]

Rahner and Vorgrimler comment that "These rules for the communication of properties are, as it were, the translation into logical terms of the reality of the hypostatic union."[20] However, regardless of one's judgment about the accuracy of the translation, the rules thus summarily stated do nothing to *explain* the hypostatic union; at most, they codify its implications for appropriate predication, as exemplified in and backed by the New Testament.

The two distinctions now noted—between analysis and understanding and between articulation and explanation—permit a sharper focus. What are the prospects, we may ask, that theological reflection might provide, not only a more *analytic explanation* or a *clearer articulation*, as at Chalcedon, but also a *clearer explanation* of the "hypostatic union"? Such a query, though doubtless repugnant to some (as betraying too great an interest in an outmoded, "ontological" style of Christology), is not idle. Cyril may have declared the union of two natures in Christ "ineffable," "inconceivable," "incomprehensible," but theologians, while disclaiming any ambition completely to resolve the mystery, have continued their efforts to explain it more fully. To this end, their attention has centered, now on one term of the hypostatic union (Jesus' humanity), now on the other (Jesus' divinity), now on their common bond (Jesus' single personhood), and now on terms and bond together. The following samples illustrate these four approaches and the difficulties which they severally confront.

Jesus' Humanity. Nowadays, a popular perspective is that stated simply, for the Masai of East Africa, by Vincent Donovan:

"But suppose the fullness of time had come and the work of God was perfect, and there appeared a man who was perfectly a man, according to the plan of God, a man completely human. If, once upon a time, there was such a man who was so completely a man, so perfectly human, then there would be no other way to de-scribe him than to say: this man is God—God appearing in the universe. Isn't that so? Jesus was that man."[21]

---

[19] Rahner and Vorgrimler, *Theological Dictionary*, 90.

[20] Ibid.

[21] Donovan, *Christianity Rediscovered*, 75.

"This man is God"—here is the kind of statement that interests us. And Donovan tries to unpack it, in a manner he evidently judges suitable not only for the Masai but also for instructed Christians. Others have sounded the same theme, "Jesus divinest when thou most art man."[22] However, to make any progress toward explaining Chalcedon, we need to clarify three points in such an account: (1) What is meant by describing Jesus as "perfectly human"? (2) Would that entail "Jesus is God"? (3) If so, would the identity thus established coincide with that stated by Scripture or Chalcedon?

With regard to the first question, evidently Donovan does not understand the word "human" as in "human, all too human." Doubtless, too, he does not have Jesus' origin, appearance, stature, health, or bodily strength in view. But what of intelligence or a sense of humor? What about curiosity, creativity, imagination, conviviality, aesthetic appreciation? Do these count as aspects of being "perfectly human"? Of many, varied human excellences, doubtless Donovan has moral perfections primarily in mind, as have others. In Jesus, writes Robinson, we are shown "how a man, and an utterly humiliated man, could nevertheless *be* the self-expression of the wisdom and the power, the freedom and the triumph, of the love that 'moves the sun and other stars.'[23]" It is by being "full of grace and truth" (Jn 1:14) that he reflects the Father's glory.

What, then, of the second question? Does moral perfection, by itself, entail divinity? According to Christian tradition, the angels of God are morally perfect. Further, as spiritual beings, they resemble God more closely than does even a sinless being of flesh and blood. Nonetheless, they are creatures; they are not God. If, then, we try applying the Criterion of Relative Similarity, which of these incompatible terms—"angel" or "God"—should we pick to characterize Jesus? In this confrontation, "angel" comes closer, for Jesus, too, is a creature; but in the confrontation between "angel" and "human being," the latter comes closest of all, for Jesus is a man of flesh and blood. Thus, though flexible, CRS does not endorse Donovan's inference, or others like it.

Jesus' Divinity. In *Christ's Person and Work*, termed the "most persuasive statement" of kenoticism,[24] Gottfried Thomasius explains his position as follows: "I am unable to hold both things firmly together, namely the full reality of the divine and human being of Christ (especially the full truth of his naturally human development of life) on the one hand, and on the other hand the full unity of his divine-human person, without the supposition of a self-limitation of the divine Logos coincident with the incarnation."[25] Treating the unity of human and divine as

---

[22] Myers, *St Paul*, 20; Moule, "The Manhood of Jesus in the New Testament," 98; Robinson, *The Human Face of God*, 208. Cf. Relton, *A Study in Christology*, xix-xx; Serenthà, *Gesù Cristo*, 486.

[23] Robinson, *The Human Face of God*, 208.

[24] Macquarrie, "Kenoticism Reconsidered," 116.

[25] Thomasius, *Christ's Person and Work*, in Welch, *God and Incarnation*, 89.

an irresolvable mystery would not "hold both things firmly together," whereas having the transcendent Word become less transcendent avoids "inner contradiction" and brings the two terms of the human-divine polarity into closer proximity. Nonetheless, Thomasius explains, God does not thereby cease to be God. For the divine attributes willingly surrendered (omnipotence, omnipresence, omniscience) are relative and nonessential, whereas those retained (absolute power and freedom, eternity, absolute holiness, truth, love) are immanent and essential.[26]

In this account, the basic mystery of how God and man form a single person or subject of attribution remains, while other mysteries are added to it: whether and how the Word can surrender omnipotence, omnipresence, and omniscience; whether and how the Word can reclaim the attributes once surrendered; whether, why, and in what sense the one set of traits is "essential" to Godhead and the other set not.[27] One critic of this view may betray too great assurance when, defining God differently ("The work of God in creation, redemption and sancti-fication constitutes a comprehensive statement of the triune being of God"), he concludes that Thomasius's distinction between relative and immanent traits lacks validity.[28] But Thomasius enjoys no more privileged insight into the divine nature, and his distinction is indeed problematic. Consider, for example, his characterization of omniscience as a mere "appearance or outward activation" of the divine essence.[29] The essence is the power, the knowledge is its activation. Now, for humans, who may show no interest in knowledge and spend their days on drugs, this distinction between power and activation makes some sense. But does any similar possibility exist for God, and if it does not, in what sense is the power "essential" and its activation not? Such murky metaphysics cannot mitigate mystery.

More recent formulations of kenoticism have a less metaphysical sound, yet raise similar difficulties. John Macquarrie, fusing the present type of perspective with the preceding, writes:

> The idea of *kenosis* acquires a new relevance and a fuller meaning when we begin with the humiliation of Christ in his earthly and human life, with the self-abasement of the human Jesus as he goes obediently to the cross. For it is this utter self-outpouring that constitutes his glory and that transfigures him so that God-language becomes a necessity if we are to speak of him with any adequacy.[30]

One wonders. Must the language take Chalcedonian form? Does Jesus' human grandeur warrant an identity statement? "When we use God-language about him," Macquarrie replies, "we mean that the self-emptying of Jesus Christ has not only opened up the depth of a true humanity but has made known to us the final reality

---

[26] Ibid., 94.

[27] Cf. Feenstra, "Reconsidering Kenotic Christology," 133-44.

[28] Sykes, "The Strange Persistence," 355.

[29] Thomasius, *Christ's Person and Work*, in Welch, *God and Incarnation*, 94.

[30] Macquarrie, "Kenoticism Reconsidered," 123.

as likewise self-emptying, self-giving, self-limiting."[31] Such resemblance might warrant a certain sort of God-talk (we might call Jesus "God-like"), but it would not warrant the language of identification: his being God-like in his self-surrender would not legitimize the assertion "Jesus is God." Furthermore, whether and how the "final reality" might freely empty or limit itself is no clearer in Macquarrie than in Thomasius. And Scripture does not endorse surmises about whose very possibility it offers no assurance.[32] The ease with which such speculations are often advanced betrays the "words suffice" syndrome noted at the end of Chapter 1.

Jesus' Personhood. Many favor a third course such as Gerald O'Collins charts, centering on Jesus' personhood. "Karl Rahner's now classical observation about Chalcedon being more a beginning than an end," writes O'Collins, "if it holds true about anything, bears on the notion of person. It was to evolve for many centuries: from Boethius (*c*.480-*c*.524) through Richard of St Victor (d.1173), Descartes, and Kant, down to the present."[33] Nowadays, O'Collins suggests, a working account of personhood should include at least the following items:

(a) Persons are distinct and individual beings,
(b) who enjoy rationality and freedom,
(c) exist and act in relationship with other persons,
(d) experience their self-identity in such a relational existence,
(e) and have an inalienable dignity.[34]

Of these developments, O'Collins observes: "I do not want to dramatize out of all proportion the changes which modern times have brought. But we ignore at our peril new or partially new elements in contemporary accounts of personhood."[35]

Behind such contrasting references to Chalcedon and contemporary developments, one frequently intuits a rationale which can be roughly stated as follows. Chalcedon spoke of personal union. But Chalcedon had a flawed or impoverished notion of person (*prosopon*). Therefore we, with our more adequate conception of personhood, can improve on Chalcedon; we can clarify what it means for Jesus to be a single person uniting two natures. This recurring rationale elicits misgivings on two counts. For one thing, traits such as those O'Collins cites may be accretions to our concept "person" more than to our understanding of persons. For another, the contemporary term "person" may have more a historical link than a semantic identity with the Chalcedonian term *"prosopon,"* and the connection with Chalcedon may therefore be illusory. To illustrate these misgivings, consider one such person-centered approach.

---

[31] Ibid., 124.
[32] Sykes, "The Strange Persistence," 360.
[33] O'Collins, *Christology*, 235.
[34] O'Collins, *Interpreting Jesus*, 181.
[35] Ibid., 180.

Walter Kasper appeals to contemporary phenomenology of personal experience "in order finally with the help of this to attain a deeper understanding of the hypostatic union."[36] It must be possible, he suggests, "to move forward from a phenomenology of personal experience to the ontological essence of personality," and therewith "to attain a deeper understanding, with our present-day intellectual assumptions, of the Christological dogma of one person in two natures."[37] Thus, turning from the abstract traditional concept of the person, he proposes this one:

> In the concrete, a person is only actually realized in relationships. The uniqueness of each individual *I* implies its demarcation from any other *I* and therefore a relation to him. Consequently a person only exists in threefold relation: to himself, to the world around, to his fellow men. A person is present to himself by having what is other than him present to him. In concrete terms, the essence of the person is love.[38]

Here, then, is the key to the hypostatic union. Jesus exists, above all, in loving relation to his Father; that is what defines him and fulfills him as a person.[39] ("For all considerations lead always to the same fundamental maxim: the greater the union with God, the greater the intrinsic reality of the man."[40]) Both unity and distinction can be recognized, for example, in Jesus' personal obedience to his Father.

> His utter distinction from "his Father" is expressed in it, and it is the most radical fulfilment of the first commandment, in this way the personal embodiment of God's reign. At the same time, however, his obedience is a response to God's turning in love to him. And so Jesus' radical unity with the Father is also shown here, in this way he is the Father's incarnate love. Because he is nothing as well as, apart from or before this obedience, he is also totally this self-communication of God. God's self-communicating love posits him freely in his own intrinsic human reality.[41]

Granted, Kasper acknowledges, mystery remains. Eventually, both philosophical and theological investigation come up against "an insuperable limit of thought, speech and sympathetic insight."[42] However, "In contradiction to the mystery which dawns at the boundaries of philosophical thought, theology is concerned

---

[36] Kasper, *Jesus the Christ*, 241.

[37] Ibid., 243.

[38] Ibid., 246.

[39] Cf. Sobrino, *Christology at the Crossroads*, 336: "What, then, are we talking about when we talk about the personal unity of humanity and divinity in Jesus? First of all we are saying something that is verifiable. We are saying that Jesus is a person who becomes the person he is precisely through his surrender to the Other who is the Father. The divinity in Jesus is the modality of this personal relationship with the Father, which takes place in history and amid the conflict-ridden reality of history."

[40] Kasper, *Jesus the Christ*, 248.

[41] Ibid.

[42] Ibid., 249.

with a mystery of a certain character, the mystery of an unfathomable love, the very essence of which is to unite what is distinct while respecting the distinction; for love is, in an almost paradoxical way, the unity of two who, while remaining distinct and essentially free, nevertheless cannot exist the one without the other."[43]

Kasper's account elicits the kinds of misgivings already mentioned, plus others. Clearly, if one person loves another, that person is not thereby made identical with the other. If one person loves another very much, this still does not warrant our saying that the one person *is* the other. Besides, in this instance, even if identity did result, it would be with the Father, the object of Jesus' loving obedience, whereas Chalcedon identifies Jesus with the Son, the Word. Concerning that identity, Kasper has little to say. He assures us, for example, that Jesus' humanity is hypostatically united with the *Logos* in a fully human way,[44] but he does not explicate what that way is (Jesus' openness, obedience, and love are directed to the Father, not to the Son), or what the hypostatic unity consists in.

The contrary impression might arise in the manner already suggested. After all, did not Chalcedon define the hypostatic union in terms of personhood, and does not the phenomenology of personal experience furnish us a richer, relational conception of personhood? Does it not follow, then, that a relational account of the kind Kasper suggests must be on the right track? Indeed, how can it be on the wrong track if so much of what he says about the mutual love of Jesus and the Father is correct? In response I would first note that their mutual love is not a recent discovery, uncovered by the phenomenology of experience. Furthermore, tucking that relational content into our contemporary concept of personhood does not show that that is what Chalcedon was talking about. If anything, the notable difference between the phenomenological concept of a Kasper and the metaphysical concept of Chalcedon cuts the connection between them and makes it impossible to claim the backing of Chalcedon for Kasper's explication.

Granted, this conclusion does not follow solely from the fact that one concept differs notably from the other. If Genesis tells us that water covered the earth, and modern science tells us that water is H_2O, we can conclude that (in the biblical account) H_2O covered the earth—even though the author of Genesis knew nothing about H_2O and wrote in an ancient language very different from our own. Here the connection between ancient concept and modern really does hold. And an analogy between "water" and "person" might readily suggest itself: as modern science has given scientific content to the phenomenal concept "water," so (we might think) modern phenomenology has given experiential content to the abstract concept "*prosopon.*" We now know what personhood really consists in. Accordingly, as we can give a more detailed account of the flood than could Genesis, so we can give a more detailed account of the hypostatic union than could Chalcedon.

When made explicit, such a parallel may look far-fetched; but that does not signify that such thinking, unexamined, has not influenced explications of the kind

---

[43] Ibid.

[44] Ibid., 248.

here being considered. For it is not immediately obvious just where and how the suggested parallel between "water" and "person" breaks down. An initial clue, I suggest, is this: whereas the author of Genesis knew nothing about H_2O, early Christians were acquainted with all the items O'Collins and Kasper cite—distinctness, rationality, freedom, self-identity, dignity, loving relationships—clustered in our contemporary notions of personhood. They just did not include them within the concept "*prosopon.*" This omission did not result from mere oversight, as though patristic theologians, lost in metaphysical clouds, failed to notice that people are distinct from one another, relate to one another, and so forth. For their speculative purposes, they needed an abstract concept—abstract enough to unite two very different natures. For this, either "*prosopon*" or "*hypostasis*" would do. It might even be suggested, therefore, that the Fathers at Chalcedon knowingly cut the very connection that current theologians rely on when they propose new understanding of personhood as a key to understanding Chalcedon and its classic formulation of the hypostatic union.

Prescinding from conciliar backing, it may of course be asked whether an account such as Kasper's does not improve on Chalcedon's. But how might we tell? Supposedly by the test of Scripture, and it looks implausible to suggest that any of the New Testament attestations of Jesus' divinity can best be explained in the manner Kasper proposes. (For example, when Thomas exclaims "My Lord and my God!" he is struck by Jesus' risen glory, not by his loving obedience.) Accounts of Jesus' divinity such as Kasper's derive their plausibility from their connection with Chalcedon, and that connection is more apparent than real.

Terms and Bond Together. Thomas Morris's *The Logic of God Incarnate* exemplifies this fourth alternative. He proposes that in Jesus "we must recognize something like two distinct ranges of consciousness. There is first what we can call the eternal mind of God the Son with its distinctively divine consciousness, whatever that might be like, encompassing the full scope of omniscience. And in addition there is a distinctly earthly consciousness that came into existence and grew and developed as the boy Jesus grew and developed."[45] The bonding of these two consciousnesses within a single person may be conceived as follows:

> The divine mind of God the Son contained, but was not contained by, his earthly mind, or range of consciousness. That is to say, there was what can be called an asymmetric accessing relation between the two minds. Think, for example, of two computer programs or informational systems, one containing but not contained by the other. The divine mind had full and direct access to the earthly, human experience resulting from the Incarnation, but the earthly consciousness did not have such full and direct access to the content of the overarching omniscience proper to the Logos, but only such access, on occasion, as the divine mind allowed it to have. There thus

---

[45] Morris, *The Logic of God Incarnate*, 102-03. Cf. D. Brown, *The Divine Trinity*, 260-67, and Swinburne, *The Christian God*, 201-03.

was a metaphysical and personal depth to the man Jesus lacking in the case of every individual who is merely human.[46]

Morris senses the likely reaction to such surmises: "can we really understand what it is to attribute two minds, or two ranges of consciousness, to one person?"[47] No, he replies, we cannot—at least not in the way that we know what it is like to be a human being. However, "we can fill out some significant level of understanding concerning the claim by way of some analogies."[48] Think, for example, of "cases of brain hemisphere commisurotomy, multiple personality, and even hypnosis, in which we are confronted by what seems to be in some significant sense a single individual human being, one person, but one person with apparently two or more distinct streams or ranges of consciousness, distinct domains of experience."[49]

In at least two respects, Morris's account sounds plausible. For one thing, scriptural backing can be found for the claim of both human and divine consciousness in Christ. For another, Christian tradition has consistently supposed that God has access to human consciousness, whereas humans, typically, do not have access to the divine consciousness. However, two questions remain: On the divine side of the relationship, how is it restricted to the Son? (Do the Father and the Spirit have no access to human consciousness?) On the human side of the relationship, how is it restricted to Jesus? Have other people never been vouchsafed any access to the divine consciousness? If they have, may not Morris's analogies apply to them as well as to Jesus? In what, more precisely, does the distinctive "metaphysical" depth of Jesus consist?

To invoke mystery at this point would nullify Morris's explication. What is needed is some specification of Jesus' access to the divine consciousness which differentiates it from that of even the most exalted mystics. For this, mere words will not suffice. Mystical modes of consciousness are sufficiently mysterious; the requisite, still more transcendent mode of consciousness required by Morris's theory—its nature and its very possibility—lies entirely beyond our experience and understanding. My summary judgment, therefore, is this. To some limited extent, Morris's account may *articulate* Scripture more clearly or explain the hypostatic union more *definitely*, but so far as I can discern, it furnishes nothing of the kind here being sought—namely, a clearer explanation of the hypostatic union.

Perhaps, in my review of this and previous proposals, my procedure has resembled the one Wittgenstein described: "in order to find the real artichoke, we divested it of its leaves."[50] The leaves, when joined, constitute the artichoke. Analogously, the accounts strewn along my path, when joined, may contain more

---

[46] Morris, *The Logic of God Incarnate*, 103.

[47] Ibid., 104.

[48] Ibid.

[49] Ibid., 105.

[50] Wittgenstein, *Philosophical Investigations*, §164.

truth about the hypostatic union than any one of them singly considered. Their chief defect, therefore, may be their implicit essentialism. Why, for instance, should we focus on noetic access as *the* key to Jesus' divinity when the most telling scriptural indications point in other directions? Thomas did not exclaim, "My Lord and my God, how much you know!"

Some would suggest a different explanation for the preceding search's lack of success. The right approach to the Christology of the New Testament, they would urge, is through its soteriology, not its metaphysics.[51] "The doctrine of Christ's Deity must be understood in the light of what it achieves."[52]

Saving Significance

This soteriological perspective, bracketed till this point, has marked Christian thought from the beginning. As Alister McGrath observes: "For the early fathers, Jesus had to be both God and man if salvation was to be a possibility. If Jesus was not God, he could not save; if Jesus was not man, man could not be saved. The affirmation that Jesus was both God and man came to be seen as a means of safeguarding the gospel proclamation of the redemption of mankind in Christ."[53] McGrath adds, problematically: "The early Christians were actually far more interested in *defending* this insight, rather than trying to *explain* it! We must never fall into the trap of suspecting that the fathers thought that they were explaining how Jesus could be both God and man—it is clear that they were simply trying to find ways of making sense of a *mystery*, something which in the end defied explanation."[54]

How, one wonders, could Christians intuit a necessary connection between salvation and Jesus' divinity if they did not understand in what sense Jesus was divine? Jesus' saving action has been variously conceived, and so has his divinity. Does just any conception of salvation match any conception of his divinity, and vice versa? If not, what should we make of a passage such as the following:

> Could Christ, in any case, fully and finally reveal God to us unless he were himself a "divine Insider"? Could we find in him the absolute Representative of God, Someone in whom we can know, experience, and meet God, unless he were personally divine? Could we acknowledge in him the absolute Saviour (who brings redemption for the whole human being and for all human beings, "divinizing" us through grace—to use the language of the Greek Fathers), without also acknowledging in him the genuine

---

[51] Haight, *Jesus, Symbol of God*, 283, 294; Moingt, *L'homme qui venait de Dieu*, 109; Mozley, "Christology and Soteriology," 171; Sesboüé, *Jésus-Christ l'unique médiateur*, 12; Schillebeeckx, *Jesus*, 549; Stevens, *The Christian Doctrine of Salvation*, 297-99.

[52] Creed, *The Divinity of Jesus Christ*, 93 (on Ritschl).

[53] McGrath, *Understanding Jesus*, 98. Cf. ibid., 101.

[54] Ibid., 98 (McGrath's emphasis).

characteristics of God? Could he give us eternal life without being himself eternal? An affirmative answer to these questions is, in effect, asking us to accept a Jesus who functions for us as God, without actually being God. This position seems at least as strange as asking others to accept someone who acts in every way as the President of the United States without actually being the American President.[55]

We may ask: does each of these indications—revelation, representation, salvation, redemption, divinization, eternal life—suggest, individually, an identical sense in which Jesus "is" God? Do they all do so, collectively? The concluding comparison, with the President of the United States, invites an affirmative reply to both queries. The man who vetoes the bill is probably the President. The man who delivers the State of the Union address is probably the President. The man who appoints the ambassadors is probably the President. And so forth. The evidence mounts and points to the same conclusion. In each instance, and in all collectively, the identity suggested is a strict identity. Whatever can be said of the man who so acts can be said of the President, and vice versa. So this comparison suggests the conception the last chapter critiqued, of strict identity, and should therefore be viewed with suspicion. But if these varied soteriological perspectives do not all point to strict identity, what do they indicate? Does each perspective entail the same kind of identity? Indeed, when taken singly does any one perspective entail identity of any kind?

Of the New Testament's richly varied soteriological perspectives,[56] consider for example Romans 10:9: "if you confess with your mouth that Jesus is Lord and believe in your heart that God raised him from the dead, you will be saved." The formula "Jesus is Lord" wears a halo of associations, some of them distinctly theistic. And the power here attributed to faith focused on Jesus' lordship and resurrection might appear to endorse a strongly transcendent conception of his person. Still, it does not permit us to infer his divinity. Not only does Hebrews 11:6 propose a different content for the faith that saves (whoever would approach God "must believe that he exists and that he rewards those who seek him"), but it thereby suggests a possible reading of Romans 10:9. Jesus was the one who above all others sought God and was therefore exalted above all (Phil 2:9); thus belief in his lordship and resurrection instantiates, paradigmatically, the basic belief Hebrews cites. Ephesians 1:17-23 connects similarly with Romans. In Jesus, writes the author, we recognize the immeasurable greatness of God's power for us who

---

[55] O'Collins, *Christology*, 228. Cf. McGrath, *Understanding Jesus*, 96-97.

[56] "The New Testament speaks of our redemption, or liberation in Christ. Schillebeeckx examines the key concepts of the New Testament which describe this process: salvation and redemption; being freed from servitude and slavery, liberation through purchase or ransom; reconciliation after a dispute; satisfaction and peace; expiation of sins through a sin offering; the forgiveness of sins; justification and sanctification; salvation in Jesus as legal aid; being redeemed for community; being freed for love; being freed for freedom; renewal of persons and the world; life in fullness; victory over alienating and demonic powers" (Edwards, *What Are They Saying*, 66).

believe. "God put this power to work in Christ when he raised him from the dead and seated him at his right hand in the heavenly places, far above all rule and authority and power and domination, and above every name that is named, not only in this age but also in the age to come. And he has put all things under his feet and has made him the head over all things for the church, which is his body, the fullness of him who fills all in all." Here, assuredly, is transcendent content for the faith Romans 10:9 commends; yet the passage does not say or imply that God made Jesus God.

Without reviewing all the New Testament passages which speak of saving faith and which make Jesus the object of that faith, I suggest that none of them individually nor all of them collectively entail Jesus' divinity more clearly than do the representative passages just cited. No more, therefore, can they be expected to clarify the nature of Jesus' divine identity. Indeed, even if they spoke more explicitly of faith in Jesus as divine, they might not do that. Suppose, for example, that we accorded full ontological weight to the word "Son" in John 3:16: "'For God so loved the world that he gave his only Son, so that everyone who believes in him may not perish but may have eternal life.'" Suppose, furthermore, that we equated "believing in him" with believing in him precisely as "the only Son." Therewith, the nature of his sonship, or of his identity with God, would remain as obscure as ever. The link with faith would permit no deeper insight into the incarnational relationship than does John's Prologue, with its multiple mysteries.

There and elsewhere in the New Testament a social, historical, cosmic perspective complements the personal. In Ephesians, for example, Jesus is "the head of the church, the body of which he is the Savior" (Eph 5:23). He "gave himself up for her, in order to make her holy by cleansing her with the washing of water by the word, so as to present the church to himself in splendor, without a spot or wrinkle or anything of that kind—yes, so that she may be holy and without blemish" (Eph 5:25-27). 1 Peter 2:9-10 evokes a similar perspective, as does 1 Corinthians 12: "For in the one Spirit we were all baptized into one body—Jews or Greeks, slaves or free—and we were all made to drink of one Spirit" (1 Cor 12:13). In that body, Jesus may confer authority on Peter (Mt 16:18-19), but Jesus himself is the head—the saving head—of his body, the church (Col 1:18). Now, what does such a role require of his relationship with God? Does it entail divinity?

Not at all evidently. Of Peter's role, Mersch writes: "Peter shall be the rock sustaining the whole Church; Peter shall hold the keys; he shall bind and loose; and Peter is given to understand that God ratifies in heaven every judicial sentence that he, Peter, shall pronounce on earth."[57] It is not evident why a similar relationship could not hold for Jesus himself—why, that is, if Jesus could build on Peter, God could not build on him. As Mersch notes, "Peter can do nothing except by Christ, and in Peter it is Christ alone who can do all things."[58] But might not something similar hold for Jesus himself ("Jesus can do nothing except by God, and in Jesus it

---

[57] Mersch, *The Whole Christ*, 47-48.

[58] Ibid., 48.

is God alone who can do all things")? As Peter is Jesus' vicar, might not Jesus be God's supreme vicar? Indeed, the progression in Luke 10:16 invites such thoughts: "'Whoever listens to you listens to me, and whoever rejects you rejects me, and whoever rejects me rejects the one who sent me.'" (Cf. Lk 9:48 and Mt 9:36) I am not, of course, suggesting how Ephesians 5 or Matthew 16 should be understood. I am just searching for any soteriological indications of divinity sufficiently clear to elucidate the sense in which Jesus' divinity should be understood. And I do not discover them in any of the sample perspectives so far considered. Neither do I find them elsewhere in Scripture.[59]

In search of the sort of connection not discernible that early, I therefore turn to subsequent theological developments. There, many soteriological doctrines do not allege any necessary link between Jesus' saving role and his divinity, but a few notable doctrines do and may therefore have interest for the question that concerns us—provided that one or the other such allegation is valid. Let us look and see, starting with a thought pattern already noted.

The Divine Divinizer

In response to the familiar query "How can we be divinized save by one who is divine?" consider the kindred query: how can fire be kindled save by fire? In this instance, evident alternatives—flint, lightning, matches, spontaneous combustion—come to mind and save us from being duped by mere words or persuasive paradigms (e.g., candles lit by tapers). But in realms of transcendent mystery no such counterinstances come to mind, and, viewed through our ignorance, the single instance with which we are acquainted may suggest a metaphysical necessity. If Jesus, who is divine, divinizes us, then divinity must be necessary for divinization. After all, does not a venerable principle dictate that like must be caused by like? This dictum, too, and its variants, reflect the tendency Wittgenstein described, of nourishing our thinking with too limited a diet of examples. Using the same example, of fire, we might counter: how does fire resemble flint, lightning, matches, or the conditions that occasion spontaneous combustion?

---

[59] Personally, I like, for example, to view Jesus himself as that bit of yeast placed in the dough which makes the whole mass rise (Mt 13:33). The appeal of this comparison derives in part from subsequent history (the dough of humanity has indeed risen, massively, as a result of Jesus' coming), and partly from the fact that the yeast does not act only momentarily, like flint striking fire, but works through its abiding presence. The comparison's further appeal, but also its limitation, comes from the fact that the yeast differs so markedly from the dough. Jesus is different! However, even this figure, which heightens Jesus' distinctiveness (indeed heightens it inordinately), does not go farther and suggest that, for the yeast to work its powerful effect, the yeast and the baker who mixed it with the dough must somehow be identical. Neither, a fortiori, does it suggest in what way they are identical.

To further assess the inference to divinity from divinization, consider a related strand of traditional thinking. Commenting on Aquinas, Mersch writes: "The Savior's human nature is elevated, divinized; it has this elevation and divinization from the divine nature; thereby it is made a principle of supernatural life, grace, and divinization, and hence a principle of supernatural unity in all mankind."[60] And yet, as Mersch notes, "Christ's humanity is assuredly not His divinity."[61] Why, then, might not something similar hold for Jesus and not only for his human nature? Why might he not become an agent of supernatural life through his intimate union with God, yet not be God? Why curb our metaphysical imagination in the one instance and give it free rein in the other?

One source of difficulty, previously noted, is the tendency to neglect the question that interests us—namely, the nature of Jesus' relationship with God—and focus solely on the terms of the relationship. The present relevance of this tendency appears, for instance, in these words of Bernard Sesboüé, echoing Athanasius[62]:

> Through the Son and in the Spirit the Father welcomes us as his children and communicates his own life to us. But for his gift not to be counterfeit, the Son and the Spirit must be God in the strong and eternal sense of the word. Otherwise they are merely creatures and become incapable of communicating God's life to us.[63]

Perhaps, for our divinization, the Son and the Spirit must be God in the strong and eternal sense of the word "God," but must they be God in the strong and eternal sense of the word "be"? Within a term-centered perspective, the alternatives look sharp: either God or a mere creature. But the alternatives are not, in fact, sharp; for the sense of "be," as we have repeatedly observed, is not sharp. Hence the asserted necessity is not clear. Within this soteriological perspective, the question that concerns us is not illuminated but ignored.

Wiles makes a further point. When they spoke of our divinization by one who was divine,

> the Fathers did not intend the parallelism to be taken with full seriousness. The Word, who was fully God, did not become fully man that he might make us full men become fully God. In speaking of man's divinization the Fathers intended to convey that men should become gods only in a secondary sense—"gods by grace" (θεοὶ κατὰ χάριν) was the phrase they used; it was never believed that they would become what the Word was—namely, "God by nature" (θεὸς κατὰ φύσιν). In the light of this understanding of man's destiny, it does not seem logically absurd to claim on behalf of Arianism that the Son, the supreme God's agent in creation, who in the Arian scheme is the example *par excellence* of what it is to be a "god by grace," should be able in the work of redemption to bring us to be what he already is and so make us

---

[60] Mersch, *The Theology of the Mystical Body*, 201.

[61] Ibid.

[62] Athanasius, *Contra Arian.* 2.67, 69, 70.

[63] Sesboüé, *Jésus-Christ l'unique médiateur*, 207.

also "gods by grace" with as full a fellowship with God as is pos-sible for finite beings.[64]

However it is viewed, therefore, the inference from divinization to divinity looks problematic; and from an unclear inference no clear conclusion follows regarding the nature of the divinity inferred.

The Mediating Redeemer

Isaiah 53 does not explain how the suffering servant "shall make many righteous" or "bear their iniquities." Neither do New Testament texts that echo Isaiah explain in what sense Jesus died "for our trespasses" (Rom 4:25), was "offered once to bear the sins of many" (Heb 9:28), or "bore our sins in his body on the cross" (1 Pet 2:24). Theologians have striven for deeper insight into such sayings as these, but their accounts have varied, and none is free of difficulties. Hence none can be identified as the sole possible meaning of Scripture's indications. However, the best-known account of this kind merits brief consideration, since it clearly maintains that redemption requires divinity.

According to Saint Anselm, only a human being can make satisfaction for human sin, and only God can make satisfaction commensurate to the offense, which is infinite. Accordingly, Jesus the redeemer must be both human and divine. Clearly, what holds of other soteriological models holds of this one, too: "they are not to be implemented totally literally, as if they were 'complete symbols' of the death of Christ, but rather as 'incomplete symbols,' which require us to desist before pressing them to their logical conclusions."[65] God making amends to himself differs greatly from one person making amends to another, and Jesus being both the offender and the offended notably alters the familiar scenario of satisfaction. Thus, even if Anselm's explanation has some validity, we have no clear insight into how or why it does, hence no clear insight into what sort of identity between Jesus and God it requires or permits. Clearer understanding of the hypostatic union might reveal some merit in Anselm's theory; but such understanding is what we seek and lack.

With Swinburne and others,[66] I would go farther. Anselm's *Cur Deus Homo* is a magnificent achievement, Swinburne writes, but it has its faults.[67] In particular, "It makes the rendering of satisfaction, of an amount of reparation equal to the harm done and penance required, necessary before forgiveness can be given," whereas for Swinburne,

---

[64] Wiles, *The Making of Christian Doctrine*, 107-8.

[65] McIntyre, *The Shape of Soteriology*, 31.

[66] Cf. Suárez, *De incarnatione*, 52: "I say secondly: the mystery of the incarnation was not simply necessary for the restoration of fallen humankind. This conclusion is common, and so certain that it cannot be denied without temerity and harm to the faith."

[67] Swinburne, *Responsibility and Atonement*, 155.

it is the victim of wrongdoing—in this case God—who has the right to choose, up to the limit of an equivalent to the harm done and the need for a little more in penance, how much reparation and penance to require before he will forgive. So, despite all of these considerations about man's inability to make substantial reparation and penance, God could have chosen to accept one supererogatory act of an ordinary man as adequate for the sins of the world. Or he could have chosen to accept some angel's act for this purpose.[68]

God need not insist on strict justice; he may temper justice with mercy.

Jesus the Revelation of God.

Some have thought that in order to reveal God, Jesus himself must be divine.[69] Thus Karl Barth writes:

> In distinction from the assertion of the divinisation of a man or the humanisation of a divine idea, the statement about Christ's deity is to be understood in the sense that Christ reveals His Father. But this Father of His is God. He who reveals Him, then, reveals God. But who can reveal God except God Himself? Neither a man that has been raised up nor an idea that has come down can do it. . . . To confess [Christ] as the revelation of His Father is to confess Him as essentially equal in deity with this Father of His.[70]

In response one might note that Scripture can speak to us of God, as can Peter and Paul and John. So they can, Barth might respond, but only derivatively. Very well, why might not Jesus speak to us of God derivatively—why might God not reveal himself uniquely to this man, and through him to us? Not only is Barth's inference unclear; its conclusion ("essentially equal with the Father") is as compatible with tritheism as with monotheism, so does nothing to explicate the nature of the union asserted by Chalcedon.

Jesus, God's Compassionate Presence.

For Christians, God's love is best revealed in Jesus who gave himself for those he loved. Amplifying this perspective, Frances Young writes:

---

[68] Ibid., 160. Swinburne adds in a note, "Scotus saw that very clearly," and refers the reader to Grensted, *A Short History,* 160f.

[69] R. Brown, *Introduction,* 150, and *Jesus God and Man,* 103; Brunner, *The Christian Doctrine of God,* vol. 1, 219-20, 222-23; M. Harris, *Jesus as God,* 284; Kuschel, *Born Before All Time?,* 99 (on Barth); Liddon, *The Divinity of Our Lord,* 461; Prestige, *God in Patristic Thought,* xv; Sturch, "The Metaphysics of the Incarnation," 69; Temple, *Christus Veritas,* 140.

[70] Barth, *Church Dogmatics,* vol. 1/1, 465.

It seems to me that the story acquires much greater significance and far more direct relevance to particular instances of human suffering in the present, if Jesus' humanity is taken totally seriously and the cross is regarded as the "classic case" of God's presence in the midst of human sin, suffering and death—that is to say, the mode of God's presence there is seen as potentially the mode of his presence in other desperate situations. God not only suffered and died, but suffers and dies, in and with human beings.[71]

Young sees this perspective as not only comforting but indispensable: "I would agree with Brian Hebblethwaite that 'only a suffering God is morally credible' in the face of the world's ills."[72] And only to a credible God can we respond with love, gratitude, and adoration.

One wonders: could a child not believe a parent's love—would the parent's love not be "morally credible"—unless the parent shared the nasty medicine, took the same painful inoculation, underwent the same operation, and so forth? The suggestion does not make sense. There are reasons for the medicine, the inoculation, the operation, but they do not apply to the parent. In our own case, we can hardly imagine a wise and omnipotent God explaining: "There is no reason for your suffering, but since I can do nothing about it, I will keep you company." But we can readily imagine God answering our queries as a caring parent might: "There is an explanation for your suffering, of that I assure you. And if you should ever doubt it—if you should ever question my love—look at what I have allowed in the case of my beloved, the son in whom I am well pleased. And consider what came of his suffering, consider what I did for him and through him for you." The former answer requires Jesus' divinity; the latter, more satisfactory answer does not. We can therefore conclude as before: reasoning that so unclearly demands Jesus' divinity cannot clarify the nature of his divinity.

Since the foregoing sampling, however representative, may appear incomplete, let me conclude with an observation of J. N. D. Kelly: "The development of the Church's ideas about the saving effects of the incarnation was a slow, long drawn-out process. Indeed, while the conviction of redemption through Christ has always been the motive force of Christian faith, no final and universally accepted defini-tion of the manner of its achievement has been formulated to this day."[73] It follows that no such definition, no matter how clearly or revealingly it implied Jesus' divinity, would do so at all surely. It would just indicate an interesting possibility.

---

[71] Young, "Incarnation and Atonement," 102. Cf. Sesboüé, *Jésus-Christ l'unique médiateur*, 323-24.

[72] Young, "Incarnation and Atonement," 101. Cf. Hebblethwaite, "Incarnation and Atonement," 94.

[73] J. Kelly, *Early Christian Doctrines*, 163.

The Where and Why of Mystery

Having looked in the likeliest places, we have had no success.[74] We have made no advance on the New Testament or on Chalcedon. Jesus' divine identity remains as mysterious as ever. Why is that? From these repeated failures, may we conclude inductively that the asteroid comparison is indeed apt—that there is no more prospect of explaining the hypostatic union, even partially, than there is of inferring the shape of an asteroid from the waves it generates? From the nature of the failures, can we gain any insight into the reasons for the overall negative result? If asked why the waves do not reveal the asteroid's shape, we might just point to one wave after another and ask: What help is that? But such a wave-by-wave response would furnish no insight into the general phenomenon. Why can no waves, near or far, provide the desired information? Why does an oblong asteroid not make oblong waves? Why does a jagged asteroid not make jagged waves? It is not easy to say; indeed expert knowledge would be required to provide an explanation. Yet doubtless research would yield one. So our question now becomes: if we cannot achieve a clearer explanation of the hypostatic union, can we at least discern the reason? Can we identify the where and why of the mystery?

With respect to the waves, it is clear where the mystery lies. We have no direct perception of the complex, quasi-instantaneous generation of the very first waves. All we perceive is the waves. Correspondingly, we have no direct perception of the complex, relatively rapid formation of the first scriptures we posses. They are what we perceive, they are what we must work with. Taking them (or derivative texts) as our starting point, we may proceed either backwards or forwards—backwards to a genetic explanation of the texts or forwards to conclusions based on the texts. All the accounts we have sampled have proceeded in the second, forward direction. They have reasoned:

- from Jesus' perfect humanity, as revealed in Scripture, to his divinity (Donovan);
- from Jesus' divinity to divine self-emptying (Thomasius, Macquarrie);
- from Scripture's portrayal of Jesus' relation to his Father to an explication of the hypostatic union as personal (Kasper);
- from Chalcedonian identity to Jesus' unique noetic structure (Morris);

---

[74] I have passed over as less promising the kind of connection of which Wiles writes: "In the case of Nicene orthodoxy it is tempting to suggest that it was the true development because it gave the 'highest' account of the person of Christ, because it took most seriously the worshipping tradition of the Church. But such a criterion is clearly unreliable. It was just such an approach which was responsible for the conviction of Eutyches and the Monophysites that their teaching must be the true expression of the faith" (*The Making of Christian Doctrine*, 168). Even were such an approach more reliable, if it entailed only Nicene and Chalcedonian orthodoxy, it would lead us to our starting point and not to our desired clarification of that starting point.

- from divinization to divinity (Fathers);
- from Jesus' divinity to his adequate satisfaction (Anselm);
- from Jesus' revelatory role to his divinity (Barth);
- from Jesus' saving role to his suffering divinity (Young, Hebblethwaite).

In no instance did these theologians reason back from scriptural data to their origin. In no instance did I challenge their scripture-based premise (Jesus' perfect humanity, his divinity, his loving relation to his Father, etc.). In every instance I questioned the inference drawn from that premise. Sometimes the premise was too indefinite (e.g., Chalcedonian identity was less definite than Morris supposed). More often the premise was sufficiently definite but the inference looked unsound. Several times I questioned whether the inference, even if sound, would permit fuller insight into the nature of Jesus' divinity. Thus, no single defect in the reasoning appeared, suggesting a uniform account not only of the repeated failures but also of why such failures should be expected.

In this regard, light may come from the comparable situation in philosophy. There, a chief reason for the difficulty of successful deductive demonstration is the lack of synthetic a priori principles of the kind needed as premises. And such is the lack we have here repeatedly sensed. For example, no implicit major premise warranted inference from perfect humanity to divinity, from divinity to divine or human limitations, from revelation *of* God to revelation *by* God, or from divinizing to divinity. We may sense in advance that reversing the direction of reasoning and attempting to discern the origins of scriptural data rather than their implications will not remove all such difficulties, but let us examine what form the difficulties take within this new, etiological perspective and whether they are equally serious.

With respect to even the earliest waves after impact there can be no reasoning back from the waves to the shape of the asteroid; whatever the asteroid's shape, the waves will be circular. Does something analogous hold for the New Testament expressions of Jesus' divinity, or does the comparison perhaps break down at this point? Might we determine that, in all probability, such or such is the manner in which such expressions arose and such or such are the implications of this origin for the nature of the divinity thus expressed? To be sure, we know much about the conceptual background of John, Paul, and the author of Hebrews, and we can therefore surmise what they meant when they described Jesus as "Word," "Lord," "God." But what about Jesus led them to such declarations? What original experience, theirs or others', impacting that milieu, did or could give rise to the highest, strongest forms of New Testament Christology? A simple answer would be, "The experience of his divinity." But that reply would take us no farther than our starting point, in John, Paul, and Hebrews; and how might someone *experience* Jesus' divinity? [75]

---

[75] I here pass over the response, popular till recently, that Jesus himself declared his divinity. Even were it true, this response would prove a dead end for our inquiry, since it

For guidance we might ask: how might someone experience *God*? Consider this account of a woman's childhood experience:

> My father used to take all the family for a walk on Sunday evenings. On one such walk, we wandered across a narrow path through a field of high, ripe corn. I lagged behind, and found myself alone. Suddenly, heaven blazed on me. I was enveloped in golden light, I was conscious of a presence, so kind, so loving, so bright, so consoling, so commanding, existing apart from me but so close. I heard no sound. But words fell into my mind quite clearly—"Everything is all right. Everybody will be all right."[76]

This child did not simply believe, understand, or sense that God was present thereabouts. No, God (to put the word in her mouth) *was* there, directly revealed to her. So it seemed, and so it may have been.

Jesus made much the same impression: kind, loving, bright, consoling, commanding. Yet heaven did not blaze on those who beheld him. He was not enveloped by a golden light. And his goodness was incarnate, his presence visible. The words of comfort that he spoke he spoke with a human mouth, a human voice. For he was a human being. But God is not visible, not corporeal, not a human being. In what sense, then, might it be conjectured that the disciples' experience of Jesus was an experience of God, and not, for instance, an experience of God acting in or through this man?

To broaden our perspective, let us vary our comparative example. Concerning the divine object of her mystical encounters Saint Teresa wrote: "Because it so far exceeds all that our imagination and understanding can compass, its presence is of such exceeding majesty that it fills the soul with a great terror. It is unnecessary to ask here how, without being told, the soul knows Who it is, for He reveals Himself quite clearly as the Lord of Heaven and earth."[77] To match this experience, we might recall Paul's conversion as recounted in Acts. There, heaven did blaze, and Jesus' presence was indeed of such exceeding majesty that it filled Paul's soul with terror and awe. The one who spoke to him, we feel little hesitation in saying, revealed himself as the lord of heaven and earth. Yet how could that be? Can a man be God? Even such an experience, not just of Jesus risen but of Jesus glorified—even this experience spanning heaven and earth—does nothing to clarify the sense in which that query might be answered in the affirmative. The mystery remains.

It is evident, though, how such an experience might lead Paul to speak of Jesus as he did:

---

would leave us with the very sayings (e.g., "The Father and I are one") which we seek to fathom.

[76] Hay, *Religious Experience Today*, 72.
[77] St. Teresa, *Interior Castle*, 186.

> Therefore God also highly exalted him
> and gave him the name that is above every name,
> so that at the name of Jesus every knee should bend,
> in heaven and on earth and under the earth,
> and every tongue should confess that Jesus Christ is Lord,
> to the glory of God the Father (Phil 2:9-11).

As Anthony Harvey remarks of the earliest Christians, although they were severely and passionately monotheist,

> it was clear to them that Jesus was far more than just one more in the long succession of divinely authorized prophets, kings, and teachers who had figured in the history of Israel. There was, it seemed, a finality about him, a total authority, which made one's personal decision for or against him a matter of infinitely more moment than one's attention to or disregard of the words of any of God's previous messengers. How then was one to articulate this finality, this ultimate authority? One could use a number of titles, such as "Christ" or "Son of God," to convey the idea; but since a person such as Jesus had never been envisaged in Jewish religious thought, no term was available which could serve as shorthand for the claims these Christians had to make.[78]

Their situation resembled that of my two-year-old niece when, viewing the Gulf of Mexico for the first time, she declared in awe: "Big bathtub!" She had no other terms for what she saw. Early Christians' made do with "Word," "Lord," "Christ," "Son of God," "God"—whatever seemed somehow appropriate. However, as my niece's naive, spontaneous expression was compatible with a great variety of sizes and shapes, so too these Christological titles left undefined the reality they expressed.

Enough has now been said to suggest and illustrate the following conclusion: Any experience we might envision as originating scriptural expressions of Jesus' divinity—even as transcendent an experience as Paul's on the road to Damascus—would not clarify the reality expressed by calling Jesus divine. It would not take us beyond Chalcedon. The mystery would lie there at the start, in the experience. "Who then is this, that even the wind and the sea obey him?" (Mk 4:41)

This negative verdict, for backward as for forward reasoning from Scripture, may disappoint our theological aspirations. If so, we may ask how realistic the aspirations were. How did we suppose the revelation might occur? What paradigms shaped our thinking? Which reasonably might? A comparison, homely yet apt, here suggests itself. In his *Philosophical Investigations*, Wittgenstein wrote: "It is possible to say 'I read timidity in this face' but at all events the timidity does not seem to be merely associated, outwardly connected, with the face; but fear is there, alive, in the features."[79] How can this be, we might wonder. Is not fear a feeling, or

---

[78] Harvey, "Christology," 53. Cf. R. Brown, *Introduction*, 70.

[79] Wittgenstein, *Philosophical Investigations*, §537.

a disposition? So how can fear be there, alive, in the external features? Similarly we might ask: is not God a spirit, is not God the maker of the universe? How, then, can divinity be there, alive, in Jesus of Nazareth? In this case, as in the other, the reply of witnesses might be: "I cannot say, it simply is," or later, "It simply was." And what witnesses themselves could not say if asked, we cannot say for them.

And so, from the point of impact the noetic waves spread out in their concentric circles, and from those waves no inference of either kind, backward or forward, can be drawn to the asteroid's shape—that is, to the precise sense in which it might be said, "Jesus is God" or "Jesus is God the Son." We have found no indication that the identity is strict, nor any way in which we might infer its nature. We can only make surmises, as we can for the shape of the asteroid plunging into the sea. Which leads us to wonder: What need have we to know the asteroid's shape?

Plainly, in this chapter and the preceding chapter I have not attempted a balanced, comprehensive view of Jesus' person, nature, and mission. The chapters have focused fairly narrowly on issues of identity, as will the chapters to come. Within this focus, however, theme relates to theme to form a web of interrelated issues. Evidently, for example, the Incarnational mystery just considered relates with that of the Trinity. SIS-type thinking would connect them tightly: if Jesus is the Second Person of the Trinity and the Second Person is God, then Jesus is God. If, however, neither of these premises states a strict identity (of Jesus with the Second Person or of the Second Person with God), the inference fails and matters become more complex. Conceivably, the Incarnational and Trinitarian identities might differ radically, not only in their terms but also in their kind. Conceivably, neither identity might illumine the other. With due diffidence, then, let us advance into these depths.

Chapter 4

The Trinity

One can empathize with a bewildered member of the flock who has written of "God and Jesus, who, as far as I understood it, were one and the same—and so was the Holy Spirit. It's all so confusing."[1] The doctrines of the Incarnation and the Trinity, with their multiple identities and interrelations, are indeed complex. Hick, however, spots an etiological key to all this complexity:

> I believe that Brunner's analysis is historically correct. The doctrine of the Trinity was developed as an interpretative framework to secure the prior doctrine of the deity of Christ. That is to say, if Jesus Christ was God incarnate, but if throughout the period of his earthly life God was also at work sustaining the universe, receiving prayer and otherwise acting outside the person of the historical Jesus, it follows that the Godhead is at least two-fold, namely Father and Son. This was the essential expansion or complication of monotheism required by the belief in divine incarnation. And when the Spirit of God, attested to in the Hebrew Scriptures, in the teaching of Jesus and in present religious experience, is added, we have a Trinity.[2]

"It follows"—how familiar the inference sounds after the preceding chapters. SIS again! If Jesus is identical with God and Jesus does different things than God does, strict identity will demand a different God than God the Father for Jesus to be—if possible—identical with.[3] Doubtless some such thinking has occurred. However, since SIS did not dominate incarnational thinking at any stage of its development, it is difficult to discern how much truth Hick's hypothesis may contain. I shall not attempt to trace the complicated etiology of the traditional doctrine, but shall focus instead on the doctrine itself and specifically on the issues of identity it poses, as have numerous recent writers.

---

[1] Beverly Donofrio, quoted in D. Kelly, Review.

[2] Hick, "Islam and Christian Monotheism," 7. Cf. Welch, *In This Name*, 128: "W. Norman Pittenger approaches the Trinity as a presupposition and implication of the Incarnation. This doctrine of God is, he says, the 'inevitable corollary of such an implicit belief and such an explicit assertion about the person of Jesus Christ,' as has culminated in the Nicene and Chalcedonian formulae."

[3] Cf. Welch, *In This Name*, 157: "Knudson states that the doctrine grew out of the expanded idea of deity which was necessary when 'Jesus *as well as* the traditional God came to be regarded as divine.'" (Note the word "necessary," comparable to Hick's "it follows.")

Roger Haight questions such an approach. In his view, "the only way critically to understand the doctrine of the trinity is to trace its historical development."[4] As it stands, this assertion, excluding all alternatives, sounds one-sided. More reasonably, Haight's claim could be understood as stressing the indispensable importance of acquaintance with the history of the doctrine. With regard to that history, Haight insists: "What is important here is that later doctrines of an immanent trinity not be allowed to be read into New Testament teaching. In this doctrine as in others, it is crucial that one preserve the stages in the doctrinal development in their historical integrity in order to ensure critical analysis."[5] This I grant. If, focusing on the later doctrine, I adopt a more analytic approach, it is because I find that, too, enlightening. It serves to highlight the issues of identity that here interest me and that have figured so prominently in Trinitarian debate.

For the Trinity, as for the Incarnation, observes David Brown, "The central difficulty concerns what is commonly labelled the problem of identity, namely the question of what would justify us in speaking of one entity rather than of a plurality of entities; that is to say, talking of one person rather than two in the incarnational case and of one God rather than three in the trinitarian instance."[6] Writing in 1978, A. P. Martinich adopted and sharpened the same focus. "All theologians," he asserted, "understand that the central problem involving the mystery of the Trinity is to explain the possibility that there is one God but three persons in God without falling into contradiction."[7] In his view, many solutions, analyzing the concepts of person, nature, substance, God, and the like, or envisaging ontological mechanisms within the Trinity, "mislocate the source of the problem, which is that Father, Son, and Holy Spirit are somehow identical and yet not identical. As the notion of identity is generally construed, this is incoherent no matter how 'person,' 'nature,' or what-have-you is analyzed."[8] Leibnizian identity allows no wiggle room: if each of the three persons is identical with God, who is one, then by transitivity the three persons are all identical with each other—which is to say, there are not three persons but only one, under different names.

Haight adopts a radical solution. "Even though the history of the doctrine has been obsessed with the problem of mathematical threeness and oneness," he writes, "and that obsession continues today, in reality the doctrine has nothing to do with this issue."[9] In support of this sweeping assertion, he argues: "The unicity and unity of God are a given and a constant; the discussion of three principles in the Godhead can only be seen as a discussion of possible differentiation within the one God's life. And this differentiation does not mean multiplicity, because the 'persons' cannot be counted, as counting is an operation applicable only to finite beings, and because traditionally there is always a unity of operation of the one

---

[4]   Haight, *Jesus, Symbol of God*, 471.

[5]   Ibid., 474.

[6]   D. Brown, *The Divine Trinity*, 223.

[7]   Martinich, "Identity and Trinity," 169.

[8]   Ibid.

[9]   Haight, *Jesus, Symbol of God*, 482.

God."[10] One would like to know the basis for the claim that counting applies only to finite beings. A model here developed will call all these denials into question. However, Haight does not envisage any such solution to the problem of three in one, and a debate for which he can conceive no acceptable solution doubtless strikes him as futile. Back, then, to a single God, multiply active, and away with any inner threeness! This narrowing of options, more extreme than any I shall suggest, is supported neither by Scripture nor by subsequent doctrine nor by metaphysical fiat. The problem of incoherence cannot so readily be swept aside.

As for the Incarnation so here, a simple solution might be to drop the supposition that gives rise to the apparent incoherence, namely the supposition that identity must be strict. CRS allows much leeway. However, according to one contemporary school of thought, there is no need to invoke any such principle as CRS. A more definite defense is available.

The Relative-Identity Solution

In recent years the chief debate about Trinitarian identity has centered on Peter Geach's theory of relative identity and its application to this mystery. According to Geach, "When one says 'x is identical with y,' this . . . is an incomplete expression; it is short for 'x is the same A as y,' where 'A' represents some count noun understood from the context of utterance—or else, it is just a vague expression of a half-formed thought."[11] Suppose, for example, that I hold two books, a and b, in my hands and I say, "a is identical with b." Do I mean that a is the same *copy*, or I do I mean that it is the same *book*? Once I note these alternatives, I may assert without contradiction: "a and b are the same book but not the same copy." Similarly, Geach argues, one may assert without contradiction: "Father, Son, and Holy Spirit are the same God but not the same person."[12]

Some have challenged Geach's general theory, some this particular application.[13] The distinction needs noting, for the theory might err only in its generality, in which case the specific, Trinitarian analysis might still hold up. However, critics have tended to argue that identity is never relative. Evidently, both positions in this confrontation hold interest for the present study as a whole and not solely for the present discussion. If identity statements are *always* relative, as Geach claims, or if

---

[10] Ibid., 483.

[11] Geach, "Identity," 3. Geach later noted: "Restricting the interpretation of 'A' in 'is the same A as' to count nouns was a slip of the pen on my part; I allowed mass terms as well to be such interpretations in my book *Reference and Generality*" (*Logic Matters*, 247).

[12] Geach and Anscombe, *Three Philosophers*, 118. For subsequent, kindred treatments, see Cain, "The Doctrine of the Trinity"; Martinich, "Identity and Trinity," and "God, Emperor and Relative Identity"; and Inwagen, "And Yet."

[13] Cartwright, "On the Logical Problem," 193-98; Feser, "Has Trinitarianism"; Macnamara, Reyes, and Reyes, "Logic and the Trinity," 5; T. Morris, *The Logic of God Incarnate*, 26-29; Perry, "The Same F"; Wiggins, *Sameness and Substance*, 15-44.

they are *never* relative, as critics contend, I have been neglecting a major consideration and it is high time to attend to it before we pass to further issues of identity.

In support of his blanket claim, Geach adduces what he claims are instances of relative identity, while opponents reject a relativistic analysis of these and other examples, largely in view of systematic requirements. According to one major critic, "The final test of a theory of relative identity is not its internal coherence, but how it subserves a total theory of the individuation and existence of particulars."[14] But, "If Leibniz's Law is dropped, or if classical identity is dropped in favour of some allegedly un-Leibnizian relative identity, then we need some formal principle or other, and one of at least comparable universality, to justify the valid instances of the intersubstitution of identicals."[15] Relative identity, with its shifting criteria, is too messy for system building. This objection need not detain us. Since, as noted earlier, logicians and other theorists may stipulate whatever restrictions they please for their purposes, and since any purposes that require strict identity are doubtless irrelevant for the present discussion (see Chapter 1), we can turn instead to particular examples and examine typical criticisms of Geach's relativistic analysis.

Consider the example just given. Familiar usage, according to which people who buy, borrow, or read different copies of a book are nonetheless said to have bought, borrowed, or read "the same book," suggests that objects *a* and *b* may be the same book but different copies. Here transitivity does not hold, as it would for strict, total identity. From the threeness of the copies we cannot infer the threeness of the book; from the sameness of the book we cannot infer the sameness of the copies. The reason for this, one countermove alleges, is not that identity is relative but that the names "*a*" and "*b*" pick out different referents in "*a* and *b* are the same book" than in "*a* and *b* are different copies." "The view I advocate," writes John Perry, "and which I believe to be Frege's, is that the role of the general term is to identify the referents—not to identify the 'kind of identity' asserted."[16] To illustrate, it might be suggested that in "*a* and *b* are the same book" the term "book" indicates an abstract referent, whereas in "*a* and *b* are not the same copy" the term "copy" indicates a concrete referent. Thus the affirmative statement asserts identity between an abstract entity (realized in one copy) and itself (realized in another copy), whereas the negative statement denies identity between one concrete entity (a copy) and another. In both instances the kind of identity asserted or denied is the same (namely, self-identity); only the referents vary. So goes the argument. But how might this alleged referential shift from statement to statement be shown? By the original affixing of the names "*a*" and "*b*" to these physical objects? By the constraints of context? Of what context, then? That of Geach's discussion? If not his, whose? In such a confrontation, arguments and counter-arguments tend to beg the question.

---

[14] Wiggins, *Sameness and Substance*, 23.

[15] Ibid. , 22. Cf. ibid., 39-40.

[16] Perry, "The Same *F*," 185. Cf. Wiggins, *Sameness and Substance*, 37, 43.

However, a second objection awaits. If, Perry believes, a pair of propositions adduced as evidence for relative identity does not fail in this first way, then it fails in another: "One of the conjuncts does not assert or deny identity, but one of the other relations often expressed by phrases of the form 'is the same F as.'"[17] Suppose, for example, that in "*a* is the same book as *b*" the names have the same physical, concrete referents as in "*a* is not the same copy as *b*." In that case, the denial may deny identity whereas the affirmation merely asserts that *a* and *b* "are similar in a certain respect, or have some property in common."[18] No doubt, I would say, this follows if all identity, by definition, is strict, Leibnizian identity. Otherwise, the range of relations "expressed by phrases of the form 'is the same *F* as'" may suggest the heterogeneity of identity. Criteria of identity may shift (compare "same river," "same club," "same tree," etc.). There may even be instances of identity (e.g., "God is love") for which we cannot specify criteria of identity in the manner Geach requires. (What term might we substitute for *x* in "God is the same *x* as love"?) However, this is a debate we need not enter. No Platonic form of "identity," no strict use of the word in the language, sharply specifies what does and does not qualify as a statement of "identity." Even if it did, that would not fix the meaning of the Nicene-Constantinopolitan and Athanasian Creeds, which make no reference to "identity"; neither would it pinpoint the orthodox sense of a statement such as "The Son *is* God" or "The Son *is not* the Father." Searching, then, for understanding, faith can more pertinently consider what readings are coherent and which make best sense of orthodox belief.

Most discussions accept that the orthodox doctrine of the Trinity includes the following propositions:

1. The Father is God.
2. The Son is God.
3. The Holy Spirit is God.
4. The Father is not the Son.
5. The Father is not the Holy Spirit.
6. The Son is not the Holy Spirit.
7. There is exactly one God.[19]

If (1) to (6) are taken as statements affirming or denying identity and the identity is taken as strict, mass incoherence results. The negation of (4) follows from (1), (2), and (7); the negation of (5) follows from (1), (3), and (7); the negation of (6) follows from (2), (3), and (7); the negation of (7) follows from (1), (2), and (4), from (1), (3), and (5), or from (2), (3), and (6); and so forth. So the question is, how

---

[17] Perry, "The Same *F*," 200.

[18] Ibid., 189. Cf. Wiggins, *Sameness and Substance*, 36.

[19] Cartwright, "Logical Problem," 188. Of these tenets Cartwright affirms: "When it comes to orthodoxy on the matter of the Trinity, they are inviolable" (ibid., 190). Cf. S. Davis, *Logic and the Nature of God*, 134-35; Martinich, "Identity and Trinity," 170, and "God, Emperor," 181.

might these seven propositions be read without incurring either contradiction or heresy? Arianism denies (2), modalism denies or makes problems for (4), (5), and (6), and tritheism denies (7). What model, conception, or account, if any, skirts these pitfalls, leaves all seven propositions intact, and, through its own coherence, suggests the coherence of the orthodox doctrine?

One Model

Given these parameters, Miss Beauchamp comes to mind and her "three different persons" (as Prince put it), each with "a distinctly different character," revealed to observers by what she said and did. However, these three "persons" were also at odds with one another (one, for instance, called another "the idiot"). So I propose instead the following analogy, with the same basic pattern of inner differences revealed by outer but without any hint of conflict.

My mother, whose Norwegian maiden name was Mary Lie, was a teacher and an artist. This one woman was all three—mother of me and my brothers, teacher of grade-school children, and professionally trained artist gifted in portraiture and the water-color depiction of flowers. The mother, the teacher, and the artist had much in common—consciousness, body, life history, memories, etc. She was, after all, a single woman, a single human being. And yet, what she *did* she also *was*. To her different roles there corresponded different capacities, interests, and inclinations. What made her capable of motherhood was not identical with what made her capable of teaching or artistic creation, neither was what made her capable of teaching identical with what made her capable of artistic creation, or vice versa. The outer revealed the inner. To indicate these differences, inner as well as outer, we might affix three names—Mary the Mother, Mary the Teacher, and Mary the Artist—and draw a comparison with God the Father, God the Son, and God the Holy Spirit. Such a comparison does not, of course, carry through in all respects (God the Father is not a mother, God the Holy Spirit is not an artist, and so forth). However, to borrow Rowan Williams's apt phrase, the comparison does provide an "analogical structure that may assist our thinking about God."[20] For the following parallel holds, proposition by proposition, with the sevenfold scheme above:

1. The Mother is Mary Lie.
2. The Teacher is Mary Lie.
3. The Artist is Mary Lie.
4. The Mother is not the Teacher.
5. The Mother is not the Artist.
6. The Teacher is not the Artist.
7. There is only one Mary Lie.

---

[20] R. Williams, "*Trinitate*," 846.

For reasons already noted, this is a coherent set of propositions. Propositions 1 to 3 state the evident union, while in propositions 4 to 6 the three names pick out differences which indicate both the basis for the negations and their sense. If the corresponding Trinitarian propositions are taken the same way, the result will be an equally coherent set. Furthermore, for reasons that can already be surmised, the propositions so taken may be orthodox. For they avoid Arianism (1-3), modalism (4-6), and tritheism (7).

Arianism. For Arius, only the Father is truly God; the Son and the Holy Spirit are not. Though the most perfect of creatures, the Son is nonetheless a creature, begotten by the Father. In contrast, Mary the Teacher and Mary the Artist were as truly Mary Lie as was Mary the Mother, and Mary the Mother did not bear either of them. Thus, a Trinitarian doctrine construed on this model is not Arian.

Modalism. For modalism, one and the same divine Person "is given different names according as He exercises different functions *ad extra* or outside the Trinity: creation (Father), redemption (Son), sanctification (Holy Spirit)."[21] However, *ad extra* and only *ad extra*, for in modalism these modes of external activity offer no information about God's eternal being (save that the one God is capable of exercising these roles);[22] they correspond to no inner differentiations. Thus, "while verbally admitting a Trinity, [modalism] denied the real distinction between the Persons."[23] By contrast, the above model (call it Model M), draws an inner as well as an outer distinction between Mary the Mother, Mary the Teacher, and Mary the Artist, and, by implication, between God the Father, God the Son, and God the Holy Spirit.[24]

Tritheism. Despite the outer and inner differences noted between mother, teacher, and artist, my mother was clearly a single individual, one person. Thus, though other models may threaten to split God into three distinct individuals, three gods, this one does not. Its kinship with modalism is more likely to elicit misgivings. For example, it may appear to be implicated in Claude Welch's critique. Modalism, he writes,

> limit[s] the significance of the doctrine of the Trinity primarily to the area of revelation or manifestation, with only the vague assertion that the threefoldness is truly rooted in the essential nature of God. With this assertion, modalism goes further than (e.g.) Knudson, but still stops short of the crucial question which the doctrine of the Trinity has historically sought to answer, namely, *in what way* are we to say that this threefoldness of revelation is rooted in the being of God? If the threefoldness is not simply a matter of our apprehension, what does it mean as applied to God

---

[21] Hamell, "Modalism," 988.

[22] O'Collins, *The Tripersonal God*, 104. See also Pelikan, *Emergence*, 176-77.

[23] Hamell, "Modalism," 988. Cf. Klinger, "Modalism," 88-89. (This sprinkling of citations is intended to stave off any impression of personal, ad hoc definition in behalf of a position that may appear to smack of modalism.)

[24] Although one reported comparison of Sabellius, the foremost modalist, resembles the present model, his typical and better-attested thought differs notably from it. See, e.g., Wolfson, *Faith, Trinity, Incarnation*, 596-97.

himself? If we are able to say nothing about the nature of God in himself on the basis of his mode of revelation to us, then one is entitled to ask to what extent we can speak of the full or decisive revelation of God in Christ.[25]

If Welch extended this complaint to Model M, one might wonder where the problem lay. Did my mother's mothering, teaching, painting, drawing, and the rest reveal nothing about her inner being? What might do so more effectively? Saying, for example, "I love painting" rather than devoting herself to painting? But actions speak louder than words. So what, in the case of God, might be more revealing than God's actions? Where is the vagueness?

Model M helps to distinguish and to assess realistically two possible sources of the kind of dissatisfaction ("vague assertion," "what does it mean") that Welch expresses. Stephen Davis indicates the first when he writes:

> Father, Son and Holy Spirit are three what and one what? Here, I believe (following Augustine), is the real source of mystery of the Trinity: not that God is three-in-one (lots of things—like triangles and families—can legitimately be described as three-in-one) but that with God we have no ready answer to the questions: three what? and one what? That is, we have no ready ontological categories in which to place God. It is tempting merely to repeat the classical terminology and say, "God is three persons and one substance," pretending that that solves the problem. But the patristic and medieval categories—three persons in one substance, three hypostases in one essence, etc.—seem obscure and problematical.[26]

Davis wants a suitable "ontological category" for the three "persons." So too, perhaps, does Welch. And modalism, it seems, provides none. Neither does Model M. In a sense, the model furnishes no answer to Davis's question: "Three what?" Mary the Mother, Mary the Teacher, and Mary the Artist are not, in the ordinary sense of the term, three distinct "persons." Neither, for that matter, are they three "subsistent relations" or "modes of being." Indeed, neither Latin nor Greek nor any of their derivatives furnishes any "ready ontological category" for this threesome—any count noun to substitute for the variable in "The three Mary's are three x's." Yet the distinction between the Mary's is no less intelligible on that account. And the like holds for the three divine "persons" if this model aptly suggests their relationship.

Where a notion is intelligible, the lack of a label to express it has little significance. Make one up. Call the three Mary's "Selective Selves," "Distinguishable Agents," or what have you. Do not suppose, though, that possessing a name, familiar or fabricated, does anything to diminish the mystery of the reality thus labeled. Here is a second possible source of dissatisfaction. My mother loved to paint; that was evident. But what in her inner make-up corresponded to the outer activity? In what did her "love of painting" consist, besides what she did? A feeling? Pleasant thoughts while painting? Not just that. A "disposition"? To be

---

[25] Welch, *In This Name*, 63 (his emphasis).

[26] S. Davis, *Logic*, 136 (paragraph break suppressed).

sure, but modern physiology, depth psychology, and philosophy of mind make clear that this reply merely issues a blank check. Something or other inside her gave rise, somehow or other, to much painting; and both the something and the somehow were specific for love of painting; they differed, in innerly mysterious ways, from those for alternative or complementary motives (financial need, desire for fame, imitation of a model, peer pressure, etc.). If this is vagueness, so be it. But with regard to human beings the vagueness is not likely to be remedied any time soon, and the idea that it might be remedied in God's case is a far-fetched illusion. Model M helps to bring this out; it helps to pinpoint the mystery.

In further illustration of the same points, consider the single rose we see, feel, and smell—the Red Rose, say, the Velvety Rose, and the Sweet Rose. To this triple aspect of the single object internal differences correspond, of that we feel sure—especially now that science has given us some idea what the differences are. Yet even today the ordinary person could not spell out these inner differences (the disposition of the molecules, atoms, etc.), and in the past they were an almost total mystery. However, the mystery was ontological, not semantic or logical. The *notion* "the rose in so far as it gives rise to this or that specific appearance" was roughly intelligible; the corresponding *reality* lay hidden in the complex physical object. Making up a common term for the Red Rose, the Velvety Rose, and the Sweet Rose, or appropriating some existing term for the purpose, would do nothing to reduce that mystery. Indeed, it might just mask the mystery, by creating the impression that we finally had a firmer grasp of the reality behind the appearances. Or it might beget new mysteries as a result of lingering associations with the appropriated term's customary employment. In making these remarks I have in mind, of course, such Trinitarian terms as "prosopon" and "persona"; for the early Fathers found themselves in this same semantic situation when they beat about for an existing, common term with which to designate Father, Son, and Holy Spirit.[27] When they picked "prosopon" and "persona," it is as though, for lack of a better word, they had chosen to call the Red Rose, the Velvety Rose, and the Sweet Rose three distinct "flowers," with a warning that the term should not of course be understood in its ordinary sense.[28]

I have dwelt on the difference between verbal and nonverbal difficulties because their conflation, which I sense is common, can obscure the merits of Model M.

---

[27] Cf. Hanson, *Search*, 181-82: "for most (but not all) writers in Greek at the beginning of the controversy and for a long time after it had begun, there was no single agreed word available and widely used for what God is as Three in distinction from what he is as One. All pre-Nicenes, Sellers tells us, found difficulty in expressing the Son's personality. The word *hypostasis* is virtually unknown in Classical Greek in its philosophical sense."

[28] Note the important divergence here from the viewpoint of Barth, as of Augustine whom he cites. According to Barth, a really suitable term not only does not exist but could not exist, given the transcendence of its referent (*Church Dogmatics*, vol. 1/1, 355-56). I view the difficulty differently. As a suitable term might have existed with which to differentiate the three Mary's, despite their inner mystery, so a suitable term—perhaps the same term—might have existed with which to differentiate the three divine "persons."

Conflate them, and the model's failure to furnish the desired, missing word or category may appear a serious matter. Again, conflate them, and it may appear that what the model does not and cannot provide is something within our reach. If only we had the right word! Reflection on the model suggests that, on the one hand, the lack of a word may not be a serious matter and that, on the other hand, possession of a word may signal no genuine advance in understanding. *No* model will clarify the mystery which this one leaves unresolved. And other models cause problems which this one avoids.

Alternatives

Most notably, competing accounts fail the identity test in propositions (1) to (3): the Father is God, the Son is God, and the Holy Spirit is God. This they do in two general ways which can be suggested roughly, here at the start, through comparison with Model M. In some accounts, it is as though Mary the Mother were identified with Mary's maternal aspect, Mary the Teacher with her teaching aspect, and Mary the Artist with her artistic aspect, with the result that no one of the three could any longer be said to *be* Mary Lie. For my mother was not any one of these aspects of her total self, neither was any single aspect identical with her. In other accounts, it is as though "Mary Lie" were the name for a triad of sisters, each with her own distinctive trait or traits and none identical with the total, communal Mary Lie. This latter Trinitarian approach has become common in recent times, whereas the other has figured more prominently throughout the history of theology. More prominently, but not more perspicuously. In the instances I shall cite, it is often unclear whether "Father," "Son," and "Holy Spirit" name mere aspects, modes, or relations present in God, or the God in whom they are present. Understood the latter way, such accounts may complement but do not conflict with Model M and do not fail the identity test. Understood the other way, they do.

The Cappadocians (I)

Such ambiguity characterizes not only the teaching of some Trinitarian theologians but also some accounts given of their teaching. After reviewing the particularizing characteristics of the three Persons cited by the Cappadocians, J. N. D. Kelly writes:

> Thus the distinction of the Persons is grounded in Their origin and mutual relation. They are, we should observe, so many ways in which the one indivisible divine substance distributes and presents Itself, and hence They come to be termed 'modes of coming to be' (τρόποι ὑπάρξεως). So Basil's friend Amphilochius of Iconium, after stating his belief in 'one God made known in three forms of presentation' (προσώποις), suggests that the names Father, Son and Holy Spirit do not stand for

essence or being ('God' does), but for 'a mode of existence or relation' (τρόπος ὑπάρξεως ἤτουν σχέσεως).[29]

The three Persons, it seems, are mere "ways" or "modes," hence cannot be identified with God. However, Kelly continues: "A modern theologian has aptly summarized [the Cappadocians'] thought in the sentence, 'The whole unvaried substance, being incomposite, is identical with the whole unvaried being of each Person . . . the individuality is only the manner in which the identical substance is objectively presented in each several Person.'"[30] Here, the manner is not the Person but is "presented" in each Person, so no problems of identity arise. As readily as in Model M, each Person can be identified with God.

This confusion of perspectives is not entirely of Kelly's creation. Similar ambiguity appears, for example, in Gregory of Nazianzus's third *Theological Oration* (section 16): "I should have been frightened by your distinction, if it had been necessary to accept one or other of the alternatives, and not rather put both aside, and state a third and truer one, namely that 'the Father' is not the name either of an essence or of an action, but is the name of the relation, in which the Father stands to the Son and the Son to the Father."[31] A relation is neither an essence nor an action. Neither is it God. However, the Father cannot be both the relation and the one who stands in that relation; so such a text leaves the judgment on identity in doubt.[32]

Augustine

The verdict for Augustine's psychological analogies looks clearer. Comparing the divine Three with mind, knowledge, and love in a single human being (book 9 of *De trinitate*) or with a single individual's memory, intelligence, and will (book 10), Augustine may slip between Arianism on the one hand and modalism on the other, and may claim backing in the biblical faith that human beings are made in God's image and likeness (Gn 1:26-27). Yet none of these analogies, despite their variety, permits the statement, "The Father is God," "The Son is God," or "The Holy Spirit is God." Jack's memory is not Jack, Jill's intelligence is not Jill, and so for all the rest. However, there is another side of Augustine's thinking. As William Hill has observed, "Because Christians profess 'three persons' Augustine personifies the triadic relationality in God. In consequence, he goes on to describe the Three as subjects, as distinct sources of a single agency. But the move is dictated by fidelity to the rule of faith and Augustine supplies us with no logical warrant for it in his own theology."[33]

---

[29] Kelly, *Early Christian Doctrines*, 265-66.

[30] Ibid., 266.

[31] Quoted in Meredith, *The Cappadocians*, 107-8.

[32] In Oration 40 (section 41), Gregory writes that the Trinitarian persons considered in themselves are God.

[33] W. Hill, *The Three-Personed God*, 60.

Aquinas

Similar problems linger in Aquinas, of whose thought O'Collins writes:

> At the same time, personal being in God is totally relational; in Aquinas's terms the
> divine persons are the relations expressed by generation and spiration (ST 1a 40.2 ad
> 1). They are subsistent relations, that is to say, relations that exist in themselves and
> are not mere "accidental" relations that are added to already existing substances (such
> as a business relationship that a human person takes on). Thus through the eventlike
> attributes of generation and spiration, clarified by his language of subsistent relations,
> Aquinas worked out further the second part of what we quoted above from Augustine:
> "God is everything that he has except for the relations through which each person is
> referred to each other."[34]

This is difficult. The divine persons cannot be both the relations and the terms of
the relations; and if they are the relations, they are not God. Paternity is not God,
filiation is not God, spiration is not God. Neither are they persons in any recognizable sense of the term. However, Aquinas saw things differently: "Distinction in
God is only by relation of origin, . . . while relation in God is not as an accident in
a subject, but is the divine essence itself; and so it is subsistent, for the divine
substance subsists. Therefore, as the Godhead is God so the divine paternity is God
the Father, Who is a divine person."[35] Model M helps to straighten this out. Real-
life Maryhood, we might say, is Mary; just the grammatical form differs. So far, so
good. However, her maternity is not Mary; neither is it Mary the Mother. Whether
essential or accidental, internal or external, a relation is not identical with what it
relates. The only way to save Aquinas's conclusion ("the divine paternity is God
the Father") would be to take him as saying, not just that each relation belongs to
the divine essence but that it exhaustively constitutes, or is identical with, the
divine essence. In God there are no real distinctions. But in that case Father, Son,
and Holy Spirit would be identical and differ only in name. Modalists would be
right.

Barth

"The God who reveals Himself according to Scripture," writes Karl Barth, "is One
in three distinctive modes of being subsisting in their mutual relations: Father, Son,
and Holy Spirit."[36] This identification of the three divine persons as "modes of
being" recurs frequently in Barth's *Church Dogmatics*. For example: "at the point
where earlier dogmatics and even modern Roman Catholic dogmatics speak of
persons we prefer to call the Father, Son and Spirit in God the three distinctive
modes of being of the one God subsisting in their relationships one with

---

[34] O'Collins, *The Tripersonal God*, 145.

[35] Aquinas, *Summa theologica* 1.29.4.

[36] Barth, *Church Dogmatics*, vol. 1/1, 348.

another."[37] Again: "This distinction or order is the distinction or order of the three 'persons,' or, as we prefer to say, the three 'modes (or ways) of being' in God."[38] Judging from such assertions as these,[39] one would have to conclude that none of the three persons is God, for a mode of being is not God and God is not a mode of being. Yet Barth wishes to retain all three identities, for he writes: "What are these three—apart from the fact that all together as well as each individually they are the one true God?"[40]

Barth acknowledges the consequent conundrum.

> The great central difficulties which have always beset the doctrine of the Trinity at this point apply to us too. We, too, are unable to say how an essence can produce itself and then be in a twofold way its own product. We, too, are unable to say how an essence's relation of origin can also be the essence itself and indeed how three such relations can be the essence and yet not the same as each other but indissolubly distinct from one another.[41]

Thus, where I see incoherence, Barth sees mystery. Though all three "persons" are mere relations or modes of being, and though all three are distinct from one another, each and all are identical with God. The Father is God, the Son is God, and the Holy Spirit is God! Yet how is that possible, Barth wonders. There is no need, I would say, to thus multiply mysteries. One can view the modes or relations, not as the "persons" of tradition but as their distinguishing traits. That is, one can adopt the perspective of Model M—the one suggested, for example, by the words Barth quotes from B. Bartmann: "That whereby the three persons are distinguished from one another is not to be sought in the essentiality nor yet primarily in the person in itself, which is fully equal to the others and perfect and eternal, but in the different way of possessing the essentiality."[42]

Rahner

"Karl Rahner," writes Jürgen Moltmann, "developed his doctrine of the Trinity with an astonishing similarity to Barth and almost the same presuppositions."[43] Specifically, notes Leonardo Boff, "Following Barth, but adding a further precision, Rahner defines 'person' as a *'distinct mode of subsistence.'*"[44] Others read

---

[37] Ibid., 366.

[38] Ibid., 355.

[39] E.g., ibid., 360 ("Nor can there be any possibility that one of the modes of being might just as well be the other, e.g., that the Father might just as well be the Son or the Son the Spirit").

[40] Ibid., 355. See ibid., 361 ("the one undifferentiated divine essence with which Father, Son and Spirit are, of course, identical").

[41] Ibid., 367.

[42] Ibid., 360.

[43] Moltmann, *The Trinity and the Kingdom*, 144.

[44] Boff, *Trinity and Society*, 118 (his emphasis).

Rahner similarly. "Karl Rahner," writes Ted Peters, "wants to hold on to the classical formulation, but he wants to define 'person' as a 'distinct manner of subsisting.'"[45] This apparent similarity of doctrine evokes a joint expostulation: "How could one adore and glorify Rahner's 'three distinct manners of subsisting' or Barth's 'the Revealer, the Revelation, and the Revealedness' (i.e., three modes of being)?"[46]

There are grounds for this assimilation. Rahner sounds very much like Barth when Rahner writes: "One could also, for instance, instead of speaking of three persons, speak of three distinct ways of being there (in the economy of salvation) and three different ways of subsistence (immanently) for the one God."[47] And he adds: "Father, Son and Spirit are distinct, qua oppositional, relations."[48] At this point, the same verdict seems to follow for Rahner as for Barth: if Father, Son, and Holy Spirit are relations or manners of subsisting, then the Father is not God, the Son is not God, and the Holy Spirit is not God. However, in the same paragraph Rahner goes on to state: "Father, Son and Spirit are the one and the same God in the Godhead, in its different ways of subsistence." This sounds more like Model M. So, too, do the sentences toward which a summarizing paragraph builds in a work often cited in support of a more Barthian reading:

> Let us further test the usefulness of the expression "distinct manners of subsisting" (while here and now methodically avoiding the word "person") by formulating a few basic statements about the Trinity with the help of this concept. We may say, then, that:
>   —the one God subsists in three distinct manners of subsisting;
>   —the manners of subsisting of Father, Son, and Spirit are distinct as relations of opposition; hence these "three" are not the same one;
>   —the Father, Son, and Spirit are the one God each in a different manner of subsisting and in this sense we may count "three" in God; . . .[49]

If this is Rahner's final word, his view resembles Model M more than it does Barth's position. The problem of identity is resolved much as in Model M, and with it the problem of adoration. Our adoration is not directed to three manners of subsisting but to the one God thus subsisting.

For the views so far sampled, Model M provides a clarifying term of comparison. To avoid modalism, these views stress the distinctness of the three Persons

---

[45] Peters, *GOD as Trinity*, 35. See Cunningham, *These Three Are One*, 27-28, and Marsh, *The Triune God*, 177.

[46] O'Collins, *The Tripersonal God*, 175-76, and "The Holy Trinity," 22-23. Cf. Boff, *Trinity and Society*, 118: "No one can adore 'a distinct mode of subsistence'; only Father, Son and Holy Spirit can be adored."

[47] Rahner, "Trinity," 302.

[48] Cf. Rahner, *The Trinity*, 47, which jumbles the relational and non-relational ("the Trinity, in which the Father is the incomprehensible origin and the original unity, the 'Word' his utterance into history, and the 'Spirit' the opening up of history into the immediacy of its fatherly origin and end").

[49] Rahner, *The Trinity*, 113-14.

from one another. To avoid tritheism, they tend to equate the three Persons with whatever distinguishes them from God. However, to the extent that they do so, they negate the identity of each Person with God. Model M exemplifies a way to avoid this unwanted consequence: the Persons are not distinguishing character-istics, but God so distinguished. Now, however, as our sampling of alternatives continues, Model M can no longer serve this clarifying purpose, for the remaining views that clash with propositions (1) to (3) do so differently. Their three Persons resemble three gods more than they do three aspects of a single God.

The Cappadocians (II)

For initial illustration of this difference, we can turn again to the Cappadocians. In explanation of the relationship between the single divine essence and the three coequal persons that share it, they drew a comparison with three human persons and the common nature they share.[50] The nature of the sharing therefore looked suspect. They were accused of interpreting the creedal term "homoousion" in a merely specific or generic sense. "Much more to the point," suggests Kelly, "is the related suggestion, which was advanced as much in their own day as in ours, that their doctrine, despite its sincere intention of maintaining the divine unity, was inescapably tritheistic. Admittedly certain features of their thought seem to lend colour to the charge, not least their unfortunate comparison of the *ousia* of Godhead to a universal manifesting itself in particulars."[51] Viewed through this comparison, the Father would not be God, nor would the Son, nor would the Holy Spirit. For no single person would be identical with the triune Godhead of Father, Son, and Holy Spirit. Similar implications arise, but differently, in numerous recent accounts.

Communitarians

For many today, the Trinity constitutes "a society," "a communion," "a community of three divine persons." "*Three Persons and a single communion and a single trinitarian community*: this is the best formula to represent the Christian God."[52] For some, the members of this community are persons in the full sense of the term.[53] They are three distinct centers of consciousness, three distinct I's, who can

---

[50] Cf. Basil, *Ep.* 38.3 (PG 32, 328-29), *Ep.* 214.4 (PG 32, 789), *Ep.* 236.6 (PG 32, 884); Gregory of Nyssa, *Quod non sint tres dii* (PG 45, 120).

[51] Kelly, *Early Christian Doctrines*, 267.

[52] Boff, *Trinity and Society*, 133 (his emphasis). Cf. Margerie, *The Christian Trinity in History*, 286: "The family together with the person of each of its members is incontestably the natural reality par excellence from which one can by analogy rise notably, with the gifts of the Spirit, to a very fruitful though still very imperfect understanding of the Trinitarian mystery."

[53] Hodgson, *The Doctrine of the Trinity*, 140 ("distinct Person in the full sense of that word"); Mondin, *La Trinità mistero d'amore*, 311 ("The three divine lovers are persons in the full sense [*a pieno titolo*]").

address each other as "you" and together can say "we."[54] "Beneath, behind the names, are personalities."[55] Other theorists mitigate somewhat the comparison with human persons in a human society, yet for them too the analogy remains sufficiently robust so that "there is in God a Father, a Son and a Spirit, who mutually love and commune—that is, *who enjoy personal relationships*—with each other."[56] Accordingly, the implication seems clear: if "God" is the name of the society thus formed, no single member can be identified with God. Neither the Father nor the Son nor the Holy Spirit is God, any more, for example, than a husband, wife, or child is, individually, the family formed by husband, wife, and child. Despite its variations, the social model conflicts with propositions (1) to (3).

Joseph Bracken has adverted to this problem. "Everything depends," he maintains, " . . . upon whether one accepts the antecedent philosophical hypothesis that the unity of a community is a genuine ontological unity on a higher level of being than that of individual substance. Given this premise, however, it is not inconsistent to say that the Father is God, the Son is God, and the Spirit is God in virtue of their unity as a (divine) community."[57] No matter how sublime their unity, I would say, the members of a community are not individually identical with the community. A parent is not a family, a chairman is not a committee, a citizen is not a nation, a member of the Mystical Body is not the Mystical Body. The difficulty is highlighted, not removed, by Bracken's parenthetical explanation: "Each of the three divine persons is both God (i.e., a member of this community) and a subsistent individual (Father, Son and Holy Spirit)."[58]

Peter Forrest proposes a solution that at first appears bizarre: God was one, then underwent fission, and now the resulting three persons can each be identified with God.[59] How? Why? No worldly split (e.g., of an iceberg into berglets) has such a result. And the splits that philosophers imagine (e.g., of persons, with half a brain here and half a brain there) elicit split verdicts. But Forrest has a special twist. The three persons now discernible through their loving relationships were originally

---

[54] Mondin, *La Trinità mistero d'amore*, 313; Hasker, "Tri-Unity," 5.

[55] McDonough, *The Divine Family*, 21.

[56] Hasker, "Tri-Unity," 5.

[57] Bracken, "The Holy Trinity," 179.

[58] Ibid., 182. Cf. Layman, "Tritheism and Trinity," 295: "the Father is worthy of worship, but He isn't the *community* of divine selves. And hence, He is not (strictly speaking) God. The same goes, of course, for the Son and the Holy Spirit." The problem appears so obvious that I look for some way to explain Bracken's claim. A clue may surface when he writes that the ideas "person" and "community" "are really only one complex idea, since it is impossible properly to conceive of one without simultaneously making reference to the other" (*The Triune Symbol*, 15; cf. ibid., 27). By the same logic, "touchdown" and "football," or "word" and "language," would be but a single idea. But they are not, and no one would say that a football is a touchdown, a word is a language, or the like. The identity inference works no better for the Trinitarian persons.

[59] Forrest explains: "I identify the ultimate cause of all things with the God who is the Trinity, not the First Person. Accordingly, I speculate that the Trinity arises as a result of fission by the primordial God, rather than the primordial God bringing other divine persons into existence" ("Divine Fission," 282).

indiscernible persons in the single primordial God. Lacking "thisness," they were only quasi-individuals; being only quasi-individuals, they left intact the unity of God. So the divine fission, unlike that of icebergs or imaginary persons, was not the splitting of a single individual into three individuals but rather the splitting of three quasi-individuals into the same three quasi-individuals, now differentiated by their relationships. Their identity with themselves, hence with the one God they constituted, endures.

And yet, note the past tense: "constituted." The primordial God is introduced in order to assure a degree of unity which no longer exists. So it is open to Muslim or Jew to object: "Your God may once have been our God, but no longer is. You now have three gods." There is also a problem about that earlier stage. In Forrest's account, lack of thisness achieves the desired unity in the primordial God, thereby crucially modifying social trinitarianism and making it more acceptable to Moslem and Jew. However, what is this "thisness"? Typically, the sort of primitive thisness Forrest has in mind is invoked to individuate a plurality of otherwise indiscernible entities. Its presence may be doubted when the entities are discernibly different (since that might suffice to individuate them) and its multiple presence may be doubted when plurality looks uncertain. In any case, such thisness has no other role and no other intelligibility than to individuate. Thus Forrest remarks, "By a thisness I mean an unanalysable intrinsic property necessarily unique to the thing which has it."[60] So my problem is this: how can Forrest's quasi-individuals in the primordial God be individuals of any kind if they are not somehow individuated, and how, if they are indiscernibly alike, can they be individuated otherwise than by their individual thisness—by their being this person and that person and the other? Differentiating by means of thisness looks mysterious enough.[61] Differentiating without even thisness looks too mysterious to throw any light on the Trinity.[62]

Comparative Assessment

The sampling now completed permits us to distinguish between positions that, like Model M, accommodate propositions (1) to (3) and those that do not, and to distinguish between those that do not because their accounts of the three Persons are insufficiently personal ("modes of being," "manners of subsisting," etc.) and those that do not because their accounts are too personal ("centers of conscious-

---

[60] Ibid., 284.

[61] Cf. Swinburne, "Thisness," and O'Leary-Hawthorne and Cover, "Framing the Thisness Issue."

[62] A sample of the sort of thing that elicits this quick response: "if there is no thisness then there is no fact of the matter as to whether we describe the possible world as consisting of one sphere or two qualitatively identical spheres. Hence the spheres are quasi-individuals" (Forrest, "Divine Fission," 292). They are or are not individuated, as you please. Choose one way for the Trinity, and you have the unity you need; choose the other way, and you have the plurality you need. The problem is solved.

ness," "distinct I's," etc.). Which of these three alternatives, we can now ask, is more orthodox, more firmly rooted in Christian belief?

Let us start with the obvious question: does the very fact that only Model M-type views satisfy the three identities—of Father, Son, and Spirit with God—tell decisively in their favor? Some proponents of the social analogy think not, since they regard propositions (1) to (3) as dispensable. Thus Stephen Layman writes:

> Someone might object: "On the Social view one cannot say, e.g., that the Father is God, since the Father is not a community. But don't the creeds say that the Father is God, the Son is God, etc.?" Yes, these *words* are used. The question is, "What do they mean?" The Social Trinitarian takes them to mean that the Father is divine, the Son is divine, etc. In other words, he understands the creeds to be saying that each of the divine persons is worthy of worship, and hence that they all have the same ontological status. This interpretation of the creeds certainly seems reasonable. Similarly, Christians say that Jesus is Lord, the Father is Lord, etc., and yet there are not three Lords. It seems reasonable to construe these utterances as asserting that each divine self is a member of the social entity that alone rules the cosmos.[63]

It may be reasonable, I would say, to propose this as a *possible* reading, but even that depends on the wording and the context, proximate and remote, of the utterances in question. I shall not wade through the pertinent evidence in scriptural, patristic, and conciliar texts, which is complex and appears indecisive, but will pass straightway to the principal objection urged against the social model.

"We in the West today," writes Catherine LaCugna,

> think of a person as a "self" who may be further defined as an individual center of consciousness, a free, intentional subject, one who knows and is known, loves and is loved, an individual identity, a unique personality endowed with certain rights, a moral agent, someone who experiences, weighs, decides, and acts. This fits well with the idea that God is personal, but not at all with the idea that God is three persons. Three persons defined in this way would amount to three gods, three beings who act independently, three conscious individuals.[64]

A response might focus on the word "independently." Thus, for Boff, "The error of tritheism was in affirming *just* the existence of three divine Persons, without their reciprocal inter-relatedness, the Three being juxtaposed and separated as though they were three natures or substances."[65] Going further, "social trinitarians might say that God is to be characterized as the perfect being and that what is perfect is not any one of these three gods, glorious though they be, but the

---

[63] Layman, "Tritheism and the Trinity," 295. For similar predicational reading of the apparent identity statements, see, e.g., T. Morris, *The Logic of God Incarnate*, 27; Yandell, "The Most Brutal," 210-11.

[64] LaCugna, *God for Us*, 250. See Leftow, "Anti Social Trinitarianism"; McDermott, *Word Become Flesh*, 180; O'Donnell, *The Mystery of the Triune God*, 103; Peters, *GOD as Trinity*, 35; Welch, *In This Name*, 252-72.

[65] Boff, *Trinity and Society*, 139.

community of love which they constitute."[66] And so they have.[67] To critics this still smacks of tritheism. There may be only one God with a capital G, namely the single divine community, but there are still three gods. To invoke the "perfect interpenetration of the three persons," as above, so as to downplay the threeness, would be to acknowledge the imperfection of the social analogy—or at least its utter mystery. And mysteries should not be multiplied without necessity.

The trouble with views at the other extreme is not that they portray the three Persons as too much resembling gods but that they portray them as too little resembling persons. An Augustinian psychological component did not send the Son or the Spirit into the world. A Thomistic subsistent relation or Barthian mode of existence will not instruct the disciples (Jn 14:26), bear witness to Jesus (Jn. 16:8), or convince the world of sin (Jn 16:8). As Alan Torrance urges against Barth, the biblical witness speaks "in irreducibly 'personal' terms (e.g., Father and Son) and metaphors (cf. the endless references to the purposive agency of the Spirit)."[68] Granted, the everyday usage of the traditional terms "Father" and "Son" may suggest the kind of individuation which Barth feared ("When used of different subjects, they suggest a plurality of personalities as also of self-consciousnesses, wills and intelligences"[69]); however, the terms need not be so used, of different subjects. Model M suggests a happier solution, more faithful to scriptural and traditional ways of speaking, than Barth's or any similarly reductive, nonpersonal solution.

Mystery

If the reasoning to this point is correct, the mysteriousness of the Trinity can be somewhat diminished. There is no need to puzzle how three persons, in any familiar sense of the term, can constitute a single, personal God. There is no need to puzzle how personal terms can rightly be used of relations, faculties, modes of being, or the like. A Model M-type solution can be found. Where, then, in this solution, does mystery remain, and of what kind?

Let us start with Model M itself—that is, with Mary the Mother, Mary the Teacher, and Mary the Artist. As already noted, this model traces outer differences to inner differences but ventures no account of the latter. The "economic" Trinity

---

[66] Forrest, "Divine Fission," 283.

[67] E.g., David Brown, *The Divine Trinity,* 299, and "Wittgenstein against the 'Wittgensteinians,'" 270; Bracken, "The Holy Trinity," 168: "The basic hypothesis will be that the three divine Persons are one God in virtue of their unity-in-community. The ontological unity of persons-in-community represents according to this way of thinking a higher level of being and intelligibility than that of individual substance." Cf. Layman, "Tritheism and the Trinity," 294: "Social Trinitarians will deny that there are three Lords of the universe, even though there are three divine selves. For it is the *community* of divine persons that has ultimate authority."

[68] Torrance, *Persons in Communion,* 233.

[69] Ibid., 237.

correlates with but need not, and probably does not, mirror the immanent Trinity (any more than a loving kiss mirrors an inner kiss, or an outer hug mirrors an inner, transcendent embrace). Furthermore, Model M does not pretend to explain why there are just three divine persons (after all, my mother was also a cook, citizen, Christian, etc.). Neither does it attempt to clarify the intratrinitarian relations, as have many theologians.

Rahner can serve as an example. Starting with the premise that God is spirit, he reasons:

> an authentic metaphysics of the spirit tells us that there are two (and only two!) basic activities of the spirit: knowledge and love. On the other hand, in harmony with the threefold distinct manner of subsisting of the one God, we know of two (and only two!) processions or emanations within God. . . . We are allowed, then, to combine these two data and to connect, in a special and specific way, the intra-divine procession of the Logos from the Father with God's knowledge, and the procession of the Spirit from the Father through the Son with God's love.[70]

Though much more definite than Model M (whose details merely illustrate a general structure), this account, too, leaves a residue of mystery: "we cannot further explain *why* and *how* these two basic actuations of God's essence, as present in the unoriginate Father and, on account of God's simplicity, essentially identical within him, constitute nonetheless the basis for two processions and thus for three distinct manners of subsisting."[71]

Rahner's reasoning merits scrutiny, since it exemplifies a common format (a theological conclusion deduced from a major premise of faith and a minor premise of reason) and illustrates the problems for such an approach. Concerning the premise of faith—"we know of two (and only two!) processions or emanations within God"—we may wonder, for example, how we can pass from "we know of only two" to "there are only two"—especially in view of the way the number two was arrived at. The premise of reason, alleging two and only two "basic activities of the spirit," appears still more problematic. Ignoring the characterization of knowledge and love as "activities" (which appears a misuse of the term), we can ask: What about enjoyment? What about regret? What about hope, expectation, thought, remembrance, contrition, frustration, intention, desire, compassion, hate, doubt, belief, interest, gratitude, repugnance, and the rest? "Not basic," might be the reply. "If we hope for something, it is because we *love* it. If we doubt something, it is because we *know* reasons for uncertainty. And so for all the rest." Well, not at all evidently. What is more, this reasoning might be reversed. Knowledge, the first of Rahner's two "basic activities of the spirit," has been defined as justified true belief, and can be traced to other beliefs. Love, his second "basic activity," can arise from remembrance, gratitude, belief, or desire. Perhaps, amid the welter of interconnecting psychological concepts, some sense of the term

---

[70] Rahner, *The Trinity*, 116.

[71] Ibid., 117 (Rahner's emphasis). Rahner often stresses the absolute mystery of God, but his theological practice, as here, often gives a different impression.

"basic" might be discerned which would allow us to identify "knowledge" and "love" as the only two basic psychological concepts, but I doubt it. However, it does not matter. For certainly all other psychological states or activities cannot be reduced to just these two. And if all the rest remain possibilities, then the divine persons might be characterized by admiration, intention, awe, gratitude, enjoyment, respect, compassion, or what have you, alone or variously combined (as for human persons). Or they might be differentiated in transcendent ways for which we have no appropriate terms.

The connection of Rahner's premises with his conclusion looks similarly problematic. Even were there only two processions and only two basic activities of spirit, how could we infer that one activity is paired with one procession and the other with the other? Why exclude the possibility that both activities are combined, differently, in both processions? Consider Model M and Mary's activities. Knowledge and love are present, variously, in all three—in her mothering, her teaching, and her artistic creation. Why might not love and knowledge combine in equally varied ways?

Such difficulties as these—for the premise of faith, the premise of reason, and the inference from them—seem sufficiently representative to make this genre of theological reasoning look unpromising as a means of reducing mystery, whether trinitarian or other. However, there are other forms of theological reasoning besides this one. For example, I have just employed the method of verdict by elimination. Citing reasons for favoring Model M-type accounts over alternative types, I have narrowed the mysteriousness of the Trinity. The same approach might conceivably be extended, for Model M-type accounts are more varied than this single model, with its single structure, might suggest. Thus, accounts which individuate the divine Persons solely by means of immanent relations—for instance, paternity, filiation, and spiration—but do not identify the Persons with the relations, to that extent resemble Model M. Accounts which individuate the three Persons by means of both economic and immanent relations, and connect the latter with the former, resemble Model M more closely. Again, accounts in which the distinguishing relations are of basically the same kind resemble Model M more, whereas those in which the relations differ more notably resemble Model M less. To illustrate, Basil writes: "Just because the Apostle . . . mentions the Spirit first, and the Son second, and God the Father third, do not assume that he has reversed the rank. Notice that he is speaking in the same way that we do when we receive gifts: first we thank the messenger who brought the gift; next we remember him who sent it, and finally we raise our thoughts to the fountain and source of all gifts."[72] Here, all three Persons relate to the same gifts, but differently, whereas in Model M all three persons relate to different gifts, but similarly. Other distinctions might be envisaged, and different combinations of these ones, but enough has been said to suggest what a range of possibilities the preceding narrowing, to Model M-type structures, still leaves open. So, what are the chances of further narrowing,

---

[72] Basil, *De Spiritu Sancto*, 16.37 (quoted in O'Collins, *The Tripersonal God*, 133).

through exclusion of one or the other of these alternatives? What are the chances of a verdict by elimination at this more detailed level?

Not good, it seems, since warrant for the elimination of more precise accounts (assuming the accounts' coherence) would have to come from Scripture and/or creedal formulations, and these are imprecise. How, for example, could Rahner be shown to be wrong when he links knowledge with one procession and love with the other? Or, again, consider Model M. To satisfy orthodoxy, it need not accommodate the sort of intratrinitarian personal relations (knowledge, love, etc.) that cause tritheistic problems for the social model, but what, we may ask, of the relations stated in the creeds? Does Mary the Mother "beget" Mary the Teacher? Does Mary the Artist "proceed from" Mary the Mother? Granted, Model M just illustrates a structure susceptible of endless variations. Granted, too, such expressions as "beget" and "proceed from" are, in their creedal context, extremely indefinite. Still, can a Model-M analogy accommodate them? Yes, even this specific version can. It might be suggested, for example, that if Mary the Mother brings forth children and these children elicit the attentions of Mary the Teacher, then Mary the Mother has, in a sense, "begotten" Mary the Teacher. This connection, however, is external. So we might go further and suggest that Mary the Mother's love for her children motivates Mary the Teacher to instruct them: maternal love begets the inclination which, together with her abilities, innerly defines Mary the Teacher. Thus, both externally and internally, Mary the Mother "begets" Mary the Teacher. This sample response does not pretend, of course, to define the relation between Father and Son. It just illustrates the possibilities of Model M and, more generally, of any model with the same structure (e.g., the Red Rose, the Velvety Rose, and the Sweet Rose; Peter the Israelite, Peter the Disciple, and Peter the Apostle; etc.). As Mary the Mother, Mary the Teacher, and Mary the Artist may relate to one another both externally and internally, so may the persons of the Trinity. Thus, read as intended, Model M can readily accommodate the relational aspect of the creeds.

The same model is equally open to such ordering as that exemplified by Basil's saying, "natural goodness, inherent holiness, and royal dignity reaches *from* the Father *through* the Only-begotten *to* the Spirit,"[73] or Cyril of Jerusalem's, "The Father through the Son with the Spirit gives every gift,"[74] However, to accommodate or make room for such ordering is not to clarify it. What, for instance, is the nature of Basil's or Cyril's "through"? A human being might give a gift "through" another human being by begetting the other, educating the other, supporting the other, encouraging the other, ordering the other, instructing the other, threatening the other, suggesting the gift, providing the wherewithal, removing obstacles, arranging the circumstances, and so forth; and doubtless none of

---

[73] Basil, *Liber de Spiritu Sancto* 18.47 (PG 32, 153B), quoted in Bobrinskoy, *The Mystery of the Trinity*, 237.

[74] St. Cyril of Jerusalem, *Catechetical Instructions*, 16.24 (quoted in Marsh, *The Triune God*, 170).

these and other possibilities, as realized in humans, provides a very close analog to whatever in the inner life of God might verify the same preposition, "through."

At best, theology can encroach only slightly on the mystery of God. Thus Henri de Lubac has remarked, "Knowledge of God's works cannot fail to throw some indirect light on God himself, a light which eliminates many unworthy or insufficient ideas rather than providing us with positive enlightenment."[75] The insufficient ideas I have set aside, consulting Scripture and conciliar orthodoxy, are first the extremes of modalism and tritheism, then their modern kin, Barthian aspectivalism and communitarian personalism. The remaining type of position, illustrated by Model M, might be termed "aspectival personalism": personalism because all three "persons" are identified with the single, personal God; aspectival because they are differentiated through multiple aspects of the single God. Just how these aspects should be understood, I have not ventured to say. Though Model M may illustrate a general alternative to some inadequate conceptions, at the same time it suggests how slow we should be to give definite content to the indefinite expressions of fathers, councils, and creeds. If the inner depths of my mother or of any human being remain so mysterious, what of the unsearchable depths of God?

---

[75] Lubac, *The Christian Faith*, 107.

Chapter 5

The Body of Christ

"This is my body," says Jesus, "this is my blood." These words—pregnant, mysterious—sound as though they might identify one thing with another. And so they do in certain readings, but not in what became two chief understandings of the utterances, claiming between them a majority of Christian believers.[1] According to the Catholic doctrine of transubstantiation as traditionally understood, the bread and wine cease to exist; so they are not identified with the body and blood of Christ. Neither are the appearances of bread and wine—which, in this view, are all that remains of the consecrated elements—identified with Christ's body and blood. The words' import, therefore, is this: "This bread and this wine which I hold in my hands cease to exist as I speak and become instead my body and blood."[2] On the other hand, in what appears the foremost Protestant perception, the bread and wine remain and the "is" that might identify them with Jesus' body and blood should, for instance, be read: "This bread *represents* my body, this wine *represents* my blood." In neither case, then, is there any identification of one thing with another.

This dichotomy requires explanation, for it has no parallel in comparable Christian beliefs—for instance in the one which Chapters 2 and 3 considered, the Incarnation. True, with respect to that belief docetists denied the humanity of Christ much as Catholic doctrine denies the bread and wine, and Arians denied the divinity of Christ much as many Protestants deny the real presence of Jesus in the Eucharist. But the dominant, Chalcedonian understanding of the Incarnation has

---

[1] Bellarmine, after citing a list of two hundred "heretical" interpretations of the words of institution which had already appeared in his day, reduced them to ten principal kinds (*De sacramento eucharistiae*, 261). Though still current, the reading he characterized as then "commoner among heretics" (namely, "This bread is my body") appears to have ceded first place among Protestants to the kind of reading exemplified in Bellarmine's list by Zwingli ("This signifies my body") and Oecolampadius ("This bread is a figure of my body"). Nowadays, many Protestant exegetes simply take such a sense for granted, while "in the minds of many laypeople the presence of Christ in the Eucharist is often understood, when it is articulated, in a kind of Zwinglian 'spiritual' sense" (Mackenzie, "Reformed and Roman Catholic Understandings," 75). Some years ago, Arthur Crabtree reported that among Baptists "the trend toward Zwinglianism has been reversed" ("The Eucharist," 108), but none of the evidence he then adduced suggests a preference for the intermediate reading, "This bread is my body."

[2] A. J. B. Higgins characterizes as a "widespread and erroneous opinion" the "Catholic view that . . .the bread and wine are in fact, if not in appearance, the actual body and blood of Christ" (*The Lord's Supper*, 51). It is, rather, this misstatement of the Catholic, Tridentine view which is widespread and which therefore needs to be noted.

maintained an intermediate position, retaining both the human and the divine and asserting their mysterious identity. The corresponding Eucharistic position, asserting a mysterious identity of the consecrated bread and wine with the body and blood of Christ, has not enjoyed similar prominence.

Other comparable beliefs contrast still more pronouncedly with the dominant forms of Eucharistic belief. Paul could write: "Now you are the body of Christ and individually members of it" (1 Cor 12:27). Ephesians speaks of the Church "which is his body" (1:23). "Thus," Augustine notes, "if you are the body of Christ and His members, it is your mystery which has been placed on the altar of the Lord; you receive your own mystery."[3] Lucien Cerfaux becomes still more explicit: "In the mystical order, nothing opposes a veritable identification of the Church with the glorious body of Christ. The Church and Christ are the same body, in virtue of an equation by (mystical) identity of the Church with the risen body."[4] Now, despite the strength of such assertions, no one has gone farther and inferred that the Church, if identified with Christ, must therefore cease to exist. Neither, on the other hand, have believers concluded that Paul's meaning was purely figurative, that the Church simply images or represents Christ. "Whatever special meaning Paul [or the author of Ephesians or Colossians] gives to the Church by calling Jesus Christ its head, it is clear that no image could be more suggestive of intimate and mysterious unity than this one."[5] A similarly balanced understanding of the Eucharist, joining image and reality, has not won similarly widespread acceptance.

In further contrast, consider the patristic theme of divinization.[6] We pray, we are told, that, fed by the Word, we may "be transformed into God."[7] Through the Spirit we not only acquire a likeness to God but we "become God"[8]—"God himself."[9]

---

[3] Augustine, *Serm.* 272 (PL 38: 1247), quoted from Powers, *Eucharistic Theology*, 20.

[4] Cerfaux, *La théologie de l'Église*, 258. Cf. Moule, *The Origin of Christology*, 82, paraphrasing Ernst Percy ("The community as *soma Christou*, accordingly, coincides ultimately with Christ himself"); Powers, *Eucharistic Theology*, 163: "the body of the Lord, that 'bit of the world in which He lives personally,' is not simply the individuality of His human reality but is, in the real bond of the Spirit, the whole of the Church. It is essential to note, of course, that this fact does not eliminate the human individuality of Jesus; it does not mean, in Schoonenberg's words, that Jesus coincides personally with the Church or that His personal reality is absorbed by the Church. What it does mean is that Jesus personally subsists not only in His own human individuality, but also in a union with His Church which, in the personal reality, action, and function of the one Spirit in Jesus and in the Church, transcends even the unity of body and spirit in man."

[5] Smedes, *All Things Made New*, 219.

[6] "This doctrine of divinization or apotheosis became a commonplace in Athanasius and the Cappadocian Fathers, it was accepted as orthodoxy in the Eastern Church, and today, especially after the work of Pseudo-Dionysius in the sixth century and Gregory Palamas in the fourteenth, is championed strongly by contemporary Eastern Orthodox theologians" (R. Hanson, *The Continuity of Christian Doctrine*, 75). Many contemporary Roman Catholic theologians speak in similar terms.

[7] Origen, *De orat.* 27 (PG 11, 515C).

[8] Basil, *De Spir. Sancto* 9.23 (PG 32, 109).

"The whole body with its head is Son of Man, Son of God, and God . . . When all are united with God, they become one God."[10] Such assertions might invite either an eliminative or a figurative reading. Yet here too, in contrast with the Eucharistic dichotomy, Christians have supposed neither that such union with God implied their ceasing to exist, nor, on the other hand, that "becoming God" was a figurative substitute for "becoming good people."

Vatican Council II evokes a still broader contrast when it thus frames Jesus' Eucharistic presence:

> Christ is always present in His Church, especially in her liturgical celebrations. He is present in the sacrifice of the Mass, not only in the person of His minister, "the same one now offering, through the ministry of priests, who formerly offered Himself on the cross," but especially under the Eucharistic species. By his power, He is present in the sacraments, so that when a man baptizes, it is really Christ Himself who baptizes. He is present in His word, since it is He Himself who speaks when the holy scriptures are read in the church. He is present, finally, when the Church prays and sings, for He promised: "Where two or three are gathered together for my sake, there am I in the midst of them."[11]

For the Council, each of these presences is real; it is not merely figurative. Yet the Council does not deny the reality of the Eucharistic minister, the sacramental water or oil, the one who baptizes, the spoken word, or the Church that prays and sings. In Catholic doctrine, the Eucharistic elements alone are singled out for transubstantiation. No bread and wine remain to be identified in any sense with the body and blood of Christ.

What explains this contrast? How might we account for the singularity of Eucharistic teaching? A likely reply would be: "Only of the bread and wine did Jesus say 'This *is* my body' and 'This *is* my blood.' That is what makes the doctrine special." However, as it stands, this reply does not suffice. John said that the Word *was* God, that the Word *became* flesh. Paul said, "It is no longer I who live, but it is Christ who lives in me" (Gal 2:20). Neither the evangelist nor Paul was speaking merely figuratively. Neither, on the other hand, meant to deny the existence of either term in the relationship asserted. And neither, for the most part, has been so understood. In some sense, the Word was God. In some sense, the Word became flesh. In some sense, Paul identified himself with Christ. So the mystery remains: why has the understanding of Jesus' Eucharistic words proved such an exception in the history of Christian belief? Why have dominant interpretations denied identity, of any kind, between the Eucharistic elements and Jesus' body and blood?

Doubtless a full, adequate explanation of this development surpasses human comprehension. Too many factors have been involved, in too intricate, complex a

---

[9] Gregory Nazianzen, Oratio 7, *In Laudem Caesarii fratris* 23 (PG 35, 785).

[10] Blessed Isaac of Stella, *Serm.* 42 (PL 194, 1831).

[11] Vatican Council II, "Constitution on the Sacred Liturgy," in Abbott, *The Documents of Vatican II*, 140-41.

weave of influences, some of which may transcend our historical awareness. As Jaroslav Pelikan has observed, "Causes and influences are notoriously elusive, and both historians and theologians have often been more informed about them than they have had a right to be."[12] However, there is reason to wonder whether one influence may not have played a more decisive role than any other single factor in begetting the sharp schism in Eucharistic doctrine.

An Etiological Hypothesis

Chapter 2 introduced SIS—the strict-identity supposition. In this assumption, an utterance that appears to state an identity either states a strict, Leibnizian identity, of indiscernibility; or it states no identity at all but is merely figurative or metaphorical. Applied to Jesus' words at the Last Supper, this "either-or" mentality yields a result of the kind just noted. For it is not at all evident how bread and wine might be strictly, indiscernibly identical with Jesus' body and blood; and that possibility has typically been dismissed out of hand. But if the identity is not strict, then—given SIS—the two terms of the relation are not identical at all. Hence only two possibilities remain. Either one of the terms must be eliminated, leaving only the other, or the words must be taken as purely figurative. Transubstantiation exemplifies the first option (the bread and wine cease to exist and are replaced by Jesus' body and blood), whereas the popular Protestant position exemplifies the second.

But why only here, in this hypothesis, has SIS effected such a sharp dichotomy? Why only here and in none of the comparable instances just cited has it led to the denial of any dual identity? Because, as noted earlier, SIS is a default setting and can be overridden. In those other instances—Incarnation, mystical body, divinization, Paul's identity with Christ—too much was at stake for SIS to have free play; so SIS was overridden, the setting was altered. Jesus survived his identification with God, and so did God. Paul survived his identification with Christ, and so did Christ. The Church survived its identification with its Lord, and so did its Lord. How horrendous to suppose the contrary! Mere bread and wine, however, are expendable. It is no great loss if a few wafers or drops of wine go out of existence. On the other hand, bread and wine, if they do remain, can more readily be viewed as mere symbols of the divine than can Jesus, his church, or his members. Thus, in this and only this instance, no need was felt to override SIS and it continued to exercise its influence, in the dominant, majority positions I have cited.

In further illustration of this response, consider Jesus' declaration: "As often as you did it to one of these my least brethren, you did it to me" (Mt 25:40). These words have traditionally been viewed as indicating an identity, and the identity has often been conceived as strong and close. "Christ, the eternal Son of God, the Judge of all nations, is literally incarnate in the most worthless tramp, the most

---

[12] Pelikan, *Development of Christian Doctrine*, 118-19.

ragged beggar, the vilest criminal."[13] Yet no one has suggested that in this incarnation, the human term of the relation ceases to exist—that Jesus' concern takes the form of annihilation! Clearly there are limits to SIS's influence. Mere bread and wine, however, put up much less resistance to SIS's "logical" demands. Bread and wine are dispensable, whereas human beings are not. If, however, the appearance of bread and wine without there being any bread and wine seems too much to accept, there is always the figurative alternative to fall back on. So long as the setting remains fixed on SIS, these appear the only alternatives—either no bread and wine, or bread and wine but no identity with Jesus' body and blood.

This account may seem too neat to be true, and so it is. I just wished to state the hypothesis initially in clear, simple terms. Realism requires recognition not only that other influences have complemented this one but also that SIS, like most assumptions, typically operates less overtly than in my explicit analysis. Historical examples illustrate such covert operation, as do more recent ones, on both sides of the Eucharistic doctrinal divide. Thus, in opposition to transubstantiation, an Anglican divine has written:

> In arguing against this doctrine, we may first observe, that it is contradicted by our senses, since we see and taste the bread and wine after consecration, and, when we actually receive them, they still continue to be bread and wine, without any change or alteration whatever. And again, was it possible for Christ, when he instituted the Lord's Supper, to take his own body and his own blood into his own hands, and deliver them to every one of his apostles? Or, was it possible for the apostles to understand our Saviour's words, as a command to drink his blood, literally, &c. . . . The bread and wine must have been considered by them as symbolical; and, indeed, the whole transaction was evidently figurative in all its parts.[14]

Here, a basic assumption explains this quick transition from one extreme to the other. Identity would require indiscernibility, but the bread and wine do not look or taste at all like the body and blood of Christ! Surely the identical person cannot both carry and be carried! Hence (SIS dictates, implicitly) the only possibility that remains is a figurative understanding of the sacrament. With equal vigor, and with an equal show of logic, Catholic theologians have argued on the other side. Their reasoning often takes the following form:

> It is, above all, in the postnicene period that the Fathers explicitly affirm, as does the liturgy, that the bread and wine change into the body and blood of Christ. . . . They express this change with a variety of terms (*gignomai, poiein, metapoiein, metasqueuazein, methistanai, metaballein, metarizmisein, fieri, convertere, mutare, cotransiri, transmutare, transfigurare, consecrare*, etc.). The terminology is not yet fixed, but all these expressions have the same sense. What the Fathers wish to express with them is that the bread and the wine cease to be such, since they are the body and blood of Christ.[15]

---

[13] Simcox, *First Gospel*, 273.

[14] George Pretyman, quoted by Wiseman, *The Real Presence*, 216.

[15] Sayes, *El misterio eucarístico*, 149.

The Fathers do not explicitly state the doctrine of transubstantiation, but such must have been their meaning (the author quoted explains) since the bread and wine have become the body and blood of Christ, and they cannot be the body and blood of Christ and also be bread and wine. That would be a contradiction—given SIS. (As another writer has stated more explicitly, "we know that two material objects cannot be identical; and therefore we are compelled to fly, by a positive repugnance and contradiction, to another sense."[16]) To this standard argument from patristic writings, a standard reply has been:

> All arguments from words, implying *mere* change are, as Thorndike observes, and Bishop Pearson implies, beside the mark. The whole question is, not whether there be a change, but whether that change be one, through which the natural substances cease to be. Before consecration, the elements are, of course, *mere* natural substances. After consecration, they are not (in the language of S. Cyril and S. Athanasius) "bare, mere, bread and wine." It is the belief of the ancient Church, that after consecration, they are in a Divine, ineffable, supernatural way, the Body and Blood of Christ. They *are* then what they *were* not. And since they *are* what they were not, they *become* by consecration what they were not. It is but saying the same thing in different words. But it does not follow, that they are *in no sense* what they were.[17]

With this I agree. Not only should we not accept SIS unquestioningly in our own thinking, but neither should we assume its presence throughout patristic literature.

SIS often reveals its presence through a sharp contrast between a "literal" reading on one side and a "figurative" reading on the other, with no room for analogy in between. Rahner, for instance, writes: "If the words of consecration are to be taken in their strict and literal sense, and if they bring about the event of the presence of the body of Christ, then what Christ offers his Apostles is not bread, but his body. This statement, as it stands, must be accepted by all who refuse to give a vague, figurative meaning to the words of Christ."[18] Rahner would not write this way about the Incarnation. He would not speak of a "strict, literal" sense in which Jesus is divine or draw from it the conclusion that either Jesus' divinity precludes his humanity or his divinity is merely "figurative." But here he can and

---

[16] Wiseman, *The Real Presence*, 195. Cf. Bellarmine, *De sacramento eucharistiae*, 378 ("So the proposition cannot be true if its subject refers to the bread but its predicate refers to the body of Christ, for the bread and the body of Christ are very different things"), 379 ("Notice, too, that the Lord never expressly said: this bread is my body, thereby so constraining the intellect that, notwithstanding the evident contradiction, we would be forced to believe that wheat bread is the body of Christ").

[17] Pusey, *The Doctrine of the Real Presence*, 170-71 (Pusey's emphasis).

[18] Rahner, "The Presence of Christ," 297. Cf. Bossuet in Batiffol, *L'Eucharistie*, i ("The real presence . . . is solidly established by the words of institution, which we understand to the letter; and there is no more need to ask us why we stay with the proper, literal sense than to ask a traveler why he follows the main road"); Badham, "Meaning," 93-94; Bruner, *Matthew*, vol. 2, 961; Hagner, *Matthew 14-28*, 772; Wiseman, *The Real Presence*, 177, 181-82, 187-88, 211, 260, 291-92.

does argue in this "either-or fashion"—the one SIS demands. Such reasoning does not merely suggest the hidden operation of SIS;[19] in its inarticulate fashion it exemplifies SIS. It draws the SIS dichotomy and just fails to state it in terms of identity.

As already noted and as might be expected, occasionally SIS thinking becomes quite explicit. Thus Cyril Vollert writes that for J. de Baciocchi the dogma of transubstantiation "formulates the only possible way of establishing complete accord between the Eucharistic gift and the testimony of the senses on the one hand, and the principle of identity on the other."[20] One may surmise in advance what "the principle of identity" here signifies, and indeed Vollert elaborates as follows:

> The doctrine of transubstantiation avoids both extremes, total transmutation and purely extrinsic modification. It also avoids a compromising alternative which admits that the Eucharistic bread remains bread and becomes besides the body of Christ. Such a duality is simply unintelligible. Either the bread remains bread or it becomes the body of Christ. To affirm consubstantiation is to affirm that bread is Christ's body. In good logic, such a proposition, with two singular terms, is convertible; if the proposition is true, then it is also true that Christ's body is the bread, and if it is this bread, it is of bread. The absurdity of the consequent obliges us to discard the antecedent.[21]

We have noted similar reasoning with regard to the Incarnation. ("There are, irritatingly, certain difficulties in claiming either that the 'is' in 'Jesus is God' is one of identity or that it is one of predication. If it is one of identity, the statement should be reversible.") In both instances, the underlying assumption is the same: identity is reversible, because it is strict. If Jesus is Elijah, then Elijah must be Jesus. The relation's two terms must be mutually indiscernible from one another.

Recent illustrations such as these, which might be multiplied, suggest already the a priori plausibility of the hypothesis I have proposed. The type of influence here revealed may be discernible in the past as in the present. Indeed, it would be surprising if it were not, for these examples are the mere tip of a much larger body of thought. Chapter 1 noted how the traditional doctrine of analogy focused on predicates rather than expressions of identity, and how in recent centuries an essentialistic conception of identity has risen to explicit prominence: the only genuine form of identity is that of a thing with itself. Such thinking, I suggested, betrays tendencies operative in many areas of thought. Chapter 2 observed how powerfully the assumption of strict identity has affected discussion both for and against the doctrine of the Incarnation. That chapter's task was to note, document,

---

[19] Rahner's dichotomy might be partly explained, but not wholly, by his truistic observation: "if what is given is *also simply* bread, hence bread from *every* aspect . . . it would not be the body of Christ, but bread" ("The Presence of Christ," 299; his emphasis).

[20] Vollert, "The Eucharist," 418.

[21] Ibid., 417. In like vein, cf., e.g., Bellarmine, *De sacramento eucharistiae*, 378 and 379, quoted above in note 16.

and challenge this way of thinking, specifically with regard to that doctrine. Such will be an incidental result of the present discussion. In the course of testing the explanatory hypothesis just advanced for the major split in Eucharistic under-standing, the chapter will note, document, and challenge the same SIS-type thinking as appeared in discussion of the Incarnation, but will do so now with regard to Eucharistic doctrine, where it has exercised equally pervasive and often decisive influence. More than any other single factor, such thinking may explain the rise of the opposed views—Catholic and Protestant—which agree in reading "This is my body, This is my blood" as stating no identification of one thing with another. To test this surmise, let us examine in some detail when and how each of these views did in fact arise.

Transubstantiation

For the doctrine of transubstantiation, the eleventh century proved decisive—not the apostolic age or the patristic period or the ninth century, earlier; nor the Fourth Lateran Council or Council of Trent, later; but that one century.[22]

First, the apostolic and patristic periods were far from offering decisive support for transubstantiation. Most of the pertinent expressions then employed were of the noncommittal variety just noted (*mutare, cotransiri, transmutare, transfigurare,* etc.). Further, in apparent conflict with the doctrine of transubstantiation, not only did various authors—Paul,[23] Ignatius,[24] Justin,[25] Irenaeus,[26] Ephrem,[27] Tertullian,[28] Augustine,[29] John Damascene,[30] and others[31]—refer to the Eucharist as "bread," but they repeatedly identified the bread with the body,[32] so that later defenders of transubstantiation were forced to suggest a "mystical" or "figurative" reading of their words: the Fathers spoke this way, for example, "either because [the sacra-ment] is brought about from bread, and retains some of its qualities, or because it nourishes the soul, and supplies it the stuff of eternal life, or because it is the bread

---

[22] Cf. Powers, *Eucharistic Theology,* 21; Vernet, "Eucharistie," 1223 ("the real battle . . . breaks out, for the first time, with Berengar"); Jorissen, *Die Entfaltung der Transsubstantiationslehre,* 155.

[23] 1 Cor. 10:16-17, 11:26-27.

[24] Ignatius of Antioch, Letter to the Romans 7.3 (*The Apostolic Fathers,* 234-35).

[25] Justin, *Apol.* 1.65-66 (PG 6, 428).

[26] Irenaeus, *Adv. haer.* 4.5.18 (PG 7, 1028), 5.2 (PG 7, 1124-27).

[27] Ephrem, *Adv. haer.* 47, quoted in Pusey, *The Doctrine of the Real Presence,* 79.

[28] Tertullian, *De corona* 3 (PL 2, 80).

[29] Augustine, *Serm.* 227 (PL 38, 1099); *Serm.* 272 (PL 38, 1246-48).

[30] John of Damascus, *De fide orth.* 4.13 (PG 94, 1144A).

[31] E.g., *Apothegmata Patrum* 189, Daniel 7 (PG 65, 157A-160A).

[32] Pusey, *The Doctrine of the Real Presence* 258-59, quoting Irenaeus, Tatian, Tertullian, Origen, Cyprian, Chrysostom, Augustine, Jerome, Theodoret, and others.

of angels."[33] Certain sayings of Cyprian,[34] Nestorius,[35] Theodoret,[36] and Gelasius,[37] asserting the continuance of the bread and wine, have proved more difficult to explain away. On the other side, it is true, a passage of Cyril of Jerusalem[38] suggests that the consecrated elements cease to be bread and wine, but his words can be read in the light of numerous assertions, by him and by other authors, that the Eucharist is not "just bread," "mere bread," or "common bread."[39] Thus, overall, the verdict of patristic evidence might seem to go against transubstantiation. However, as Darwell Stone has remarked, in these early centuries "there is but little attempt to explain the method of the relation of the presence of the body and blood of Christ to the elements of bread and wine."[40]

In the ninth century this began to change, when Paschasius Radbertus more clearly denied the continued presence of bread and wine and Ratramnus of Corbie challenged his position. However, their debate centered more on the real presence and on the relationship between the heavenly and the Eucharistic Christ than on the elements' cessation, and it resulted neither in magisterial pronouncements as did the debate of the eleventh century, nor in a theological discussion comparable in depth and intensity with the one that then occurred. So I shall pass on, just noting as I do so Edward Schillebeeckx's pertinent summation:

> It was essential and fundamental to the dogma of faith that there should be no *reality* bread after the consecration, since, if the ultimate *reality* present in the Eucharist were to be called bread, there would be simply bread (a reality cannot at the same time be two realities!) and the eucharistic presence could only be conceived symbolically. The whole of the Catholic life of faith was opposed to this.[41]

---

[33] Alger of Liège, *De sacramentis corporis et sanguinis dominici*, 755-56. Cf. Peter of Ailly, in Pusey, *The Doctrine of the Real Presence*, 24 ("if any such be found in the sayings of the saints, they are false in matter of language, but are to be understood in a good sense"); Wiseman, *The Real Presence*, 298 ("as Christ is said to be an inferior, or a man, from the outward form in which he subsisted, so is this called bread, from the appearances under which the body of the Lord is veiled").

[34] Cyprian, *Ad Caecilium* (Epistle 62.2, *Ante-Nicene Fathers*, vol. 5, 359).

[35] Nestorius, *The Bazaar of Heraclides*, in Bethune-Baker, *Nestorius and His Teaching*, 145-46.

[36] Theodoret, *Eranistes*, Dial. 1 (PG 83, 56) and 2 (PG 83, 168).

[37] Gelasius, "De duabus in Christo naturis adv. Eutychen et Nestorium," quoted in Pusey, *The Doctrine of the Real Presence*, 88-89, and Stone, *History*, vol. 1, 102, who cites several sources.

[38] Cyril of Jerusalem, *Catech.* 4.9 (PG 33, 1104).

[39] Stone, *History*, vol. 1, 98-102; Pusey, *The Doctrine of the Real Presence*, 91-93.

[40] Stone, *History*, vol. 1, 98.

[41] Schillebeeckx, *The Eucharist*, 74. For suggestions of such thinking—both SIS and its implications—see, for example, Ratramnus, *De corpore et sanguine domini*, 160 ("things that differ from each other are not the same . . . For they differ from one another, and therefore are not the same") and 151: "For [Ambrose] says: 'Christ is in that sacrament.' He does not say: That bread, and that wine, is Christ. If he did, he would state that Christ is

"A reality cannot at the same time be two realities!" The influence of SIS could hardly be more succinctly stated. Since one reality cannot be identical with another (SIS forbids it), there are only two possibilities: either no bread and wine or no body and blood; either transubstantiation or mere symbol. But the latter alternative is unacceptable, so the former must be adopted.

Behind this sharp split, Edward Kilmartin discerns the shift from a Hellenic to a Germanic mindset.

> Introduced into the new cultural and historical situation, the ancient patristic understanding of reality was naturally "received" in a differentiated new way. In this milieu, thingly realism was contrasted radically with the symbolic. Whereas the idea of participation of the image in the prototype was taken for granted in the ancient Greek worldview, the image now took on the role of signaling a reality to which it can be related only externally. This resulted in a basically different approach to the understanding of the eucharistic mystery.[42]

The ninth-century debate, like that in the eleventh century, now faced the problem: "How can one express the symbolism and realism of the Eucharist, when contemporary thought no longer understands the implications of the ancient image theology?"[43] The answer officially adopted in the eleventh century, for reasons which we shall consider, did not recover, discover, or postulate a nonstrict form of identity, nor show itself open to such a possibility. The bread and wine must cease to exist.

Looking later, beyond the eleventh century, we see that the arrival of Aristotelian thought in the West furnished new tools for stating this doctrine but not new reasons for holding it. Neither did the pronouncements of the Fourth Lateran Council (1215), the Second Council of Lyons (1274), and the Council of Trent (1551) introduce new reasons or arguments besides those that surfaced in the eleventh century; they just added decisive weight to the argument from authority already established then. There was no going back, no reversing the direction taken by the Councils of Vercelli (1050), Paris (1051), and Rome (1050, 1059, and 1079). The repeated condemnations of Berengar of Tours left no doubt where orthodoxy lay. There, then, in the eleventh century, came the moment of decision. There, if anywhere—in the thought of Berengar and in that of his critics—we may test the suggestion that SIS played a major, perhaps uniquely important role in the rise of the doctrine of transubstantiation.

Berengar denied transubstantiation; and his denial, clear and constant, brought the issue to a head: did the bread and wine persist? At the same time, he strongly professed his belief in the real presence of Christ in the Eucharist. Yet, despite his protestations, contemporary criticism centered primarily on his alleged denial of

---

corruptible (perish the thought) and subject to mortality; for whatever in that meal is seen and tasted bodily is evidently subject to corruption."

[42] Kilmartin, *The Eucharist in the West*, 79. See McKenna, "Eucharistic Presence," 302-3.

[43] Kilmartin, *The Eucharist in the West*, 143-44.

the real presence. For this allegation and this focus, various explanations can be offered, besides the indefiniteness of some of Berengar's expressions in a time of still fluid terminology.[44] One reason was his insistence, with Augustine, that the Eucharist, like any sacrament, served as a sign; to some, this suggested that the Eucharist was nothing but a sign. Another likely explanation was Berengar's resistance to the extreme realism—the SIS-type realism—widely prevalent at the time. According to the view he was made to sign,[45] if the Eucharist was Christ's body, then the priest broke Christ's body and the faithful chewed Christ's body. A third explanation, of similar interest for our theme, is the one still reflected in the comments of some recent scholars. Félix Vernet perceives an "apparent contradiction" in Berengar's assertion that the bread and wine do not cease to be what they were yet are changed into something else (in Berengar's words, "non ut desinant esse quae erant, sed ut sint quae erant et in aliud commutentur").[46] Without SIS, there is not even an appearance of contradiction here; with SIS, the contradiction is real. Bread and wine cannot be body and blood, body and blood cannot be bread and wine. So if Berengar affirms the bread and wine and really means what he says, he must deny the body and blood.[47]

Just such rigid thinking appears in Berengar's first major critic, Lanfranc. Observe how he sums up Berengar's position: "You believe that the bread and wine of the Lord's table, when consecrated, remain substantially unchanged, that is, that bread and wine existed before the consecration and bread and wine exist

---

[44] In his letter to Adelmann (*Purgatoria epistola contra Almannum*, 532), Berengar writes for instance that "after the consecration, the bread and wine themselves become, for faith and understanding, the very body and blood of Christ" ("post consecrationem ipsum panem et vinum factum esse fidei et intellectui verum Christi corpus et sanguinem"). Jean de Montclos here perceives a "volatilization" of the real presence (*Lanfranc et Bérenger*, 132). Perhaps so. However, Nathan Mitchell gives a plausible account of the offending phrase, "for faith and understanding," when he writes, "These two, sacrament and reality, are essentially related, but the relation can be grasped only through the power of faith and intellect" (*Cult and Controversy*, 143). "For faith and understanding" may contrast, not with "in reality," but with "for the senses," or with the extreme realism of the "flesh-eaters," or perhaps with both together. Cf. *Purgatoria epistola contra Almannum*, 534.

[45] DS 690.

[46] Vernet, "Bérenger de Tours," 733. Cf. Berengar's response to the Council of Rome: "the consecrated bread on the altar, its substance intact, is the body of Christ, thus not losing what it was but acquiring what it was not" (ibid., 732). R. P. Redmond comments, revealingly: "the elements, since they remain exactly what they were, cannot be the real, physical Body of Christ. Yet he frequently uses current realist language, so that his denial of the Real Presence is not always clear, and there has been a heated controversy amongst scholars as to his real meaning" ("Real Presence," 443).

[47] Cf. Sayes, *El misterio eucarístico*, 163-65; Whalen, *The Authentic Doctrine*, 2 ("Berengar's blatant denial of transubstantiation did seem to be tantamount to a denial of the real presence"); Moloney, *The Eucharist*, 118: "[Berengar's] basic position was a denial of the Eucharistic Change: after the consecration you may refer to the Eucharistic gifts as Christ's body and blood, but in reality they remain bread and wine."

after the consecration, and that hence ["propterea"] they are called Christ's body and blood because they are celebrated in the Church in remembrance of the cruci-fied body and the blood shed from his side."[48] The inference here is Lanfranc's, not Berengar's. From the affirmation of the bread and wine there follows, Lanfranc assumes, the denial of any but a symbolic presence (Germanically diluted) of Jesus in the Eucharist. For bread and wine cannot be body and blood. In view of this dichotomy in his thinking, one can understand Lanfranc's accusations that Beren-gar had perjured himself. If Berengar persisted in asserting the presence of bread and wine, how could he truthfully swear, as was demanded of him: "I, Berengarius, anathematize the heresy of which I am accused, which tries to maintain that the bread and wine that are placed on the altar, after the consecration are only a sacrament and not the true body and true blood of our Lord Jesus Christ"?[49]

One can also understand the confidence with which Lanfranc invoked Scripture and the Fathers. To read them as Berengar proposed, Lanfranc protested, would impose an incredible sense on their words. "For what sane person," Lanfranc expostulated, "would believe that one thing is changed into another yet does not therewith cease to be what it was?"[50] Who would believe, for example, that when snow turns into ice it does not cease to be snow?[51] In response, Berengar cited other kinds of change. When, for example, a pillar is formed of marble or a table of wood, the pillar is still marble and the table is still wood.[52] These comparisons, as Berengar realized, were far from perfect (Jesus' body and blood are not brought into being as the pillar and table are). But we can sense that their intent was legitimate: the comparisons were meant to suggest wider possibilities than Lanfranc envisaged.[53]

Guitmond of Aversa, Berengar's other principal contemporary critic, sensed somewhat better the nature of Berengar's position. Jesus is "impanate," so to speak, in the bread, as the Word is incarnate in Jesus.[54] Against this hypothesis, intermediate between transubstantiation and pure symbolism, Guitmond urged both negative and positive arguments. No impossibility precludes transubstantiation, he argued, and no evidence supports impanation: "Neither prophets foretold, nor Christ indicated, nor apostles preached, nor the world, save these few heretics, has believed" any such thing as Berengar was suggesting.[55] Berengar might have countered that neither did they foretell, indicate, preach, or believe any such thing as the elimination of the bread and wine. However, Guitmond read the evidence differently. Like Lanfranc, where the Fathers wrote "change" he read "transub-

---

[48] Lanfranc, *De corpore et sanguine Domini*, 440.

[49] Ibid., 415 (with Lanfranc's abbreviated version of the fuller text, found for instance in MacDonald, *Berengar*, 130).

[50] Lanfranc, *De corpore et sanguine Domini*, 419D. Cf. Hugh, *Tractatus*, 1327AB.

[51] Lanfranc, *De corpore et sanguine Domini*, 416.

[52] Berengar, *Rescriptum contra Lanfrannum*, 71.

[53] For different examples and fuller discussion of Berengar's insistence on ana-logy, see Geiselmann, *Die Eucharistielehre der Vorscholastik*, 344-45.

[54] Guitmond, *De corporis et sanguinis Christi veritate*, 1430.

[55] Ibid., 1482.

stantiation." Ambrose, for example, did not teach that the Lord's body and blood lie hidden in the bread and wine, but that the bread and wine are changed into the Lord's body and blood. Note carefully, Guitmond insists: Ambrose says the bread and wine are changed "in aliud"—into something else. Guitmond dwells on this point and evidently sees it as decisive.[56] For this, a likely explanation is the one now grown familiar. If one thing is changed into another, it cannot remain what it was. Either it is one thing or it is the other; it cannot be both. SIS, it seems, is still operative.

"But why speak of SIS?" some may query. "Why introduce the question of identity? Guitmond may have had a simple-minded conception, not of identity, but of change. Recall Lanfranc's question: 'Who in his right mind would believe that one thing is changed into another yet afterwards does not cease to be what it was?'" So, for Guitmond and Lanfranc, did all change entail the total elimination of the antecedent entity? No, they were well aware of partial changes. Indeed, with respect to the Eucharist, they distinguished between the bread and wine that ceased and the appearances that remained. But in no instances of change, or none that came most readily to mind, could one say that the antecedent *is* the consequent. The child that becomes an adult is not an adult. The block of marble that becomes a pillar is not a pillar. The caterpillar that becomes a moth is not a moth. And so forth. The "is" makes all the difference, or so Guitmond evidently believed: "These impanators the Lord Jesus himself slew with the word of his mouth when, taking bread, blessing it, and giving thanks, he said: 'This is my body.' He did not say: 'Here my body lies concealed.' Nor did he say: 'My blood is in this wine.' No, he said: 'This *is* my blood.'"[57]

"Is" indicates an identity. But for SIS, there is just one kind of identity—the kind that precludes one thing being identical with another. What is bread cannot also be Christ's body, what is wine cannot also be Christ's blood. Accordingly, to retain the bread and wine is to exclude the body and blood, and, conversely, to assert the body and blood is to exclude the bread and wine. So when Jesus says, "This is my blood," that decides the matter. The wine has ceased to exist. Such is the viewpoint that governs the reasoning of both Lanfranc and Guitmond. Neither envisages the possibility that the words of institution might indicate a non-strict identity, allowing the bread and wine to persist. Berengar is therefore mistaken. SIS refutes him.

Lanfranc and Guitmond have historical interest as Berengar's two chief eleventh-century critics, revealing reasons for the eleventh-century pronouncements which determined the subsequent course of church teaching. But their interest also transcends that century. If we pass to the time of Trent, we encounter

---

[56] Ibid., 1482-83.

[57] Ibid., 1484 (emphasis added). Cf. Kilmartin, *The Eucharist in the West*, 148-49: "According to Albert, the Lord 'did not say: "*Accipite in hoc, vel cum hoc corpus meum*" [Receive my body in this, or with this]!' Thomas Aquinas (d. 1274) and Bonaventure (d. 1274) also hold that the wording of the institutional account of institution of the Eucharist is a decisive argument for transubstantiation."

the same major thrusts as in their writings. The Council Fathers, too, leaned heavily on the witness of Scripture[58] and the Fathers[59] as evidence for the doctrine of transubstantiation; and they did so in the same way and for the same reason as their eleventh-century predecessors. A first indication of the conciliar Fathers' thinking can be discerned in the succinct statement which issued from their deliberations:

> But since Christ, our Redeemer, said that what he offered under the appearance of bread is truly His own body, it has always been a matter of conviction in the Church of God, and now this holy Synod declares it again, that by the consecration of the bread and wine a conversion takes place of the whole substance of bread into the substance of the body of Christ our Lord, and of the whole substance of the wine into the substance of His blood.[60]

Here, the opening "since" ("ideo") has the same revealing significance as Lanfranc's "propterea" (and as Sayes's "since" in an earlier quotation): if there is a conversion, it must be a substantial conversion, so that bread and wine do not remain. For Christ, the Council Fathers argue, said that the Eucharist "is" his body.[61] They do not indicate how this premise leads to the stated conclusion, but by now we may surmise their likely reasoning. Since dual identity, of one thing with another thing (bread with body and wine with blood), is inconceivable, it need not be mentioned as an alternative possibility blocking the Council's inference. This surmise is supported by the fuller exposition in the Catechism of the Council of Trent, which reflects the thinking of the time:

> The substance of bread and wine does not remain after consecration. This, though it rightly calls out the greatest wonder, yet is a necessary consequence of what has already been shown. For if the real body of Christ is under the species of bread and wine after consecration, it is absolutely necessary, since it was not there before, that

---

[58] Wohlmuth, *Realpräsenz und Transsubstantiation*, vol. 1, 445-50.

[59] Ibid., 429-40.

[60] DS 1642 (my translation).

[61] Cf. Marín-Sola, *La evolución homogénea*, 378-81 ("The Council of Trent itself clearly indicates that this is the argument or reasoning which the Church used to know and define this dogma"); Franzelin, *Tractatus de ss. eucharistiae sacramento*, 259 ("the Church herself understood the dogma of transubstantiation from the words of institution, as the Council of Trent teaches"); Sayes, *La presencia real*, 235-36 (his emphasis): "*Since* Christ said that what he offered under the appearance of bread was really his body, *therefore* the Church holds the conversion of the bread and wine into the body and blood of Christ. Transubstantiation is implicit in the words of Christ and has its origin in them. Only through this substantial conversion can it properly be asserted: 'This is my body, this is my blood.'" Sayes highlights the significance of this conciliar argument: "If we consider that Luther's principal objection against the doctrine of transubstantiation was that it is nothing but a mere Thomistic opinion used to coerce Scripture itself, we shall understand that the Council's basic intention was precisely to argue that the doctrine of transubstantiation emerges from the very words of Christ and is their consequence or implication. Otherwise, Luther's principal objection in this matter would have remained without any response." (ibid., 259).

this comes to pass either by change of place or by creation or by the conversion of another thing into it. Now it certainly cannot be that the body of Christ is in the Sacrament by coming from one place into another; for in that case it would happen that He would be absent from His abode in heaven, since nothing is moved without leaving the place from which it is moved. And it is still less credible for the body of Christ to be created, and this cannot even be imagined. Therefore it remains that the body of the Lord is in the Sacrament by the conversion of the bread into it; wherefore of necessity no substance of bread remains.[62]

What is the nature of this "necessity" backing the Catechism's "wherefore"? The likeliest logical link, serving as missing premise, is the "principle of identity": one thing cannot be another thing. So if the bread and wine become the body and blood, they cannot still be bread and wine. SIS precludes it.

Records of the Council's deliberations tend to confirm these surmises. Concerning the Council's canon 1, condemning the denial of the real presence,[63] and its canon 2, condemning the denial of transubstantiation,[64] Schillebeeckx observes:

No separate justification was provided for the error of canon 2, for many bishops maintained that the opposite was apparent from the falsehood of the first thesis (canon 1). The second canon was only a different formulation of what had already been said in the first canon. In other words, the canon dealing with transubstantiation added nothing new, as far as its *content* was concerned, to the canon dealing with the specifically and distinctively real presence in the Eucharist. Eucharistic "real

---

[62] Stone, *History*, vol. 2, 102. Cf. Nichols, *The Holy Eucharist*, 70, on Aquinas: "Well, then, do the substances of bread and wine remain in this sacrament after the consecration? Thomas replies that such co-existence of Christ's real presence with the substances of bread and wine is impossible. He argues that Christ's body can only come to be in this sacrament by one of two ways. Either it is brought in from outside, or something already there is changed into it. But there can be no question of Christ's body moving through space: among many difficulties, this would entail that body ceasing to be in heaven. This leaves only the possibility that the substance of bread changes into it: and this explains why Christ said not 'Here is my body' but 'This is my body,' for the latter proposition would be false were the substance of bread still present." Here, at the end, is the crucial move, backed by SIS. See *Summa theologiae* 3.75.2.

[63] "If anyone denies that the body and blood, together with the soul and divinity, of our Lord Jesus Christ and, therefore, the whole Christ is truly, really, and substantially contained in the sacrament of the most holy Eucharist, but says that Christ is present in the Sacrament only as in a sign or figure, or by his power: let him be anathema" (*The Church Teaches*, 286; DS 1651).

[64] "If anyone says that the substance of bread and wine remains in the holy sacrament of the Eucharist together with the body and blood of our Lord Jesus Christ, and denies that wonderful and extraordinary change of the whole substance of the bread into Christ's body and the whole substance of the wine into his blood while only the species of bread and wine remain, a change which the Catholic Church has most fittingly called transubstantiation: let him be anathema" (*The Church Teaches*, 286; DS 1652).

presence" and "transubstantiation" were, in the minds of the fathers of the Council, identical as affirmations.[65]

SIS and only SIS makes the two doctrines logically equivalent. Loosen the requirement of strict identity, as elsewhere in theology and Christian belief, and the bread and wine might, in some sense, become the body and blood without ceasing to be bread and wine. SIS being so prevalent, in general and specifically in Eucharistic thinking, it therefore seems plausible to divine, again, its pervasive, powerful influence at Trent as in preceding centuries.[66] What, though, of the suggestion that SIS's influence may have been the primary one?

Doubtless other factors, large and small, worked in the same direction. Thus, recalling the tale of how the loss of a nail in a horse's shoe nail led to the loss of the realm, we may wonder how the Berengarian controversy might have turned out had Berengar been less bitterly polemical in his writings, or had he presented sounder arguments for his own views, or had the theological issues been less entwined with ecclesiastical policy and political intrigue. Recalling, too, that then, as now, the Eucharist was celebrated more often than it was analyzed, we may wonder what influences of Eucharistic devotion perhaps underlay the play of dialectic. "The doctrine of transubstantiation," notes Michael Gaudoin-Parker, "would be a mere refinement of subtle scholastic thought and of academic interest unless it led us to be united in deeper love for the presence of Christ our Savior, through whom we experience the joy of being in communion with his Mystical

---

[65] Schillebeeckx, *The Eucharist*, 46 (his emphasis). In the references which Joseph Powers cites, I can detect no basis for either part of his claim: "it seems to have been Melchior Cano's opinion that one could accept the real presence without affirming transubstantiation which eventually led to the incorporation of this [second] canon" (*Eucharistic Theology*, 156). According to Raymond Moloney, Schillebeeckx "neglects the significance of the Council's implicit *rejection* of the view of Archbishops Nausea of Vienna and Campeggio of Feltre, who held that canon 2 was sufficiently contained in canon 1" (*The Eucharist*, 173). A reply is readily discernible in Schillebeeckx's words. Often, as clearly in this instance (think of Luther), it is advantageous to express the same content in different ways. Separate wording might be desirable even if separate justification was neither desirable nor necessary. Of interest here is the fact that such linking of the two canons was explicitly expressed and not explicitly or implicitly contested. See, e.g., *Concilium Tridentinum*, 149, lines 26-27; 153, lines 10-12; 156, lines 17-18; 158, lines 11-12; 161, line 13; 170, lines 25 and 32-34.

[66] Cf. Sobrino, "Sobre la discusion moderna," 11: "According to various authors (Rahner, Schillebeeckx, Baciocchi, Neunheuser), the first and second canons are identical in content; the canon on transubstantiation 'is a distinct formulation of what was said in the first canon'; 'it adds no truly new affirmation to the meaning of Christ's words at the Last Supper. It appears the only possible way to make the truth of the Eucharistic gift entirely agree with the testimony of the senses on the one hand and the principle of identity on the other.'" Clearly, the "principle of identity" here alluded to is the principle of *strict* identity, as in SIS. To Sobrino's list add Powers, *Eucharistic Theology*, 37-38, 40, 141-42, and Jorissen, *Die Entfaltung der Transsubstantiationslehre*, 9-10.

Body."[67] Thus this development, too, "must be seen and interpreted according to that solid principle of living Christianity which Cardinal Newman so finely illustrated in *The Development of Christian Doctrine*. It is ever a question of the realization of doctrine following or, at least, keeping apace with the life of prayer: *Lex orandi, lex credendi* [the law of prayer is the law of belief], as the Fathers of the Church tersely put it."[68] No doubt this principle contains much truth, but how does it apply in this instance? How is love for Christ in the Eucharist deepened by the conviction that he alone is present and not bread and wine? I can conceive only one answer, and therefore sense again the influence of SIS: if the bread and wine were present, people might suppose, Christ would not be present, and that would indeed affect their piety.[69]

Casting about for alternative sources of the doctrine of transubstantiation, I spot one or two more general influences than personal, ecclesial, or political factors of the kinds just mentioned,[70] but they still do not match the massive, enduring influence of SIS. Perhaps, however, my gaze has been too confined. Lewis Smedes evokes a larger perspective:

> To isolate the bread and to ask how eating a piece of bread recreates the body of Christ is to miss the dynamics of the sacramental event. Concentrating on the bread itself, in isolation, the Church in the past was frequently caught in truly fantastic controversies. It was this neglect of the total sacramental action that created the vocabulary of transubstantiation, consubstantiation, and all the other theological doctrines created to assure the real and effective presence of Christ in the sacramental bread.[71]

---

[67] Gaudoin-Parker, *The Real Presence*, xxx.

[68] Ibid., xliv-xlv.

[69] On the religious significance of real presence versus merely figurative or sacramental presence, see for instance a third major critic of Berengar, somewhat later than Lanfranc and Guitmond: Alger of Liège, *De sacramentis corporis et sanguinis dominici*, 815-16.

[70] For example, the realistic alternative to transubstantiation has often been conceived on the model of the Incarnation, as impanation, and that conception has elicited objections such as those of Guitmond, *De corporis et sanguinis Christi veritate*, 1490 ("What need, what utility, what honor would there be for Christ our Lord futilely to be impanated or inwined?"), and Alger, *De sacramentis corporis et sanguinis dominici*, 765: "It would be no great thing that the Apostle said, to commend God's love to men, and the dignity of human nature, that 'the Son of God did not take hold of angels but of the descendants of Abraham,' if he who did not deign to be personally united with angelic nature, wished instead, united with the brute substance of bread, to become bread. His embodiment, no longer restricted to humans but shared with bread, would both diminish the dignity of human nature and demonstrate less God's love for humans."

[71] Smedes, *All Things Made New*, 244. Cf. Robert Sokolowski's related remarks, which raise an identity issue which I shall not pursue: "Two of the major theological issues concerning the Eucharist are that of the Real Presence of Christ in the sacrament and that of the identity of the sacrifice at the altar and at Calvary. The two issues are obviously related, but it does seem that an ontological theology is more immediately focused on the former, and a theology concerned with manifestation on the latter. In the thought of St. Thomas

No doubt this suggestion, too, contains some truth. Berengar's opponents did slight the sacramental aspect of the Eucharist, often viewing with suspicion any talk of symbolism. However, it was not neglect of the sacramental action that fixed attention on the words of institution or begot a realistic understanding of Christ's Eucharistic presence in John, Paul, Ignatius,[72] Justin,[73] Irenaeus,[74] and succeeding generations. And, given that realistic understanding, it was not mere historical chance that eventually gave rise to the doctrine of transubstantiation. SIS, I have suggested, had a great deal to do with it.

This does not signify, automatically, that the doctrine is mistaken. In the history of thought, inadequate grounds have sometimes led to what now appear correct conclusions. And God can write straight with very crooked lines. Besides, as so often in dialectical developments, the same influence that helped beget the doctrine of transubstantiation then contributed to the rise of the doctrine at the opposite extreme. It was Protestants' turn to exemplify the power of SIS.

Mere Figure

For a figurative conception of the Eucharist, denying both transubstantiation and real presence, the most seminal century to consider is the sixteenth, not the eleventh; and the sixteenth-century figure most associated with such a view is Ulrich Zwingli. Briefly stated,

> [Zwingli] understands the words of Christ, "This is my body" to mean "This signifies my body," in the sense that the bread and wine are symbolic pictures of something to which they are not essentially related. They are reminders of Calvary, not vehicles through which the divine life is mediated. The words of Christ are to be construed as we would construe the statement in Exodus 12.11, "This is the Lord's Passover." The paschal lamb of each recurrent festival was not itself the "Passing-over," but rather signified a redemption that happened long ago in the Exodus, as the Eucharist recalls the redemption of Calvary.[75]

This reductive view opened a split between Zwingli and Luther, who maintained a real presence of Christ in the Eucharist. The reasons for this split are far from

---

Aquinas, for example, the focus is on the Real Presence, and the identity of the sacrifice is understood derivatively . . . . The sacrifice is the same because of the identity of Christ. In contrast, in some of the more recent theologies of the Eucharist, such as those of Vonier, Journet, and Casel, the emphasis is on the identity of the sacrifice and the Real Presence is seen in reference to that identity: for the sacrifice to be the same, Christ must be truly present" (*Eucharistic Presence*, 96-97).

[72] Ignatius of Antioch, *Smirn.* 7.1 ("the Eucharist is the flesh of our Lord Jesus Christ").

[73] Justin, *Apol.* 1.66.

[74] Irenaeus, e.g., *Adv. haer.* 5.2.2-2.3.

[75] Richardson, *Zwingli and Cranmer*, 18. Cf. Zwingli, *On Providence and Other Essays*, 52-53.

obvious. Luther, like Zwingli, was opposed to Rome and what it stood for, including the doctrine of transubstantiation; and he recognized that a position more radically at variance with that doctrine, such as Zwingli's, might offer polemical advantages.[76] Luther, like Zwingli, was imbued with the nominalistic philosophy which has been cited in explanation of Zwingli's more extreme view.[77] Doubtless Luther too, like Zwingli, was put off by the excesses of popular Eucharistic piety ("Hold it higher, Sir!"). Again, Luther, like Zwingli, was aware of the possibility of a purely figurative interpretation (Zwingli exemplified it). Why, then, did Zwingli seize on that possibility, whereas Luther did not?

The most important explanation may be that Zwingli's thinking, unlike Luther's, was locked into an "either-or" dichotomy. Zwingli saw only two alternatives: either a "literal" reading of Jesus' words or a figurative one.[78] But the former seemed clearly excluded. If the bread was "literally" Jesus' body, then the priest would not be able to lift it.[79] If the bread was "literally" Jesus' body, we could see his body—face, limbs, and all.[80] If the bread was "literally" Jesus' body, the priest would break that body, and communicants would chew it and tear it apart when they masticated the host.[81] Horrendous! Absurd! "All believers know very well that they do not eat the body of Christ in that way. Hence the very nature and truth of the matter will not allow us to take the words literally."[82] A figurative reading follows ineluctably, "for there is no alternative way of avoiding a figurative interpretation."[83] There is no third alternative, that is, given the underlying assumption that governed Zwingli's dialectic. What repeatedly created the impression of absurdity, we can discern, was precisely SIS—that is, Zwingli's unquestioning assumption that the identity had to be strict. He left no room for analogy.

A secondary argument, stressing the sacramental nature of the Eucharist, also betrays signs of SIS: "But the very body of Christ is the body which is seated at the right hand of God, and the sacrament of his body is the bread, and the sacrament of his blood is the wine, of which we partake with thanksgiving. Now the sign and the thing signified cannot be one and the same. Therefore the sacrament of the body of Christ cannot be the body itself."[84] One wonders.[85] Is not Jesus a sign of God's mercy, yet is he not also God's mercy incarnate? For the Eucharist, however, Zwingli allows no such analogical leeway. There the only identity he envisages is "literal"—that is, strict.

---

[76] Rupp, *Patterns of Reformation*, 23.

[77] Richardson, *Zwingli and Cranmer*, 8-9.

[78] Zwingli, "On the Lord's Supper," 190-95, 199.

[79] Ibid., 194.

[80] Ibid., 190, 192. Cf. Congar, "*Lutherana*," 173-74: "Karlstadt said he could not admit that Christ is in the sacrament with his height, his size, his length."

[81] Zwingli, "On the Lord's Supper," 190.

[82] Ibid., 199.

[83] Ibid., 192.

[84] Ibid., 188.

[85] Dulles, *Models of Revelation*, 157.

The kind of symbolic, anti-realist thinking that Zwingli, Oecolampadius, and Karlstadt propagated on the continent, Nicholas Ridley and Thomas Cranmer advocated across the Channel at roughly the same time. Ridley was important, in part, for his influence on Cranmer;[86] and Cranmer was important, in part, as the chief architect of the Book of Common Prayer. Whether through contagion or natural bent, in both Ridley and Cranmer tell-tale signs of SIS appear—as also more broadly.

Ridley writes: "What is the matter of the Sacrament? . . . if it be Christ's own natural body born of the Virgin, then . . . (seeing that all learned men in England, so far as I know, both new and old, grant there to be but one substance) . . . they must needs grant Transubstantiation, that is, a change of the substance of bread into the substance of Christ's body."[87] In this progression, Ridley contests the first premise ("if it be Christ's own natural body"), accepts the second premise ("one substance"), and draws a different conclusion:

> if, I say, the true solution of that former question, whereupon all these controversies do hang, be that the natural substance of bread is the material substance in the Sacrament of Christ's blessed body; then must it follow of the former proposition (confessed of all that be named to be learned, so far as I do know in England) which is that there is but one material substance in the Sacrament of the body, and one only likewise in the Sacrament of the blood, that there is no such thing indeed and in truth as they call Transubstantiation, for the substance of bread remaineth still in the Sacrament of the body.[88]

Here, sharply drawn, is the antinomy that interests us: either the one substance or the other, either transubstantiation or no real presence. So crucial interest attaches to the shared principle that underlies both antithetical positions. Whence this common agreement that there "be but one substance" in the Eucharist? Doubtless others would reply as Ridley did: "the very bread which He took, brake, and gave them could not be in any wise His natural body, for that were confusion of substances."[89] Not "in any wise"—not by any manner of analogy: genuine identity leaves no such latitude. Hence the harshness of Ridley's polemic, leading to his figurative conclusion:

> these false thieves and jugglers have bewitched the minds of the simple people . . . and make them to believe that to be Christ our Lord and Saviour which indeed is neither God nor man, nor hath any life in itself, but in substance is the creature of bread and wine, and in use of the Lord's Table is the Sacrament of Christ's body and blood, and for this holy use, for which the Lord hath ordained them in His Table to

---

[86] "Largely owing to the influence of Ridley, he abandoned the belief that the consecrated Sacrament is the body and blood of Christ" (Stone, *History*, vol. 2, 125).

[87] Ibid., 190.

[88] Ibid., 190-91.

[89] Ibid., 192.

represent unto us His blessed body torn upon the cross for us and His blood there shed, it pleased Him to call them His body and blood.[90]

Cranmer, like the other "learned men of England," envisaged the same two alternatives as Ridley and reached a similar conclusion by similar reasoning. On one side, Cranmer noted, Catholics allege the words of institution in support of transubstantiation.

> For these words of Christ, say they, be most plain and most true. Then forasmuch as he said, *This is my body*, it must needs be true, that that thing which the priest holdeth in his hands is Christ's body. And if it be Christ's body, then can it not be bread; whereof they gather by their reasoning, that there is Christ's body really present, and no bread.[91]

On the other side, however, "when Christ gave bread to his disciples, and said, *This is my body*, there is no man of any discretion, that understandeth the English tongue, but he may well know by the order of speech, that Christ spake those words of the bread, calling it his body, as all the old authors also do affirm."

> Wherefore this sentence cannot mean as the words seem and purport, but there must needs be some figure or mystery in this speech, more than appeareth in the plain words. For by this manner of speech plainly understood without any figure as the words lie, can be gathered none other sense, but that bread is Christ's body, and that Christ's body is bread, which all Christian ears do abhor to hear. Wherefore in these words must needs be sought out another sense and meaning than the words of themselves do bear.[92]

Cranmer's allusion to "figure *or mystery*" might suggest some alternative to a figurative conception, but his exposition contains no trace of analogy or metaphysical mystery. In the Eucharist, he insists, we do not eat and chew a present thing but "by a lively faith in heart and mind" chew and digest an absent thing, ascended into heaven.[93] As in the Old Testament the lamb was not the Lord's passover but a figure of the passover, "likewise in the New Testament, the bread and wine be not Christ's very body and blood, but they be figures, which by Christ's institution be unto the godly receivers thereof sacraments, tokens, significations, and representations of his very flesh and blood."[94] The Eucharist is not itself a mystery but connects us with the mysteries of our salvation. "These things

---

[90] Ibid., 194. Note the misrepresentation of the Catholic view, illustrating note 2 above.

[91] Cranmer, *Defence*, 120. Cf. ibid., 72: "Then reason they after this fashion. If the bread which Christ gave be his flesh, then it cannot also be material bread; and so it must needs follow, that the material bread is gone, and that none other substance remaineth but the flesh of Christ only."

[92] Ibid., 121.

[93] Ibid., 131.

[94] Ibid., 160.

we ought to remember and revolve in our minds, and to lift up our hearts from the bread and wine unto Christ that sitteth above. And because we should so do, therefore after the consecration they be no more called bread and wine, but the body and blood of Christ."[95]

From such an account of the scriptural "is," it is evident why Cranmer spoke of needing and seeking "another sense and meaning than the words of themselves do bear." Yet he perceived no alternative; for, as just seen, a realistic reading would require us to believe "that bread is Christ's body, and that Christ's body is bread, which all Christian ears do abhor to hear." In good logic, the identity would have to be reciprocal. If Jesus is Elijah, then Elijah is Jesus. If the bread is the body, then the body is the bread. The risen Christ is made of flour! Cranmer did not apply the same logic to "Jesus is God," "The Word is God," or "God is love." But with respect to the Eucharist, he was locked as firmly as Ridley into the SIS dichotomy.

This sampling of influential theologians—Zwingli, Ridley, and Cranmer—suggests SIS's role in eliciting the figurative conception of the Eucharist and not just the Tridentine view at the opposite extreme. But it does not yet suggest the strength of this influence relative to others. And indeed there were other influences. In particular, strong soteriological motivation worked against a realistic understanding of the Eucharist. Thus Zwingli writes: "As the body cannot be nourished by a spiritual substance, so the soul cannot be nourished by a corporeal substance. But if the natural body of Christ is eaten, I ask whether it feeds the body or the soul? Not the body, hence the soul. If the soul, then the soul eats flesh, and it would not be true that spirit is only born of Spirit."[96] Justification comes through faith alone, and what do flesh and blood have to do with faith?[97]

> Since, therefore, this [Eucharistic] presence amounts to nothing without the contemplation of faith, it belongs to faith that the things are or become present, and not to the sacraments. For, how ever much they lay hold on the senses and lead to reverence for the things that are done, these handmaidens can yet effect nothing unless their mistress, faith, first rules and commands on the throne of the heart. Hence it is apparent that the sacraments cannot justify nor give grace, for we know no other justification than that of faith.[98]

Such considerations weighed heavily with others besides Zwingli in favor of a figurative understanding of the Eucharist, as they have since, and helped to create the polarization between a figurative, anti-realistic conception on the one hand and

---

[95] Ibid., 154.

[96] Zwingli, *On Providence and Other Essays*, 53. "'The flesh is of no avail' (John 6:63) is the key text for Zwingli. It is a wall of bronze which nothing can shake, let alone shatter" (Stephens, *The Theology of Huldrych Zwingli*, 232).

[97] "The underlying concept is that religion has to do with mind and spirit. The relationship of faith is the central issue; and while this has, as we have seen, strong objective elements, its apprehension is conceived in terms that have primarily to do with mind and consciousness" (Richardson, *Zwingli and Cranmer*, 10).

[98] Zwingli, *On Providence and Other Essays*, 113.

transubstantiation on the other.[99] However, Luther, too, held justification by faith alone, yet believed in the real presence. And clearly, such soteriological thinking did nothing to generate the even more opposed conception of transubstantiation. Accordingly, it seems plausible to suggest that, overall, SIS was still more influential than soteriology in bringing about the dominant dichotomy between the figurative view on the one hand and transubstantiation on the other. For, as we have seen, SIS's influence has extended, powerfully, to both sides of the divide. There remains, however, one further factor of which the same might perhaps be said.

Mystery

Two principles enunciate a longstanding tension in theology: Mysteries are not to be multiplied without necessity; and mysteries are not to be eliminated without necessity. The latter principle, stronger in ages of faith, is reflected in the doctrine of transubstantiation.[100] The former principle, stronger in recent times, helps to account for the rise to dominance of a Zwinglian rather than a Lutheran, more realistic view of the Eucharist.[101] Symbolism is more readily intelligible than impanation or companation. What I now wish to suggest is that, even without the influence of SIS, positions of these latter kinds, midway between mere symbolism on one hand and transubstantiation on the other, may appear more mysterious than either of these opposed extremes and may have been avoided for this reason, too, by those at both extremes.

First, paradoxical though it may appear, a middle position has seemed more mysterious to some than even transubstantiation. They have regarded the denial of bread and wine as a clear, decisive position in comparison with the nebulous suggestion that, in some inconceivable sense or manner, the consecrated bread and wine may be the body and blood of Christ. They have possessed intellectual

---

[99] Leenhardt sums up a widespread attitude: "Reification—if one can sum up everything with this word—is intolerable because it transforms the personal relation between Jesus Christ and the believer into a physical relation: it treats persons as things and grace as a sort of fluid flowing from one to the other; it ends in a doctrine of the sacrament's effects which can scarcely be distinguished from the workings of magic. Is it to these lamentable abuses that we shall be led by the desire to assure Jesus' word and deed all their concrete density?" (*Ceci est mon corps*, 37). Still more succinctly: "Such a myopic concentration on the substance of bread and the substance of the body of Christ ends up with a cosmological miracle devoid of any significant religious setting" (Powers, *Eucharistic Theology*, 175).

[100] "In the view of the opponents of Berengar, the Eucharist has been given by God to mankind in such a mysterious form precisely in order that we may have the opportunity to exercise our faith, and thus more surely attain to the reward of faith" (Sheedy, *The Eucharistic Controversy*, 42, citing Guitmond).

[101] Cf., e.g., Staehelin, *Das theologische Lebenswerk Johannes Oekolampads*, 278 ("Oecolampadius undertakes to show that 'there is no miracle here, hence nothing beyond our grasp'").

tools—"substance," "accidents," "appearances," and the like—to deal with transubstantiation, but none to articulate an in-between analogy. Modeling a Eucharistic identity of bread and body on the incarnational identity of God and man hardly seemed appropriate, but if that model did not fit, what model did?[102] "Thus [one author revealingly comments] the catholic dogma escapes that incomprehensible hypothesis of the duality of substances in which Luther found himself imprisoned and that he had vainly tried to make acceptable."[103]

True, in the traditional conception we have been considering, transubstantiation leaves the appearances mysteriously suspended, with no substance to possess or support them. However, to proponents this consequence has often appeared more miraculous than mysterious. The chief problem resided in the "how" and not the "what." Even God, to be sure, cannot draw a square circle, but proponents have not seriously entertained, or often even envisaged, the possibility that the hypothesis of substanceless accidents, or objective appearances which are not appearances of any object, harbors a contradiction.[104] The more usual outlook has resembled Cardinal Wiseman's:

> Can we suppose that the apostles would think, "It is true that he once changed water into wine; it is true that he deprived his body of gravity; it is true that he multiplied a few loaves, so as to satisfy a crowd; but the change here proposed, the destruction of the essential qualities of a body, the *multipresence* of one substance here designed, meets the laws of nature at a point so nicely different from the former cases, that *here* we must, for the first time, doubt whether his power can go so far, and must understand him figuratively?"[105]

Some Catholic thinkers, it is true, have viewed transubstantiation not only as multiplying miracles but also as more difficult to grasp than an intermediate con-

---

[102] Cf. Suárez, *De eucharistia*, vol. 21, 119; Franzelin, *Tractatus de ss. eucharistiae sacramento*, 262-63; Bellarmine, *De sacramento eucharistiae*, 380: "Second: Because [Kemnitz] says that there is not a personal union between the bread and the body of Christ, yet he maintains that 'This bread is the body of Christ' is just as true as 'This man is God.' For either he wants to deny that there is a personal union between God and man in Christ, which is clearly Nestorian, or he doesn't know what he is saying, since he asserts a similarity and at the same time removes the basis of the similarity." In this connection, I have not encountered necessary observations such as these: (1) the supposition that all non-strict identities would have to resemble the Incarnational identity disregards the dissimilarity of non-strict identities such as those noted at the start of this chapter; (2) the reasonable supposition would be that non-strict identities between pairings as diverse as God-man and bread-body would *not* be similar. (Is color identical with wave lengths the same way that ice is identical with water? Is Jesus identical with the Word the same way that the Word is identical with God?) The contrary supposition has kept much eucharistic thinking locked within the SIS dichotomy.

[103] Godefroy, "Eucharistie," 1347.

[104] At least one author goes so far as to say that in every body there is an "aptitude" for such separation (Pourrat, "Le développement historique," 105).

[105] Wiseman, *The Real Presence,* 227. Cf. Aquinas, *Summa theologiae* 3.77.1.

ception retaining bread and wine.[106] So I do not want to overstress the avoidance of mystery as a contributing factor on this side of the Eucharistic divide. I just want to suggest its presence here too, where it is less evident. Despite its difficulties, the Tridentine doctrine has been described, for instance by Wiseman, as a simple, straightforward understanding of Christ's words.[107] "He tells his dear friends and brethren, that the time is come when he would speak plain and without parables to them. These reflections ought surely greatly to strengthen our preference, on this occasion of the plain, intelligible, natural signification of his words, when instituting the great sacrament of his religion."[108]

For Zwingli, on the other side of the Eucharistic divide, God is the only mystery,[109] and other mysteries he rejects as chicanery: "they defend themselves with this weapon, 'Faith is of things invisible; these things take place in some inexplicable and incomprehensible way.' As if any juggler and even the Roman pontiff could not say of any juggling of his own, 'This that I promise takes place, but invisibly and incomprehensibly. For faith is of things invisible and incomprehensible!'"[110] The advent of scientific thinking, the Enlightenment, and modern rationalism strengthened such resistance to mystery. "The true Religion," wrote John Toland in 1696, "must necessarily be reasonable and intelligible."[111] But, "what is evidently repugnant to clear and distinct Idea's [*sic*], or to our common Notions, is contrary to Reason."[112] Judged by such standards, only the figurative conception of the Eucharist can survive; real presence and transubstantiation, whatever their scriptural or traditional credentials, harbor too much mystery.[113] Thus, when Jesus said "This is my body," "he could mean no more than this, *viz.* that the bread which he was now breaking *represented* his body, which, in the course of a few hours, was to be crucified for them. Common sense, unsophisticated with superstition and erroneous creeds; and reason, unawed by the secular sword of sovereign authority, could not possibly take any other meaning than this plain, consistent, and rational one, out of these words."[114]

---

[106] E.g., Scotus, Ockham, Peter d'Ailly. See Pusey, *The Doctrine of the Real Presence*, 18-19, 25; Jones, *Christ's Eucharistic Presence*, 98-99.

[107] Wiseman, *The Real Presence*, 214.

[108] Ibid., 243.

[109] Zwingli, *On Providence and Other Essays*, 196.

[110] Ibid., 195.

[111] Toland, *Christianity Not Mysterious*, xxvii.

[112] Ibid., 23 (emphasis omitted).

[113] Betz (*Die Eucharistie*, 44) highlights a complementary perspective: "If one removes God to an absolute transcendence; if one conceives the relation between God and the world as the greatest possible contrast and contradiction; if, accordingly, one views a divine influence on the realities of this world as an inadmissible worldly involvement of an other-worldly God; if one therefore denies the possibility of God's interfering with causal connections within the world, then basically only a figurative understanding of the Eucharist is possible and, to be sure, no room at all remains for a Real Presence."

[114] Clarke, *Discourse*, 50. Cf. Jeremias, *The Eucharistic Words of Jesus*, 224 (on Jesus' "double simile"): "Its meaning is quite simple. Each one of the disciples could

This claim contrasts piquantly with Wiseman's view that "the plain, intelligible, natural signification" of Jesus' words points to transubstantiation. Perhaps matters are more complex than supposed. More pertinent, perhaps SIS has a rival. The interest both sides manifest in what is "plain," "intelligible," and "rational" suggests a further factor, besides SIS, that helps to explain the Eucharistic dichotomy: faith that seeks understanding seeks to mitigate mystery. However, SIS appears a still stronger explanation of the dichotomy. For one thing, I detect no indication that avoidance of mystery (as distinct from contradiction) played any considerable role, historically, in first begetting the doctrine of transubstantiation. Moreover, as we have seen, SIS itself has figured importantly in each side's claims to greater clarity. Because of SIS, transubstantiation appears more intelligible than any realistic, nonfigurative alternative. Because of SIS, transubstantiation appears the only rival and—given its difficulties—a weak rival to a straightforward figurative understanding. Clearly, bread and wine cannot be *identical* with Jesus' body and blood!

Synthetic Identities

Whereas, thanks largely to SIS, in past centuries majority views of the Eucharist polarized, excluding any identity of the Eucharistic symbols with what they symbolize, some contemporary thinking has moved toward middle ground, from both sides. Starting in the middle of the last century, theologians began to develop an approach pioneered by Yves de Montcheuil which, while retaining transubstantiation, permits an identity reading of Jesus' Eucharistic words. Empirically, these theologians agreed, nothing happens to the bread and wine. However, things are not defined empirically but by their function, significance, or finality. Thus, for Franz Leenhardt:

> The final reality of things is not in themselves, not in what they convey to our senses, even when those are improved by the most intricate laboratory instruments. In order to apprehend the substance of reality, it is necessary to have a knowledge in depth, attaining, beyond what the things are, the why of their existence. The essence of a reality lies in the divine intention which is realized through it. Only faith apprehends this dimension of things, their invisible and eschatological reality (cp. the definition of faith in Heb. 11:1). Faith alone is capable of knowing what things are in the will of God, what their object is, their reason for being; faith alone knows that there is the essence of their being, their final substance.[115]

What, then, from the perspective of faith, is the final reality of the bread which Jesus offers to his disciples, saying "This is my body"? Leenhardt replies:

---

understand it. Jesus made the broken bread a simile of the fate of his body, the blood of the grapes a simile of his outpoured blood."

[115] Leenhardt, "This Is My Body," 48.

Jesus inserts this bread into a precise intention. This intention is explicitly formulated by Him and the framework of the Paschal ritual confirms its scope. At the instant of leaving His disciples, He wishes that, after the arrest and all that follows, His presence shall continue to be real and active as before. The Paschal rite is intended to assure this permanent actuality of the redemptive acts of God. Henceforth this rite will be related to the presence of Christ, who while yet with His own is soon to be taken from their sight. Jesus wishes that, despite the efforts of the Power of Darkness, His presence shall continue. It is for this that, taking bread, He declares: "This is my body." He inserts this bread in this explicit intention of His.[116]

Given the new finality thus conferred on the bread, and given the constitutive power of divine intention, Leenhardt suggests that we may speak of Eucharistic "transubstantiation." For this term "preserves two affirmations which are essential to faith, in which everything can be summed up: (1) The substance of things is not in their empirical data, but in the will of God who upholds them. And (2) Jesus Christ declares in the upper room, in a sovereign manner, His will that the bread should be His body; He transforms the substance of this bread."[117]

Other theologians, defining reality similarly, in terms of meaning, function, or finality, reached a similar conclusion. For de Baciocchi, "Things are purely and simply what they are for Christ, for his understanding is the absolute norm of our understanding."[118] In the view of Édouard Pousset, "What makes bread and wine substances is not their weight, nor their resistance to touch, nor their physico-chemical constitution, nor their atomic or nuclear structure. . . . What defines them as substances is the fact that they are *food*."[119] According to Charles Davis, "bread has an ontological reality . . . not as a physical substance, but as a human object. The unity and intelligibility it possesses is a unity and intelligibility inseparable from its relation to man."[120] Similarly, for E. L. Mascall what, for instance, defines a five-pound note is not its consisting of paper. "What is supremely important about an object, in the place which it holds and the finalities to which it is directed and the energies which it exerts in the total order of God's creation, can rightly be called its substance."[121] From such premises as these, it follows that if the words of consecration alter the elements' finality—if they "totally change their social and religious destination,"[122] conferring on them "a new purpose and a new relation to man"[123]—they effect a substantial transformation. "There is a change in the reality of the object, which ceases to be bread and becomes the body of Christ. The

---

[116] Ibid.

[117] Ibid., 49-50.

[118] Baciocchi, "Présence eucharistique," 151. See Baciocchi, "Le mystère euchar-istique," 576 ("Things *are* then purely and solely what they are for Jesus Christ").

[119] Pousset, "L'Eucharistie," 199.

[120] Davis, "Understanding the Real Presence," 174.

[121] Mascall, "Egner on the Eucharistic Presence," 541.

[122] Baciocchi, "Présence eucharistique," 150.

[123] Davis, "Understanding the Real Presence," 175.

presence is thus by transubstantiation, not by consubstantiation. We affirm that the consecrated host is Christ, not just that he gives himself with it."[124]

Notice: "The consecrated host *is* Christ." Still more explicitly, for Davis, "Christ is present in the Eucharist *by identity* with the consecrated bread."[125] Davis can speak this way because the Eucharistic elements are no longer mere appearances. The physical reality persists, providing a real, distinct referent for the subject pronoun in "This is my body." As Schillebeeckx notes, in such a perspective "*What* appears, in our experience, as bread and wine *is* the 'body of the Lord' appearing to us (as sacramental nourishment). The significance of the phenomenal forms of bread and wine changes *because* by the power of the creative Spirit, the reality to which the phenomenal refers is changed—it *is* no longer bread and wine, but nothing less than the 'body of the Lord,' offered to me as spiritual nourishment."[126]

This emergence of a two-term identity where previously, at the extremes, there was none, may be viewed as the outcome of a dialectical development in which transubstantiation figures as thesis, Zwinglian symbolism as antithesis, and "transignification" or "transfinalization" as synthesis, combining something of both the thesis and the antithesis positions. Kinship with the latter, symbolic view appears in the redefinition of reality in terms of function or meaning. Kinship with the former view, eliminating bread and wine, appears in the change of natures which the elements undergo. Indeed, in this modern perspective, the bread and the body do not merely succeed one another, with one eliminated and the other replacing it, but (as Trent stipulates) the whole substance of the bread is changed into the whole substance of the body of Christ. Only the physical objects endure from start to finish, not bread as bread or wine as wine.

These recent attempts and subsequent variants invite varying reactions. From a Protestant perspective, they may be seen as improving on Luther's middle position, through their greater definiteness, or as marking a regression, through their introduction of suspect metaphysics. ("For my part," declared Luther, "if I cannot fathom how the bread is the body of Christ, yet I will take my reason captive to the obedience of Christ, and clinging simply to his words, firmly believe not only that the body of Christ is in the bread, but that the bread is the body of Christ."[127]) From a Catholic perspective, the attempts may be seen as improving on Trent, through their removal of free-floating appearances and their adoption of more existential, dynamic categories, or as marking a regression, through their introduction of new word meanings and therefore new doctrines, replacing those of Trent and Catholic tradition. Transignification or transfinalization, it may be objected, is not the same thing as transubstantiation.

Fidelity to Scripture, not to Luther, concerns the Protestant; fidelity to Church teaching as well as to Scripture concerns the Catholic. Both concerns evoke larger

---

[124] Ibid., 172. Cf. Durrwell, *L'Eucharistie, sacrement pascal*, 113-14.

[125] Davis, "Understanding the Real Presence," 171 (emphasis added).

[126] Schillebeeckx, *The Eucharist*, 149.

[127] Luther, *Babylonian Captivity*, 34.

questions, beyond the scope of this chapter. I believe that the New Testament, with its Johannine and Pauline realism and its Pauline references to "bread," is open to a reading that, one way or another, identifies the consecrated bread with the body of Christ. It does not stop short at a pure figure, nor does it go as far as transubstantiation. How ready a person is to accept this evidence and how transcendent a view of the Eucharist a person is prepared to embrace will depend, in part, on two considerations which Adelman of Liège noted long ago. With regard to the words "This is my body," he observed: "Who disbelieves that this is so, unless he does not believe Christ or does not believe that he said it?"[128] Conversely, who shares Paul's Eucharistic realism without also sharing his belief that "Jesus Christ is Lord" (Phil 2:11) and that "the Lord Jesus, on the night when he was betrayed, took bread, and when he had given thanks, he broke it and said, 'This is my body that is for you. Do this in remembrance of me'" (1 Cor 11:23-25)? Thus, the present chapter connects importantly with the preceding two, on Jesus' divinity. It also connects with the next chapter, on doctrinal identity. Whether the modern, existential readings retain the "same" meaning as Trent, whether the Tridentine teaching retains the "same" meaning as the faith of the apostles, what such claims of sameness might mean, how they might be assessed—these are questions of such complexity and far-reaching significance that I shall leave them for separate consideration.

---

[128] Adelman of Liège, *De eucharistiae sacramento*, 1292.

Chapter 6

The Word of God

In his Eucharistic encyclical *Mysterium Fidei*, Pope Paul VI lamented those who proceed "as if everyone were permitted to consign to oblivion doctrine already defined by the Church, or to interpret it in such a way as to weaken the genuine meaning of the words or the approved import of the concepts involved."[1] It is not permissible, for example, "to discuss the mystery of transubstantiation without mentioning the marvelous changing of the whole substance of the bread into the Body and of the whole substance of the wine into the Blood of Christ as stated by the Council of Trent, so that it consists [only] in 'transignification' or 'transfinalization' as they put it."[2] True, it is licit and desirable to elucidate the Tridentine formulae, "but only in the same meaning they originally had so that as the knowledge of the faith increases the truth of the faith remains unchanged."[3] This stress on doctrinal sameness of meaning, like that of Pius XII,[4] Pius IX,[5] Vatican Council I,[6] and others back through the centuries, echoes Vincent of Lérins's early saying: "The intelligence, then, the knowledge, the wisdom, as well of individuals as of all, as well of one man as of the whole Church, ought, in the course of ages and centuries, to increase and make much and vigorous progress; but yet only in its own kind; that is to say, in the same doctrine, in the same sense, and in the same meaning [*in eodem scilicet dogmate, eodem sensu eademque sententia*]."[7]

Today, this traditional prescription has come to appear problematic. If, as Wittgenstein remarked, "only in the stream of thought and life do words have meaning,"[8] and the stream of thought and life shifts from century to century, how can the words of contemporary theologians have the same meaning as those of

---

[1] Paul VI, *Mysterium Fidei*, 3 (n. 10).

[2] Ibid., 3-4 (n. 11).

[3] Ibid. 7 (n. 25).

[4] Pius XII, DS 3886.

[5] Pius IX, "Inter gravissimas," 260.

[6] "It also follows that any meaning of the sacred dogmas that has once been declared by holy Mother Church, must always be retained; and there must never be any deviation from that meaning on the specious grounds of a more profound understanding" (*The Church Teaches*, 34; DS 3020). In *Mysterium Ecclesiae* the Congregation for the Doctrine of the Faith similarly insists: "The *sense*, however, of dogmatic formulas always remains true and consistent in the Church, even when it is more clearly enunciated and more fully understood" (403; emphasis in the original).

[7] Vincent of Lérins, "The Commonitory," 148 (23.54).

[8] Wittgenstein, *Zettel*, §173.

Trent?[9] How, in turn, can the words of Trent retain the same sense as the words of the Fathers, or the Fathers' sayings retain the same sense as Jesus' original message or that proclaimed by the Apostles?

This issue of doctrinal identity, on which the present chapter will focus, pervades Christian faith and thought. Passages such as the following, from various sources, attest to the issue's significance and also furnish data for initial reflection. (Thus the sampling, though long, is not a mere smorgasbord; its length and its variety serve a double purpose.)

> We are involved in history and only in this ongoing process do we possess the eternal truth of God which is our salvation. The truth retains its identity in this history, but it is an identity which had a history and continues to have one. We have always this same, identical truth, but never in such a way that we could detach it completely from its historical form.[10]

> The truth of revelation, in a mysterious way, preserves its dynamic identity amid the changing formulations. Each of the formulations must justify itself as an authentic articulation of the one gospel to which Christians are committed in faith.[11]

> The whole message, the whole of the faith remains the same, but the approach, the light in which the faith is seen, is new.[12]

> Neither St. Paul nor St. John can possibly have been unaware that their own teaching represents a *development* of the explicit teaching of the Master, nevertheless each regards his own teaching as *identical* with the original Gospel preached by Christ.[13]

> This sense of tradition—a deposit—a rule of faith—a gospel unchanging through the centuries—became part of faith. It was the clearest way in which the uneducated layman or laywoman could understand what was authority in the Church. Being deep within the idea of authority, it was deep inside faith. It was part of Christian devotion.[14]

> The church, then, following the example of St. Paul, becomes all things to all men. It communicates what God has revealed both in the manner appropriate to the various differentiations of consciousness and, above all, in the manner appropriate to each of the almost endless brands of common sense. Still, these many modes of speech

---

[9] "Words only have meaning insofar as they are used in a concrete cultural situation. Two different words, arising in different languages and periods of history, cannot have identical meanings (so, for example, a renewed interest in the bible is making people increasingly aware of how difficult it is to convey the meaning which words such as 'water' and 'light' had for a primitive Middle Eastern nomad, to a contemporary European city-dweller)" (Lash, "Dogmas and Doctrinal Progress," 19).

[10] Rahner, "The Historical Dimension in Theology," 35.

[11] Dulles, *The Survival of Dogma*, 183.

[12] *A New Catechism*, v.

[13] C. Harris, *Creeds or No Creeds?*, 23 (Harris's emphasis).

[14] Chadwick, *From Bossuet to Newman*, xvi.

involve no more than a pluralism of communications for, though they are many, still all can be [in Lérins's words] *in eodem dogmate, eodem sensu eademque sententia.*[15]

The exegete attempts to establish precisely how this word was spoken to and heard by the Jewish people and the early church. The dogmatic theologian, on the other hand, attempts to establish how this same word, heard by Israel and the apostolic church but nonetheless addressed to us as well, should be heard in a pure form by us in the twentieth century.[16]

It is too clear that the different notions to which theologians have had recourse to express the same truth are *equivalent* notions; otherwise they would not be suitable to sustain the same affirmation.[17]

If the concepts are allowed to keep their plain, original simple meaning, we are bound to say that an explication of what is formally implicit in a revealed proposition is present only when the new proposition really states the *same thing* as the old in other words, has the same content as the old one, however useful and necessary it may be for various reasons to formulate the new proposition.[18]

The point to be ascertained is the unity and identity of the idea with itself through all stages of its development from first to last.[19]

Dogmatic fixity has lost its traditional role as the chief expression of the invariability of the faith, but the claim to invariability has not been abandoned. Instead, the theological understanding of faith has been revolutionized in such a way that its self-identity through change can be plausibly maintained in the face of the modern emphasis on historical relativity.[20]

Common to all forms of Modernism is the denial of the fact (and in most cases also of the possibility) of a fixed Deposit of Faith retaining an absolutely identical meaning throughout the process of its development.[21]

The heresies of liberal Protestantism and modernism on the one hand, with their denial of the identity throughout the ages of Church dogma, by an appeal to the results of the history of the human spirit and of dogma; the insufficiency of much current apologetics on behalf of this identity, on the other hand, conceding only a minor change in verbal formulas—both show how difficult and how little mastered the question still is.[22]

---

[15] Lonergan, *Method in Theology*, 329.

[16] Schillebeeckx, *Revelation and Theology*, vol. 1, 176.

[17] Bouillard, "Notions conciliaires," 254 (Bouillard's emphasis).

[18] Rahner, "The Development of Dogma," 59 (Rahner's emphasis).

[19] Newman, *Essay*, 206.

[20] Lindbeck, "Reform and Infallibility," 348 (on developments in the Catholic Church).

[21] C. Harris, *Creeds or No Creeds?*, 29.

[22] Rahner, "Considerations on the Development of Dogma," 5.

These recurring references to identity and sameness and the varying perspectives in which they occur—history, gospel, faith, revelation, development, tradition, church, exegesis, theology, dogma, apologetics—appear to leave no doubt about the importance of this chapter's chosen topic. Doctrinal identity is indeed a major issue for Christendom. Yet notice how differently, in an often-quoted passage, John Courtney Murray words his kindred observations:

> Leaving aside the issue of what Catholic and Protestant respectively mean when they say, "Credo," I consider that the parting of the ways between the two Christian communities takes place on the issue of development of doctrine. That development has taken place in both communities cannot possibly be denied. The question is, what is legitimate development, what is organic growth in the understanding of the original deposit of faith, what is warranted extension of the primitive discipline of the Church, and what, on the other hand, is accretion, additive increment, adulteration of the deposit, distortion of true Christian discipline? The question is, what are the valid dynamisms of development and what are the forces of distortion? The question is, what are the criteria by which to judge between healthy and morbid development, between true growth and rank excrescence? The question is, what is archaism and what is futurism? Perhaps, above all, the question is, what are the limits of development and growth—the limits that must be reached on peril of archaistic stuntedness, and the limits that must not be transgressed on peril of futuristic decadence?[23]

"Legitimate development," "organic growth," "warranted extension," "valid dynamisms," and the like, versus "accretion," "adulteration," "distortion," "rank excrescence," and "archaistic stuntedness"—such are Murray's categories. The terms "same," "sameness," "identical," and "identity" make no single appearance in his remarks. So my collection of sample statements, all stressing identity, may look carefully selective. The same issues may be addressed in other terms.

No doubt the issues may be differently formulated, but they need not be; and discussion in terms of identity can cast light on all of Murray's questions, plus others. Furthermore, such questions as his lead to, and often require, closer analysis in terms of identity or sameness. What, for instance, will count as "legitimate development" or "warranted extension"? Does it require no sameness of any kind? If so, what kind? If, however, no identity of any sort is either needed or discernible, why have so many supposed the contrary? The very frequency with which questions of faith, revelation, tradition, dogma, theology, and apologetics have been stated in the manner exemplified attests to the importance of the issue this chapter will address.

The same sampling also serves a second purpose, suggesting the issue's complexity as well as its significance. Sameness varies for different classes of things. Whereas a regiment can change all its members and remain the same regiment, a book cannot change all its words and remain the same book. Whereas a river can momentarily run dry yet remain the same river, a jet of water cannot

---

[23]   Murray, *The Problem of God*, 53 (paragraph break omitted).

momentarily cease and remain the same jet of water. And so forth. To know the criteria of identity, you must know the class of things identified. Here, however, in these sample texts, sameness is asserted of a dozen different referents—truth, gospel, message, teaching, dogma, sense, belief, word, thing, content, affirmation, idea, meaning—all bundled together. In this respect, too, the sampling is apt. Even the most detailed studies of such a topic as doctrinal development have made little effort to sort out these different categories, identify their respective criteria of identity, and determine how the criteria interrelate. The varied terms—truth, gospel, message, faith, dogma, content, sense, etc.—have appeared interchangeable. And so they doubtless are to some extent. But here as elsewhere, we may rightly fear the pervasive influence of essentialism of the kind identified in Chapter 1.

Essentialistic Simplifications

Preceding chapters traced and critiqued the essentialistic notion of identity. Reappearing here, with respect to doctrinal sameness, it comes tightly bound with other such notions. Essentialistic conceptions of thought, speech, revelation, and doctrinal development conspire to make the issue of doctrinal identity appear much simpler than it is, and they therefore merit preliminary attention.

Revelation and Development

In his once-classic work, *La evolución homogénea del dogma catolico*, Francisco Marín-Sola proposed in detail one form of essentialistic simplification—the long-dominant "propositional" concept of revelation. "In divine revelation," he observed, "two elements must be well distinguished: a) the revealed formulas, whether verbal or mental; b) the revealed sense of these formulas."[24] With regard to the latter he explained:

> For there to be true revelation and true divine faith, it is indispensable for God to have given *some* explicit sense to the revealed formulas; it is likewise indispensable for the prophet or apostle to have explicitly understood at least *something* of this divine sense; finally, it is indispensable for the hearers of the prophet or apostle, which in our case is the primitive church, to have understood from the first moment *some* sense, indeed some *explicit* sense, of the apostolic formulas.[25]

Here, for Marín-Sola, is "the true starting point of all dogmatic or theological development."[26]

In this perspective, there need be no fear that, in seeking an initial term of comparison for a claim of doctrinal identity, one might find a person, event, or experience rather than a doctrine, or find a metaphor, parable, or story rather than a

---

[24] Marín-Sola, *La evolución homogénea*, 169.

[25] Ibid., 170.

[26] Ibid., 169.

statement of fact. Revelation is propositional from the start; it takes this single form. But surely, many have recently objected, revelation does not always take the form of propositions, statements, or revealed truths. Did the Apostles learn nothing from the person of Jesus as well as from his words? Did they learn nothing from his resurrection? To such objections, Swinburne has replied:

> It is . . . very hard to see how God could reveal himself in history (e.g. in the Exodus or the life, death, and resurrection of Jesus) without at the same time revealing some propositional truth about himself. For events are not self-interpreting. Either God provides with the historical event its interpretation, in which case there is a propositional revelation; or he does not, in which case how can anyone know that a revelatory event has occurred?[27]

With equal right, one might wonder how, in the former supposition, one can know that a divine interpretation has been supplied. And why must the interpretation occur in apostolic times? In Matthew 11, the Baptist inquires, "Are you the one who is to come, or are we to wait for another?" and Jesus replies: "Go and tell John what you hear and see: the blind receive their sight, the lame walk, the lepers are cleansed, the deaf hear, the dead are raised, and the poor have good news brought to them." Go, that is, and tell John about me and my doings, and let him draw his own conclusion. Why might not revelation function, at least on occasion, in somewhat similar fashion? Why might it not act like a seed, planted and watered by God and bringing forth new fruit in due season? The traditional answer, simply put, is that God might, no doubt, effect such growth but the result would not qualify as "revealed truth."[28] Thus, in the classical viewpoint espoused till recently, there can never be any improvement on the Apostles' understanding of revelation.[29] Full knowledge of revelation would amount to a knowledge of all the revealed propositions in their minds. Doctrinal fidelity consists in matching present proposition with past proposition. And doctrinal development takes a corresponding form.

---

[27] Swinburne, *Revelation*, 4.

[28] "The assertions of the Magisterium, which declare the content of revelation, are not a new revelation. For this reason all comparisons with the growth of biological organisms, even when defended by the great name of Vincent of Lérins or of Newman, are open to criticism" (Rondet, *Do Dogmas Change?*, 116).

[29] "For St Thomas, as for later Thomists, the apostles had possessed the fullness of divine revelation. This was owing to their position as *capita*, 'heads' or 'leaders' of the New Testament Church. By an infused divine light, they enjoyed an explicit knowledge of divine revelation greater than that of all later theologians or even of the whole later Church" (Nichols, *From Newman to Congar*, 180). Cf. Chadwick, *From Bossuet to Newman*, 43 (on Suarez and Lugo); Walgrave, *Unfolding Revelation*, 130-31 (on the Port-Royal theologians); Marín-Sola, *La evolución homogénea*, 173. Some have allowed a bit more leeway: "All dogmatic progress consists either in the explicit data of revelation finding an apter formulation or in the implicit data finding a formulation they lacked" (Batiffol, *L'Eucharistie*, 501).

"A theory of development," writes Jan Walgrave, "provides a general model to explain and justify what the history of the several dogmas reveals."[30] Given the diversity of dogma and of its history, one may wonder about the adequacy of any single model. However, descriptively Walgrave's account sounds accurate enough. "Theories of development" have often aimed to furnish a universal, uniform account. With a propositional conception of revelation, for example, they have often combined a logical conception of doctrinal development. What later doctrine declares, must be present already, at least implicitly, in the original revelation. The later doctrine may clarify, make more precise, state in other terms. However, to quote Charles Journet, "If the implicit is really contained in the explicit, we must say without hesitation that the making explicit of a divine truth, that is, its passage from the state in which it is unformulated and obscure to the state in which it is formulated and clear, occurs in conformity with a logic which is intrinsic, rigorous and unescapable."[31] The process and its logic might, for instance, be given syllogistic form.[32] However, such a logical theory of development must be distinguished from a historical, etiological theory of development.[33] What might have been inferred with rigorous logic need not have been. Thus Journet prudently adds: "However rigorous it may be, the process by which a truth of the faith is derived from one that precedes it takes place wholly in the night of faith." Even when the development has occurred, we need not be able to demonstrate the logical relationship between revelation and its dogmatic expression; but such a relationship there must be.

Why? One motive for such a stance is epistemological: if subsequent doctrine were not logically identical with "divine truth" at the start, its truth would not be assured by its derivation from that truth. Extra, fallible content might creep in, whereas revealed truth is infallible, as are the principles of logic that link the later teaching with the apostolic doctrine. (For the same reason, the later teaching cannot be just "more or less identical" with revealed truth, for then it might be just

---

[30] Walgrave, *Unfolding Revelation*, 4-5.

[31] Journet, *Esquisse*, 53-54 (translation in Rondet, *Do Dogmas Change?*, 117-18). See Marín-Sola, *La evolución homogénea*, e.g. 148 ("The sense of a doctrine across various formulations remains the same when the sense of later formulations does not come from without but was already *implicitly contained* [original emphasis] in the earlier formulations").

[32] Cf. Marín-Sola, *La evolución homogénea*, 353 (best left in the original Spanish): "Entremos ya a poner ejemplos históricos y concretos de verdaderos desarrollos dogmáticos, después de los Apóstoles, verificados por la vía especulativa de raciocinio propiamente dicho . . . . en cada ejemplo señalaremos las majores de fe y las menores de razón inclusiva que han intervenido en esos raciocinios . . ."

[33] The two perspectives are often not distinguished, and confusion results. A handy sample: "Putting it differently: an explicit proposition has been contained in another proposition as something formally implicit only when it results from the latter in consequence of a *hermeneutic* and exegetical operation, not involving (as a necessary feature) the use of a properly deductive procedure" (Rahner, "the Development of Dogma," 59; his emphasis).

"more or less true.") To be sure, nowhere, early or late, has divine truth assumed a pure, nonhuman form; nor has anyone, to my knowledge, ever demonstrated satisfactorily the strict logical identity between subsequent doctrine and God's original word. But I speak here of a motive, a psychological influence inclining to this form of essentialism, not of a sound argument. If the Church's assurance of perseverance in the truth rests on continuing divine assistance, that assistance might occur in other ways than that dictated by the logical theory. God is not bound by our theoretical requirements.

A second motive, noted above, for insistence on strict logical identity with revelation is largely conceptual. "Revelation," it is held, ended in apostolic times, hence any accretions would not be revealed truth. If, then, "doctrine" is restricted to revealed truth, it cannot develop otherwise than in the way prescribed: change can occur only in the formulation and not in the content. The doctrine cannot grow and still count as "revealed" truth. Granted, the church may not have ascertained such logical identity when formulating doctrine, and individual Christians need not restrict their belief to any such hypothetical content. They may freely and rightly believe, for example, that if Jesus is with his people through all ages, he is with them in the twenty-first century—even though the apostles knew nothing about the world's lasting that long (and neither, according to Mt 24-36 and Mark 13:32, did Jesus). Thus, though the theory—floating free in an abstract realm of interlocking definitions—has a reassuring sound, it tends to obscure the facts of development.

Reinforcing these motives, we may also surmise the underlying influence of an essentialistic conception of human thought and speech, without which the theory's stipulations would appear less plausible.

Concepts and Statements

If the basic role of the intellect is to abstract eternal, universal essences and thereby to form universal concepts, expressed by universal terms, and if the constructive role of the intellect is to combine these concepts in judgments, expressed by statements, there should be little problem about the transtemporal or transcultural identity of statements. "Just as all men have not the same writing," said Aristotle, "so all men have not the same speech sounds, but the mental experiences, which these directly symbolize, are the same for all, as also are those things of which our experiences are the images."[34] If, in addition, as these words suggest, the contents of judgments, statements, propositions, beliefs, doctrines, dogmas, and so forth are all are equally essentialistic, equally definite and uniform, it should make little difference which of these mental and linguistic units one cites in stating the

---

[34] Aristotle, *De interpretatione* 16a. Cf. Marín-Sola, *La evolución homogénea*, 104: "Human understanding also has fixed and immutable elements. They are the first principles, the first notions. Principles and notions in which the essences of things are reflected. The essences are immutable and eternal, they never change. And if understanding is to be genuine, it will always tend to adapt itself to them, it will always be identical, it will never change."

question of doctrinal identity. As the concepts and propositions of one people, epoch, or culture match those of another, so the contents of judgments or beliefs match those of statements, doctrines, or propositions, and vice versa. "These concepts: proposition, language, thought, world, stand in line one behind the other, each equivalent to each."[35] Once, however, we recognize that concepts do not match concepts from language to language, culture to culture, or century to century, the problem of doctrinal identity appears more complex.[36]

"For example," observes Rahner, "we would only have to ask what the words *spirit, logos, flesh, blood, justice, redeemer, sinner* and so on really and precisely mean in the NT. That meaning includes all the aspects, nuances, various applications, and meaningful undertones that they have. It involves the proximate and remote environment and the whole 'field' of meaning in which these concepts exist."[37] What, we may therefore ask, are the chances that a term in one culture, language, or epoch will match some term in another in all these respects? However, Rahner's account retains something of the essentialism against which it reacts. Philosophers do not agree on this all-inclusive account of "meaning," neither does common usage back it for all occasions; indeed, usage does not clearly establish it in any standard context. When, for instance, we state that this English word has the same meaning as that German word, we do not mean to include "all the aspects, nuances, various applications, and meaningful undertones that they have." More importantly, and word usage aside, not every context of discussion or inquiry requires such inclusive coverage. Most discussions of doctrinal identity do not. And yet, the main thrust of Rahner's remarks is valid and important. Concepts are more rich, varied, and indefinite than essentialistic accounts suggest.[38]

So are statements. Some utterances report "how things stand," as the younger Wittgenstein put it, but many do not. Some, for instance, are tautologies, others are performatives, still others are avowals. Of those that state "how things stand," some are empirical and some are not, some are abstract and some are concrete,

---

[35] Wittgenstein, *Philosophical Investigations*, §96 (on his former way of thinking).

[36] Whereas I speak of "essentialism," Lonergan speaks of "classicism": "The classicist is no pluralist. He knows that circumstances alter cases but he is far more deeply convinced that circumstances are somehow accidental and that, beyond them, there is some substance or kernel or root that fits in with classicist assumptions of stability, fixity, immutability. Things have their specific natures; these natures, at least in principle, are to be known adequately through the properties they possess and the laws they obey. Over and above the specific nature there is only individuation by matter, so that knowledge of one instance of a species is knowledge of any instance. What is true of species in general, also is true of the human species, of the one faith coming to us through Jesus Christ, through the one charity given through the gift of the Holy Spirit. So it was concluded that the diversity of peoples, cultures, social arrangements can involve only a difference in the dress in which doctrines are expressed, but cannot involve any diversity in church doctrine itself" (*Method in Theology*, 301-2).

[37] Rahner, "The Historical Dimension in Theology," 33.

[38] See Hallett, *Essentialism*, ch. 1, and *Language and Truth*, ch. 2.

some are temporal and some are atemporal. None, however, functions in the way that essentialism has considered typical. Essentialistic meanings do not run through the speaker's mind, get translated into shared words, and thereby reappear, intact, in the minds of all and sundry hearers. If, for instance (to adapt Wittgenstein's example), a speaker makes a statement about Moses, each hearer will understand the statement in accordance with his or her beliefs about Moses—"for example, as 'the man who led the Israelites through the wilderness,' 'the man who lived at that time and place and was then called "Moses,"' 'the man who as a child was taken out of the Nile by Pharaoh's daughter' and so on."[39] And these beliefs are likely to vary, perhaps radically, from person to person (e.g., fundamentalist or scholar) and from epoch to epoch (e.g., believing or unbelieving).

Identity

For the essentialist, synonymy—sameness of meaning—is relatively unproblematic, both for concepts and for statements. Essences are definite and invariant, and so are the concepts that capture them, and so, accordingly, are the meanings of the words that express the concepts. Given all this invariance, the doctrinal identity typically supposed in this viewpoint is strict identity. Grounded in indistinguishable essences, the content of concepts and statements remains indiscernibly the same across speakers, cultures, and epochs.

Something of this viewpoint lingers in the definition which Swinburne stipulates:

> Two sentences express the same proposition if and only if they are synonymous. "Rex mortuus est," uttered by a Latin speaker of the fourteenth century, "Le roi est mort," uttered by a French speaker of the eighteenth century, and "The king is dead," uttered by an English speaker of the twentieth century, express the same proposition. If you take into account only what dictionaries would tell you that the words mean, and forget the context of utterance, the three sentences mean the same.[40]

Anyone inclined to Wittgensteinian misgivings about the equivalence of the Latin, French, and English expressions might have similar misgivings about the terms—Latin, French, and English, or all English?—employed in the dictionary definitions. And theorists have offered the most varied accounts of word and sentence meanings. However, let it pass. As Wittgenstein remarked, "The sign-post is in order—if, under normal circumstances, it fulfils its purpose."[41] Swinburne's definition and accompanying example sufficiently differentiate one sense from others in which a given sentence might be said to have the same meaning as

---

[39] Wittgenstein, *Philosophical Investigations*, §79.

[40] Swinburne, *Revelation*, 10. Cf. Pitcher, *Truth*, 5: "If one person says 'It is raining,' another 'Il pleut,' and a third 'Es regnet,' a correct answer to the question 'What did he say?' would in each case be 'He said that it is raining'—for each would have said *the same thing*" (Pitcher's emphasis).

[41] Wittgenstein, *Philosophical Investigations*, §87.

another. For future consultation, and to counteract the influence of essentialistic blinkers, let us note a few alternative senses and examples of sentence synonymy.

Swinburne speaks of ignoring context. If, instead, we take context into account and attend to the message of an utterance rather than its medium, a different sense of sameness results. Suppose, for example, that a history professor asked a pupil, "When a Frank declared in 814 'Rex mortuus est' and a Frenchman declared in 1743 'Le roi est mort,' did their words have the same meaning?" The pupil would probably reply in the negative, on pain of betraying her ignorance of history. "No," she might say, "the first statement meant that Charlemagne was dead, the second that Louis XIV was dead." Much depends on context, and how the question is posed.

The like may hold even for verbally identical utterances within the same language. If, for example, one inquired: "Do the words 'It's raining' used on different occasions to report the weather on those occasions—now a drizzle, now a downpour—have the same meaning?" the reply might be negative. If, instead, one asked: "Does the identical sentence 'It's raining' used in the same way—to report the weather—and with the same sense of 'rain' have the same meaning?" the reply would more likely be positive.

These varied samples differ from Swinburne's further illustration: "'I am ill,' spoken by me, 'you are ill,' addressed to me, and 'he is ill,' spoken of me."[42] Here, both the words and the sentence structures vary. But the truth-conditions do not: what verifies one sentence verifies the other. Thus, in a clear sense the sentences or statements all "say the same thing." In this sense and for this reason, we might say they all "have the same meaning."

Something similar may hold for even more varied utterances—for example these varied reports of a single event: "The king has died," "We've lost our king," "The king's soul has departed," "The king has joined his ancestors," "The king has gone to his reward," "The king has become one with the One." In a sense, these announcements all say the same thing, and we might therefore agree with them all, even if we did not believe that the king joined his ancestors or had a soul or went to his reward or became one with the One. For here, "saying the same thing" signifies something like "making the same point." These are all reports of the king's death. The various ways of making the report do not affect its basic truth.

Other variations might be added, but let these suffice for the moment. Enough has been said to illustrate how, in multiple ways, essentialism may oversimplify the issue of doctrinal identity. No single account is likely to fit all doctrines, all contexts, and all analytic purposes. I therefore propose that for deeper, clearer insight, it will be profitable to focus on some single doctrine in some single context of discussion, where questions of broad interest arise. For this purpose the doctrine of transubstantiation has several advantages. The last chapter has already laid the basis for discussion, further reflection will remedy somewhat the incompleteness of that discussion, and this example will introduce questions of general significance. Eventually, I shall introduce other examples. However, neither in this

---

[42] Swinburne, *Revelation*, 11.

chapter nor in the next shall I venture to offer a comprehensive view of all varieties of doctrinal identity, actual or possible.

The Eucharistic example is made intriguing as well as instructive by the sharpness with which it poses a common type of dilemma. Can Paul VI and like-minded theologians have it both ways: can the doctrine of Trent be both definite enough to rule out transfinalization or transignification as an acceptable reading, on the one hand, and indefinite enough to qualify as the teaching of Scripture or the Apostles, on the other? Won't success in either direction preclude success in the other? Let us examine both horns of this dilemma—first the relation between the modern theories and the teaching of Trent, then the relation between Trent's teaching and that of the Apostles.

Identity with Dogma

At Trent, as we have seen, the Council Fathers declared that "by the consecration of the bread and wine a conversion takes place of the whole substance of bread into the substance of the body of Christ our Lord, and of the whole substance of the wine into the substance of His blood."[43] Since the Fathers were imbued with Scholastic philosophy of various forms (largely Aristotelian), they would have understood the word "substance" accordingly. And it might therefore appear that the Council obliges the faithful to understand the word the same way. To embrace the doctrine, they must embrace the philosophy of those who defined it. However, most theologians judge otherwise. "Even when the Church makes use of terms drawn from particular philosophical or theological systems, she does not employ them in all the strictness of their technical sense, and in consequence does not bind our faith to any philosophic system."[44] Thus at Trent, for example, "it is evident that the use of the words *substantialiter* and *substantia* does not rest on the Aristotelian categories of substance and accident."[45] The Council, it is commonly held, employs these terms "in a current, vague, and indeterminate sense."[46]

This seems basically correct. Given the diversity of the Council Fathers' philosophical views,[47] what definite sense would be acceptable to all who approved the Council's decrees? However, were the sense completely indeterminate, there could be no conflict between the Council's teaching and the recent theories which Paul VI questions. What, then, is left, after the Council's terms are stripped of their specifically Scholastic or Aristotelian content? In what might the underlying nucleus consist, establishing the doctrine's identity? Responses vary greatly, yet two general directions can be discerned, often within

---

[43] DS 1642 (my translation).

[44] Lebreton, *The Encyclical and Modernist Theology*, 64.

[45] Ghysens, "Présence réelle eucharistique," 428.

[46] Egender, "Vers une doctrine eucharistique commune," 176.

[47] Jedin, *History*, 180 ("only Nominalism . . . no longer found a defender at Trent").

the same response. Some accounts cite common *word meanings*, while others cite common *opinions* ("common sense"). The importance of this split appears from the fact that, whereas word meanings are not true or false, opinions are. Yet many recognize no difference between these two alternatives, but bundle meanings and opinions together.[48] Clarity demands that the difference be noted, for it is as basic in the present context as elsewhere. Here, then, are samples of the two approaches, in relatively pure form.

Ambroise Gardeil takes the second, shared-belief direction when he asks:

> What can be the meaning *common to all* that the Church wishes to define? Evidently it is the meaning that relates to what is fixed and permanent in the natural understanding of human beings, beneath all the accidental differentiations of races and mentalities. It is the understanding of assertions accessible to human common sense . . . Here is what is revealed, here is what is defined, here is the sense that does not change.[49]

It would seem, then, that, though agreement with Trent does not demand that believers become Scholastics or Aristotelians, it does require that they accept a common-sense philosophy of some unspecified variety. Yet what variety? What does this natural philosophy have to say, for example, about physical reality? Does it espouse mediate realism or immediate realism? If so, what kind? What are its views about primary and secondary qualities, or does it admit any such distinction? What does it say about essences or universals? Is it Platonic, Aristotelian, nominalist, conceptualist, Wittgensteinian? I need not belabor the point. If the philosophy in question takes no stand on any of the most basic questions of philosophy, in what does it consist? How could any account of the Eucharist or

---

[48] Cf., e.g., Powers, "Mysterium Fidei," 33 ("distinguishing the substance of the faith of the church from its time-bound clothing in language of a particular natural philosophy"); Masi, "La conversione eucaristica," 296 ("The terms employed by dogmatic formulas express human concepts and categories known to everyone, at every time, in every place, according to the immediate and evident first principles of natural knowledge"); Sayes, *La presencia real*, 266 ("the philosophy implicit in the dogma of transubstantiation is the everyday philosophy we use in our common language"); O'Neill, *New Approaches to the Eucharist*, 92: "These formulas, states the encyclical, express concepts which are not tied to any particular civilization or stage of scientific development or theological school. On the contrary, they signify what the human mind perceives of things 'by necessary and universal experience.'"

[49] Gardeil, *Le donné révélé*, 83 (Gardeil's emphasis). Cf. O'Neill, *New Approaches to the Eucharist*, 97 ("It must be insisted once again: only common sense is being appealed to"); Godefroy, "Eucharistie," 1349: "whatever the terms employed, they need not be understood save in the light of the *philosophia perennis*, of that very simple and rudimentary philosophy that is as indispensable in the exposition of dogmas as in any rational knowledge, that can be understood without any study, that remains apart from all systems, or rather, that should underlie all systems since without it they would only defy good sense."

transubstantiation conflict with it? If, however, it does take a stand on controverted philosophical issues, how could the Council impose it as revealed truth?

I shall need to return to this question, but let us now sample the alternative, linguistic perspective, centered on word meanings rather than opinions. "Even technical terms," we are told, "such as person or substance, that have entered these or those dogmatic formulas, there have no other sense than the one the Church gives them, which is not a technical sense borrowed from a determinate philosophy, but the sense of ordinary language."[50] For example, "The phrase *substantia panis et vini* as it occurs in the decree on the Eucharist at Trent was not designed to sanction any philosophical theory of substance, but indicates the reality which is ordinarily signified by the word 'substance,' that by which bread is truly bread and wine is truly wine."[51] In this view, the conciliar phrase is entirely noncommittal; "substance" signifies merely whatever, however described, makes a thing what it is and not something else.[52] In contrast with "appearances" or "accidents," it designates the "deepest level of reality,"[53] the "true, basic reality of a thing,"[54] the "true, profound reality of a thing,"[55] the "profound, solid, fundamental reality of things,"[56] etc.—but leaves the nature of that reality for philosophers to debate. Thus, if we wish to make Trent's doctrine explicit, suggests Baciocchi, "we have satisfactory translations of the pair *substantia-accidens* in the following: 'thing' and 'qualities, properties,' or perhaps 'being' and 'presentation,' or again 'that which exists' and its 'way of existing.'"[57]

If the issue is thus defined, proponents of transignification or transfinalization should have no problem claiming agreement with Trent. They may have their own existential or phenomenal view of what makes something be what it is—of its true, basic, profound reality; and their view may differ from others'. But what Trent means by "substance" they mean by "substance"; what Trent means by "bread" and "wine" they mean by "bread" and "wine"; what Trent means by "substantial conversion" they mean by "substantial conversion." It is as though all parties agreed that a reported object was red, but one believed it was scarlet, another believed it was crimson, a third believed it was magenta. Each account would clash with the others and only one account could be true. But the clash would be factual, not semantic. The meaning of the word "red" would not shift from account to account.[58]

---

[50] Batiffol, *L'Eucharistie*, 496.

[51] Vollert, "The Eucharist," 392.

[52] Ghysens, "Présence réelle eucharistique," 428; Sayes, *La presencia real*, 74.

[53] Schoonenberg, "Transubstantiation," 80.

[54] Vollert, "The Eucharist," 392.

[55] Ghysens, "Présence réelle eucharistique," 428; cf. Sayes, *La presencia real*, 263.

[56] Ghysens, "Présence réelle eucharistique," 429.

[57] Baciocchi, "Le mystère eucharistique," 572.

[58] Notice the difference in Schoonenberg's analysis: "if the broader interpretation is the official one, then such notions as 'transfinalization' (transposition of the aim) and 'transignification' (transposition of meaning) may mean the same thing as 'transub-

Such a result, so arrived at, would exemplify and support a general view of dogmas: "In practice they appear to be relatively empty shells which can be filled with any one of a number of concrete religious meanings; they can be given an indefinitely large variety of theological interpretations."[59] If it is so for the canons of Trent, it may be so in other instances. But is it so for Trent? Specifically, are transfiguration and transfinalization, in the typical versions I have cited, compatible with the Council's teaching?

Their compatibility may be challenged either with respect to what the Council affirms (Christ's real presence) or with respect to what it denies (the bread and wine) after the consecration. Paul VI takes the first tack when he insists that the Eucharistic conversion occurs "not only because of the faith of the Church, but in objective reality."[60] I shall take the second approach and focus on the claim that the transfinalized or transignified elements remain physically the same but are no longer bread and wine.

In this connection, I recall an episode from the Chaplin film *Modern Times*. When Charlie arrived at his girlfriend's ramshackle house and, grabbing a broom, started to do some sweeping, the house almost fell down. The broom was a pillar. Notice how I put that, naturally: the *broom* was a pillar. In its new function as a pillar it did not cease to be a broom. Similarly, I suggest, bread and wine do not cease to be bread and wine simply because they acquire new, Eucharistic significance or finality. In support I cite countless other examples—books used as doorstops but still called books, white shirts used as flags of surrender but still called shirts, smoke used for signals but still called smoke, and so forth. That is, I cite usage, not a theory. No theory can flout usage without running the risk of vacuity ("To be sure, people still call the broom a broom, but it really isn't, you know").[61]

In any case, such was not Trent's use of terms. "With the term 'substance,'" as Antonio Piolanti observes, "the Council of Trent intends everything that consti-

---

stantiation'" (Schoonenberg, "Transubstantiation," 82; cf. ibid., 90). This is misleadingly put (at least in translation). It is as though, upon identifying the object's redness as scarlet one were to conclude that "red" and "scarlet" mean the same thing. "Transignification" and "transfinalization" are not synonymous with "transubstantiation," broadly understood, but are more specific. It is the broader meaning of the Tridentine expression that, in the analysis just suggested, permits these narrower terms to be employed, not as synonyms, but as factual analyses. These things, too—transignification and transfinalization—can count as "transubstantiation."

[59] Lindbeck, "Reform and Infallibility," 352.

[60] Paul VI, *Mysterium Fidei*, 14 (n. 46).

[61] Sayes's challenge to these theories' denial of the elements cites the theories themselves, not usage: "Indeed, if we consider that in modern existential phenomenology relations have an ontological, not an accidental, character and that a change of relation amounts to a change of being, we can ask whether in these theories a genuine change of the reality of the bread and wine is possible: after the consecration do not the eucharistic elements of bread and wine in fact retain the same relationality that they had before the consecration? Do they lose their capacity to nourish naturally?" (*Presencia real*, 86; cf. 122, 239, 248).

tutes the bread, except the appearances."[62] For Scholastics, that would include prime matter and substantial form. For the present-day populace, it would include the molecular and atomic constituents. For proponents of transfinalization and transignification, it would include the physical reality and something more. But the physical reality suffices to establish conflict with Trent. If bread and wine (however understood—commonsensically, hylomorphically, or scientifically) remain, the "substance" of bread and wine remains. Bread and wine are not mere "appearances." No one, then or now, would say they were—save, perhaps, theorists who redefine Trent's terms. However, redefinition is not interpretation. What Trent denied, the new theories admit. The disagreement cannot be papered over.

The same verdict results if we take the Council's term "species" in the sense of "accidents" rather than "appearances." For the stuff that the transfinalists and transignificationists recognize as enduring in the Eucharist is no mere "accident" of what they or anybody else calls bread. It is not an accident in the Aristotelian sense of belonging to one of the categories Aristotle contrasts with "substance." It is not an accident in the sense of being eliminable while bread remains. It is not an accident in any of the senses Baciocchi contrasts with "substance": "quality," "property," "presentation," or "manner of existing." It—the stuff the rest of us call bread, regardless of its finality—is more than that, so more than Trent allows for after the words of consecration. For according to Trent only the "species" remain. To sum up, then, whether one considers the term "bread," "wine," "substance," or "species," and whether one takes the last term in the sense of "appearances" or of "accidents," the disagreement remains. These theorists in fact affirm what Trent denies (bread and wine after the consecration) and deny what Trent affirms (the cessation of all but the "species" of bread and wine).

Let me make explicit the distinction here relied on between theories that redefine terms and theories that do not, and let me illustrate the difference with a simple example. A theory that tells me what a house-supporting broom consists of (e.g., atoms) does not redefine the term "broom," whereas a theory that tells me it is not really a broom, since it is holding up a house, does redefine the term. It does depart from common usage. Hence this type of theory begets problems about genuine agreement or disagreement, whereas the other kind does not. Thus if, for instance, I say that a broom is holding up the house and a theorist denies it, I need to know what kind of theorist he is before I can determine whether he really disagrees with me. Similarly, if Trent says that the bread and wine cease to exist and only their appearances remain, and these modern theorists express agreement, I need to know what kind of theorists they are before I can determine whether their agreement is genuine. In my judgment, it is only verbal.

---

[62] Piolanti, "La transustanziazione," 260. Cf. Kenny, *Reason and Religion*, 17, on the Tridentine doctrine: "in the Eucharistic *conversio* there is no parcel of stuff which is first bread and then Christ's body; not only does one form give way to another but one bit of matter gives way to another." In transfinalization and transignification, there is such a perduring "parcel of stuff."

I see no way to avoid this conclusion. In the absence, therefore, of any more serious attempts than those I have encountered,[63] I shall terminate this dialectic and take stock. Where have we arrived? First, Trent's formulas do not appear as wide open as some have proposed. Second, this example does not support the view of dogmas as, in general, relatively empty shells susceptible of "an *indefinitely* large variety of theological interpretations." Transfinalization and transignification fail as interpretations. Third, it now appears that the other horn of our initial dilemma may be the sharper one. If Paul VI is right about Trent's exclusion of modern readings, can he be right about Trent's identification with revelation? A doctrine indefinite enough to accommodate such widely divergent interpretations would more readily coincide with the original deposit than would a doctrine definite enough to exclude them. We must therefore now inquire: In what sense, if any, might Trent's teaching, negating the bread and wine, be identical with the faith of the Apostles?

Identity with Revelation

"It could be argued," writes Colman O'Neill, "that the dogma is no more than a verbal clarification of Christ's statement within the context of a realist epistemology."[64] And so it has in fact been argued. Rahner, for instance, has written:

> "I should like to put forward the thesis that the dogma of transubstantiation (insofar as it is really strict *dogma*) is a logical and not an ontic explanation of the words of Christ taken literally . . . It intends to say exactly what Christ says: that what he gives is his body and no longer bread, though bread had been there, because his declaration effectively changes the reality and produces what it affirms: the reality of the body of Christ instead of the substance of the bread. . . . [T]he doctrine of transubstantiation tells me no more than do the words of Christ, when I take them seriously.[65]

---

[63] Two quotations can suffice to suggest the direction of most responses: (1) "It is a change that lets the *appearances* remain. This word is self-explanatory; appearances are everything one sees, everything one observes or experiences, everything that in any way falls under the senses" (Godefroy, "Eucharistie," 1349; original emphasis). So are bread and wine, of which all these things might be affirmed, mere appearances? (2) "Carlo Colombo seems to us to have shown that the Catholic doctrine affirms a change that is not physical but metaphysical, understanding that word of course in its etymological sense of transphysical. For the Church's dogma is situated beyond the physical domain, since it concerns nonempirical realities—not just the body and blood of Christ that are made present under the empirical appearances that persist but also the profound being of the bread and wine that are transformed" (Ghysens, "Présence réelle eucharistique," 434). Are bread and wine, of which dogma treats, not physical realities? Can they not be experienced? Yet are they therefore identical with their appearances? Does dogma affirm a realm of reality distinct from the elements' molecular and atomic constituents? Such responses, treating bread and wine as "appearances" or reading the dogma as purely metaphysical, do not look at all promising.

[64] O'Neill, *New Approaches to the Eucharist*, 98.

[65] Rahner, "The Presence of Christ," 302 (Rahner's emphasis).

Accordingly, for some the doctrine can be derived from Christ's words simply by way of analysis. "The celebrated definitions of the Council of Trent are nothing but a rendering in more precise terms of the traditional doctrine inherited from Scripture and the Fathers."[66] The Council's articles "descend logically from the analysis of the words of institution: 'This is my body, this is my blood.'"[67] Others, for instance Marín-Sola, derive the doctrine by reasoning, not analysis:

> This, then, is a revealed truth. But where and how is it revealed? It is revealed *in other* truths in which it is included and from which it emerges by reasoning. These other truths are: first, in the consecration the words of Jesus Christ "This is my body, This is my blood" must be truly verified; second, without transubstantiation these words of Jesus Christ cannot be truly verified. From these truths, one of faith and the other of reason, the defined dogma issues by reasoning.[68]

These two perspectives, one citing analysis and the other reasoning, may appear to conflict. In the first, the doctrine is logically identical with, or contained within, the scriptural datum; in the second, reason has need of a second, nonscriptural premise in order to reach its conclusion. Since this premise is not a revealed truth, it may seem that neither is the conclusion based on it a revealed truth. There is no need, however, to make heavy weather of this difference of perspective. Consider a comparison. Suppose someone tells me his sister is six feet tall. If I consider just the explicit, positive content, I may apply the principle that no one can simultaneously have two different heights, and conclude that his sister is not, for instance, five feet tall. Thus, I reason; I pass beyond the datum. If, however, I reflect that everyone else shares the same principle and understands such statements the same way I do, I may include the negative content along with the positive. Realistic analysis can find it there, implicit in the utterance and in the mind of the speaker; there is no need for inference.

If, then, Jesus said, "This is my body," and the truth of his statement was clearly incompatible with the continued presence of the bread, it would be clearly incompatible for the Apostles and not just for us. What is implicit for us would be implicit for them. What we believe, coerced by sheer logic, they would believe. We need not suppose, therefore, that in adding a premise of reason we add a non-apostolic premise. The Apostles, too, were reasonable people. They, too, hearing Jesus' words, would believe the negative part as well as the positive, with equal immediacy. Such would be the message his words conveyed to any reasonable hearer then or now, if indeed the incompatibility were equally clear to all, thanks to some shared principle.

However, the requisite principle is SIS—the strict-identity supposition. It is that which permits Marín-Sola to state with such assurance that without transubstantiation the words of Jesus cannot be truly verified. It is that which permits Rahner to suppose that he is simply unpacking the clear meaning of Jesus' words.

---

[66] Ghysens, "Présence réelle eucharistique," 420.

[67] Piolanti, "La transustanziazione," 228.

[68] Marín-Sola, *La evolución homogénea*, 378 (Marín-Sola's emphasis).

But SIS is not a truth of reason, nor is it shared by all. In particular, the abundant citations in Chapter 1 make clear that it did not coerce people's thinking in apostolic times. There is no need, therefore, to cite other difficulties—for example, the variations in the words of institution or the varied interpretations of which any single version is susceptible. The claim of strict logical identity lacks foundation. It is conceivable, perhaps, that first-century Jewish hearers of Jesus' Jewish words would take them as implying the cessation of the bread and wine, but it is not likely. Only the assumption that their belief must have been the same as Trent's teaching would make it appear likely. Or rather, only the assumption that their belief must have been the same as Trent's in the sense of being logically identical with that teaching would make it appear likely that the Apostles, too, believed in transubstantiation. But such a general assumption with regard to doctrinal identity is one which the present example calls into question.

To see how and why it does, let us return to Moses. One person says, "Moses was born in Egypt," and another person agrees. Do their statements express identical beliefs, with exactly the same truth-conditions for each? Well, suppose one believes that Moses was raised by Pharaoh's daughter and the other judges it unlikely: does that difference affect the content of their respective beliefs? Essentialism might stipulate some specific set of traits which constitute the essence of Moses, a set known and accepted by all users of the name, on pain of talking at cross purposes. But so much the worse for essentialism. Different people have different beliefs about Moses, and those beliefs give whatever cognitive content they possess to such statements as "Moses was born in Egypt." If, then, the belief expressed by identical words in an identical setting may vary from speaker to speaker and from hearer to hearer, what are we to say of statements made in different words and different languages by people of different cultures, whose beliefs vary still more notably—for example, by people some of whom assume strict identity with all its implications and some of whom do not? Given this diversity, it does not appear plausible or meaningful to claim logical identity from statement to statement or speaker to speaker.

Does it follow from this account that if two people disagree about Moses' upbringing but agree in saying "Moses was born in Egypt," one of them has made a false statement? If not, why not? Doesn't one person mean something false by "Moses" and the other mean something true (e.g., Moses reared or not reared by Pharaoh's daughter)? So doesn't the speaker who holds the false opinion in effect assert something false when he says, "Moses was born in Egypt"? How can both speakers be right? One response might distinguish between the cognitive content of "Moses" (in the realistic sense of the beliefs expressed and conveyed by that name) and the name's unique referent, who experienced no such fluctuations as do the beliefs of speakers and hearers. If that man was born in Egypt, then, regardless of what any speaker or hearer believes or has believed about Moses, the statement "Moses was born in Egypt" is true. A related response might invoke the standard, reasonable use we make of the terms "true" and "false." The point of such a statement is to indicate Moses' birthplace, not to give a comprehensive account of the man Moses, down to the last detail. And when we get that point right, we call the statement "true." If, however, we affirmed or denied Moses' being raised by Pharaoh's daughter, we would then have to get that detail right, for such would then be the point of the statement.[69]

This rough account, combining basic truth and peripheral falsehood, bears evident resemblance to one given earlier for the statements: "We've lost our king," "The king has died," "The king's soul has departed," "The king has joined his ancestors," "The king has gone to his reward," "The king has become one with the One." If these utterances all serve the same purpose, of reporting the king's demise, and if he has in fact died, then all are basically correct, regardless of whether the king had a soul, joined his ancestors, went to his reward, or became one with the One. The speakers may not agree in their beliefs and may not agree in the beliefs their varied utterances express, but they do agree on this: the king has died. And that, for the statements in question, is the important identity.

Adapted, this model has likely application to numerous doctrinal statements and not just to Eucharistic teaching.[70] To suggest this broader relevance and enrich the discussion in this chapter and the next, we can linger a moment on Nicholas Lash's example:

> Let us suppose that a theologian is studying Boniface VIII's bull *Unam Sanctam.* There he reads: "Porro subesse Romano Pontifici omni humanae creaturae declaramus, dicimus, definimus et pronuntiamus omnino de necessitate salutis" (Denzinger 469). He translates this as: "We declare, announce, define and proclaim that subjection to the Roman Pontiff is absolutely necessary for salvation, for every human being." There, surely, is an *ex cathedra* papal definition if ever there was one, and it seems to be manifestly false. Then the theologian remembers the importance of understanding any statement in its historical context. He discovers that the problem to which the pope is addressing himself is not any theoretical theorem in soteriology or even ecclesiology, but a conflict concerning the respective socio-political authority of the pope and the king of France. Boniface VIII wishes to assert the transcendence of God's kingdom—in relation to which all human community is provisional and subordinate. The theologian therefore recasts the papal definition in terms which take these considerations into account and, accordingly, is able to assess it as meaningful and true.[71]

Though roughly plausible, this account cannot be left as it stands. Lash's rendering of Boniface's intended meaning, his equation of speaker meaning with utterance meaning, his apparently favorable judgment on the original statement as well as on its recast version—all this and more appears problematic. Consider our comparative

---

[69] For similar analyses, in the vein of CRS, see Hallett, *Language and Truth,* 170-72.

[70] Note the model's difference from a familiar analog: "according to P. Fransen, the 'first rule' for the interpreting of conciliar texts is that only the central assertion in a decree or canon is defined, and all the rational, biblical and dogmatic arguments put forward to support the central assertion 'are not final, . . . may be corrected and even, with certain limits, be called into question'" (McSorley, Contribution, 73).

[71] Lash, *Change in Focus,* 174-75.

example. "The king has died" may pose no problems of meaning or truth, but what about "The king's soul has departed"? If there is no soul, the statement is at best "basically true"; it is not true without qualification. So, too, when recast in the manner Lash suggests, Boniface's statement may pose no problems, but left in its original form it does. It is at best "basically true" and, given its solemn *ex cathedra* character, that is worth noting.

Swinburne might side with Lash. To see why, consider his linguistic sample:

> Believing that the person to whom you are talking is your cousin, I may say, "I see you agree with your cousin"; my point is that you agree with the person to whom you are talking, his being your cousin is not an aspect of the situation on which I am commenting, but my belief that your collocutor is your cousin gives me a short way of referring to him.[72]

In such an instance, Swinburne argues, "Because of the irrelevance of such presuppositions to the job which the speaker is trying to do with his sentence, it is natural to understand the sentence as expressing a statement which does not state the presuppositions in terms of which it is cast, and to whose truth-value the truth or falsity of the presuppositions is irrelevant."[73] To this I answer yes and no. Yes, from the statement as it stands one might distill an utterance which states just its main point, and the truth of that utterance would not be affected by the truth or falsity of the supposition that appears in the original version. To the remark "I see you agree with the person you are talking to," the person addressed might reply without hesitation, "Yes, I do." But not to the remark: "I see you agree with your cousin." Neither would the person call that statement true, without qualification. And the like holds for Boniface's statement, with its comparable mix of basic truth and incidental error.

For transubstantiation, there is no difficulty discerning the doctrine's central thrust. Authors cited above and in the previous chapter have already indicated it. The dogma, wrote Rahner, intends to say exactly what Christ says: that what he gives is his body—and therefore no longer bread. The assertion, he assumes, demands the negation. For, as Marín-Sola typically insisted, without cessation of the bread and wine, the words of Christ, "This is my body, This is my blood" could not be "truly verified."[74] His presence would be purely symbolic, not real. That is why Trent added its negative canon 2 to its positive canon 1. Even within canon 2 the same linking of positive and negative appears, when the concluding phrases speak of "that wonderful and extraordinary change of the whole substance of the bread into Christ's body and the whole substance of the wine into his blood while only the species of bread and wine remain." First the change is affirmed, then all

---

[72] Swinburne, *Revelation*, 28.

[73] Ibid.

[74] See above. Cf. Schillebeeckx on Aquinas: "For him, it was first and foremost something that was necessary to thought—this distinctively eucharistic real presence could not be established in any other way but by proposing a change of the substance of the bread. It was also precisely the same for Bonaventure" (*The Eucharist*, 50).

but the appearances of the bread and wine is denied, with the denial viewed—mistakenly—as logically required by the affirmation. The whole point of the doctrine of transubstantiation is to permit the Real Presence.[75]

Whereas the negation of the bread and wine can with difficulty be lodged in the minds of the Apostles, for the Real Presence there is no comparable problem. Jesus' first followers may have believed that in some realistic yet mysterious sense Jesus was present in the Eucharist (think of John 6 and 1 Cor 10-11). If so, it is evident in what sense the teaching of Trent might be said to be identical with the faith of the Apostles. The logical-identity model does not help in this instance. Neither does the organic model of a seed planted in the ground. Neither does the pedagogical model of the teacher whose meaning is discerned later on. It appears that the "king is dead" model may.

This tentative conclusion permits a tentative solution of the dilemma posed by *Mysterium Fidei.* How, we wondered, could Trent's meaning be precise enough to exclude mere transignification or transfinalization yet imprecise enough to coincide with the faith of the Apostles? It seems at this point that it could not. Trent was precise enough to exclude those modern substitutes, but the very precision that excluded them precluded Trent's full identity with apostolic teaching. The added negative element begot the exclusion, the original positive core did not. This, however, as I say, is only a tentative solution, for from a Catholic perspective, evident problems remain.

Identity and Infallibility

Vatican Council I affirmed that the Bishop of Rome, when he teaches *ex cathedra,* "possesses through the divine assistance promised to him in the person of St. Peter, the infallibility with which the divine Redeemer willed his Church to be endowed in defining doctrine concerning faith or morals";[76] and Vatican II explained: "This infallibility with which the divine Redeemer willed His Church to be endowed . . . extends as far as extends the deposit of divine revelation, which must be religiously guarded and faithfully expounded."[77] Neither council went into much detail. For instance, neither envisaged analyses such as those just adduced, and determined whether a doctrine that is only "basically true" passes the test of infallibility.

---

[75] "The Council of Trent was an 'ecumenical council' testifying here, on the basis of its supreme authority, to the fact that it could not uphold the biblical affirmation of faith in its purity without at the same time affirming the change of the substance of the bread and the wine" (Schillebeeckx, *The Eucharist,* 51). "These fathers were firmly convinced that they could not safeguard this distinctively eucharistic presence of Christ unless they also insisted on the acceptance of a 'change of substances.' What has obviously emerged, then, is that the final statement was without doubt secondary and that it was there purely to explicitate the first statement in a polemical context" (ibid., 48).

[76] *The Church Teaches,* 102.

[77] "Dogmatic Constitution on the Church," 25 (Abbott, *The Documents of Vatican II,* 48).

Neither specified how perfect the identity must be between infallible teaching and the "deposit of divine revelation." So no clear conflict appears between these official teachings and the preceding discussion. That discussion, however, examined only the positive statements, first about papal authority, then about the Real Presence. It did not examine negative statements in which what was implicit or peripheral in the positive formulations became explicit and central. It did not consider canon 2's opening words, which deny that the substance of the bread and wine remains. It did not consider the explicit, negative doctrine: "Outside of the church there is no salvation."

On this dictum, Francis A. Sullivan comments:

In the thirteenth century, when this was defined by the Fourth Lateran Council, and even in 1442, when it was even more rigidly asserted by the Council of Florence, the world known to the council fathers was practically limited to Christendom and Islam. With no idea of the vast multitudes of human beings living in the continents still to be discovered, they believed that everyone had had an opportunity to hear the gospel and respond to it, and so they considered those who were "outside the church," such as the Jews and Moslems, guilty of rejecting the offer of salvation. It was only in the light of new knowledge about the extent of the earth and its human population, achieved in the late fifteenth and sixteenth centuries, that Catholic theologians came to realize that they could no longer interpret that doctrine in the same way that medieval Christians had done. This led to the search for a new understanding of the necessary role of the church in the divine plan of salvation, the fruit of which one finds in the documents of Vatican II.[78]

"As I see it," Sullivan suggests, "the 'substance' of the doctrine whose history we have been following is that God has assigned to the church a necessary role in the divine economy of salvation."[79]

Given this substance, what verdict should we render on the doctrine's truth? Sullivan cites as extremely relevant the words of the Congregation for the Doctrine of the Faith: "It sometimes happens that some dogmatic truth is first expressed incompletely (but not falsely), and at a later date, when considered in a broader context of faith or human knowledge, it receives a fuller and more perfect expression."[80] It is clear how Sullivan conceives the part about "a broader context of faith or human knowledge," but what about the parenthetical remark "not falsely"? Does it apply in this instance? With utmost solemnity, the Council of Florence declared that "'no one remaining outside the Catholic Church, not just pagans, but also Jews or heretics or schismatics, can become partakers of eternal life; but they will go to the 'everlasting fire which was prepared for the devil and his angels' (*Matt.* 25:41), unless before the end of life they are joined to the Church."[81] Can this assertion be termed "basically true"?

---

[78] Sullivan, *Creative Fidelity*, 115-16.

[79] Sullivan, *Salvation Outside the Church?*, 199.

[80] Congregation for the Doctrine of the Faith, *Mysterium Ecclesiae*, 402-3, in Sullivan, *Salvation Outside the Church?*, 11.

[81] *The Church Teaches*, 78.

One hesitates to say so, for what was peripheral in Boniface's positive statement now looks central and strong. True, it is not as though "There is a One" had replaced "The king is one with the One," or "People have souls" had replaced "The king's soul has departed." These replacements retain no mention of the king or of his death, and they cannot by any stretch be construed as veiled reports of his demise. By contrast, "Outside the church there is no salvation" does mention the church and does insist, excessively, on her role. The excessiveness, it seems, is the problem. The women in 1 Samuel may sing, "Saul has killed his thousands, and David his ten thousands," but they do not really mean it; it is just their way of saying what mighty deeds their heroes have performed. If they did mean it, without hyperbole, we would not hesitate to call their statements false. With regard to the Council of Florence, however, there can be no doubt that the Council fathers really did mean every word they said. All outsiders were going to hell.[82]

I agree with Sullivan that the Council's statement must be understood in the light of their presumption that all who remained outside the Church did so guiltily. I agree that this judgment of theirs was mistaken but is not doctrine. Further, since no defined doctrine is to be identified with the reasons or motives that prompted its definition, the falsehood of the Council's assumption is compatible with the truth of the Council's pronouncement. However, it seems clear that in this instance a false premise has led to a false conclusion. All outsiders are not doomed to eternal damnation.

If the Council of Florence was fully or at least sufficiently ecumenical, a verdict of "false" on its teaching conflicts with the doctrine of infallibility. If it was not fully or sufficiently ecumenical, then neither may Vatican I and Vatican II have been, for similar reasons.[83] Either alternative raises the possibility that the doctrine of infallibility exemplifies the same limited form of doctrinal identity as does the doctrine of no salvation outside the Church and as does, perhaps, the doctrine of transubstantiation.

What are the chances that the first Christians believed in the statement-by-statement, belief-by-belief type of inerrancy asserted by Vatican Councils I and II? It can hardly be supposed that Peter, Paul, and their companions put this question to themselves or formulated an explicit answer to it. But what of their unformulated impressions? What did their experience suggest? On this question, Acts and Paul's epistles furnish pertinent evidence. As the Church later recognized that

---

[82] Compare Vatican Council I's declaration, to which similar comments apply: "This is the doctrine of Catholic truth [concerning the Roman Pontiff]; and no one can deviate from this without losing his faith and his salvation" (*The Church Teaches*, 98).

[83] I add the word "sufficiently" because of a reader's comment: "I do not think that the fact that Vatican II recognized a presence of Christ's Church beyond the Catholic Church means that Trent and Vatican I were not ecumenical councils. I would say that its statement that the Church of Christ subsists in the Catholic Church would justify seeing those councils as sufficiently ecumenical to define dogmas." (Compare the suggestion that, though the soul is not the whole person, the person survives if the soul—the "core self"—survives.) This problematic suggestion deserves more attention than I have seen it receive.

Christ's salvation extends to non-Christians who remain non-Christian, so the church had first to recognize that his salvation extended to non-Jews who remained non-Jewish. This recognition did not come easily. Peter himself, we are told, had to be jolted from his earlier way of thinking, and he then met much opposition. "Why did you go to uncircumcised men and eat with them?" (Acts 11:3) Paul undertook to clarify how full acceptance of the Gentiles was not betrayal of God's covenant with his people (the truth his critics clung to) but its fulfillment. At the heart of the narrower conviction there lay a larger truth, and it was this that established continuity from one stage to the next in the Apostles' own faith journey. If, then, the first Christians learned something from this early experience of doctrinal development, it would not likely be a lesson of strict logical identity between their later and earlier beliefs, nor a lesson of statement-by-statement infallibility. They had been wrong about the Gentiles.

How, then, and in what sense might the doctrine of papal and ecclesial infallibility be identical with the faith of the Apostles? To this query, Hans Küng has offered his well-known and much-debated response. The truth at the heart of the dogma, he suggests, is the Church's doctrinal indefectibility—that is, "the fundamental permanence of the Church in truth, a permanence which is not suspended by individual errors."[84] Such indefectibility, he notes, is supported by the New Testament as a whole, and is aptly illustrated by the Exodus: "All detours and wrong turns in wandering through the desert did not in any way alter the fact that the ancient people of God were basically on the right road to the promised land. All the false steps, false conclusions, blunders, and slips will not ultimately divert the people of God now wandering through many a desert from its destined course."[85]

In supportive parallel, Küng cites the traditional belief in scriptural inerrancy, which similarly combined basic truth with secondary error. The Church has always viewed the Bible as the Word of God and, as such, the privileged vehicle of the divine message: there is the basic truth. From this truth, Christians long inferred that the Bible contains no errors (that the Bible's genealogies, for example, are all strictly factual): there lies the error. To accurately capture the truth while recognizing the error, we may therefore say (paralleling Küng on infallibility): "Despite mistakes, the Bible unfailingly communicates the truth of salvation to men."[86] This doctrine, therefore, conforms to the same general model of identity as our previous examples. As for them, however, the verdict on any particular saying depends on the relative prominence it gives to the truth or the error in the doctrine. For example, the statement that the books of the Old and New Testament "contain undoubted truth in all things,"[87] may merit the verdict "basically true," but the statement that inspiration "excludes all error"[88] does not, and still less does the

---

[84] Küng, *The Church—Maintained in Truth*, 17.

[85] Ibid., 36.

[86] Baum, Contribution, 4.

[87] Clement VI, in Denziger, *The Sources of Catholic Dogma*, 205-6.

[88] Leo XIII, ibid., 493.

statement that "In the Scriptures not only the opinions expressed but each and every word pertains to the faith."[89] Here, as the truth quotient declines, so too, one may surmise, does the degree of identity with the faith of the Apostles.

What emerges from examples such as these, which might be multiplied, is not a general theory of doctrinal identity, but a particular model—one that, understandably, has received much less attention than the long-popular logical-identity model, with which it contrasts so strongly. For various reasons, the latter is the only developed model of doctrinal identity (as distinct from doctrinal development) with which to make comparison.[90] A full treatment of doctrinal identity would need to identify other models, realized in other examples (e.g., Chalcedon's teaching on the Incarnation), lying in the spectrum between strict logical identity and mixed-truth identity. Of these two extremes, perhaps no post-apostolic doctrine exemplifies the former, whereas the latter, mixed-truth model looks widely applicable.[91]

Too widely, some may fear. "Some profess," writes a Catholic prelate at the start of a long list, "that God has created not only the visible world, but also the angels. Others say that there are no angels and that, when Holy Scripture mentions angels, it refers only to God's tender and loving care for us."[92] There, they suggest, is the truth at the heart of the traditional teaching. Again, "Some profess that a sacramental marriage which has been consummated is indissoluble because God wills it to be so. Others say that the indissolubility of marriage is only a commandment one ought to strive to observe, so that remarriage is to be allowed during the lifetime of the other spouse, if the earlier marriage is hopelessly wrecked."[93] Such is the core of that teaching. And so the revising goes (a warning voice admonishes), case by case, down the slippery slope that leads at last, for instance, to the

---

[89] Bellarmine, *De controversiis* 2.2.12, quoted in Blackwell, *Galileo, Bellarmine, and the Bible*, 31.

[90] Development by logical inference is often paired with logical identity, and organic development is often contrasted with the former; but comparison with the growth of organisms furnishes no ready sense in which doctrines which grow remain identical, nor has any such sense, identified and developed, become a competing paradigm with logical identity.

[91] Cf. Bouyer, "Réflexions," 114 (on the Immaculate Conception and the Assumption); Sullivan, *Creative Fidelity*, 135-36 (on original sin); Schlink, *The Coming Christ*, 42 (on predestination); Rahner, "The Historical Dimension in Theology," 39-41 (on various examples). In Rahner's view, "The changes which have occurred in the last century and up to the present time cannot all be explained under the rubric of passing from the implicit to the explicit and from the less exact to the more exact. We have done more than simply acquire new and additional knowledge. There was also the passage from errors to true knowledge, and it was not accomplished without struggle, pain, and bitter personal sacrifice" (ibid., 39).

[92] Joseph Cardinal Höffner, in a letter to Hans Küng (United States Catholic Conference, *The Küng Dialogue*, 90). Though the Cardinal's examples aptly serve my purpose, in his letter they lead to the query: "By what authority do you profess your opinions?" (ibid., 91).

[93] Ibid., 90-91.

conclusion that Jesus did not rise from the dead but that, after he died, "his memory was so powerful in the disciples that they dared to say, figuratively, that he was dead no longer, but had been raised from the dead."[94]

I agree that the "basically true" model may be misapplied. However, the same holds for any model. And slippery-slope arguments can work both ways. At the opposite extreme from the demise of all doctrine through sublimation, some have believed, for example, that the teaching of Aquinas could be defined, practically *in toto*, as explicitly or implicitly revealed truth. Again, I have heard it said that everything in *Donum Vitae*, a Vatican document on varied issues such as prenatal diagnosis, surrogate motherhood, fetal research, and *in vitro* fertilization, could be proposed as infallible teaching. Somewhere between agnosticism and rampant infallibilism there lies a happy mean, but where?

Recent developments suggest that here may be another question on which Christendom is in the process of reaching greater clarity, as it did with regard to the Gentiles, salvation outside the church, and the inerrancy of Scripture. In its limited way, perhaps the present chapter can contribute to the process. Some of its analyses are new. Its sustained focus on doctrinal identity, as distinct from historical, psychological, etiological processes, is different. However, as the last chapter was incomplete without the present one, so this chapter, on doctrinal identity, is incomplete without the next, on ecclesial identity. Most Christians recognize some form of doctrinal authority within the church of Christ, but which church is that? What church, denomination, or constellation of denominations is identical, in what sense, with the church of the Apostles? And what significance or implications, doctrinal or other, does such a query have?

---

[94] Ibid., 90.

Chapter 7

The Church of Christ

Traditional thinking connects doctrinal identity, just considered, and ecclesial identity. Doctrinal identity with apostolic teaching confirms ecclesial identity with the apostolic church, and vice versa: if the doctrine is the same, then the church is the same; if the church is the same, then the doctrine is the same. The inference goes in both directions. Both ways, however, there can be problems. Thus, Vincent of Lérins could propose as a test of right doctrine the one, identical faith "which has been believed, everywhere, always, by all,"[1] but we in our day would like to know more about these "all." Told that they are members of the one true church, the church Christ founded, the church of the Apostles, we would like to know which present-day church that is and how it can be recognized.

Responses have been roughly of two kinds, one exclusive and the other inclusive. The preceding chapters raise a Roman Catholic dilemma which illustrates this distinction and its significance. On the one hand it has been argued that:

> Trent solemnly taught that the substance of bread and wine does not remain after the Eucharistic consecration.
> Vatican II taught that such teaching, of an ecumenical council, is infallible.[2]
> Therefore the doctrine of transubstantiation is infallible.

On the other hand it has also been suggested that:

> Vatican II extended the church of Christ beyond the Roman Catholic Church.
> Since only the Roman Catholic Church was represented at the Council of Trent, it was not a truly ecumenical council.
> Therefore its teaching about transubstantiation is not infallible.

Accept a pre-Vatican II conception of the church, and infallibility may follow; accept a post-Vatican II conception of the church, and the inference looks shakier—not only for transubstantiation but also for other teachings on which non-

---

[1] Vincent of Lérins, "The Commonitory," 132 (2.6).

[2] Purists would restrict the term "infallible" to the teaching authority and call its teaching "irreformable," not "infallible." For purposes of ready communication, however, extending the former term to the teaching seems no more misleading than calling an essay intelligent or a work of art imaginative.

Catholic Christians have disagreed with Catholic Christians and in whose promulgation they had no say.

These teachings include the doctrine of infallibility itself, especially papal infallibility. As Richard McBrien has noted, "If the case for papal infallibility is already difficult because of the sparseness of biblical and historical testimony, then it is made even more difficult if the only surviving argument, i.e., from the authority of the First Vatican Council, is subject to radical challenge."[3] But many agree with McBrien that that argument is in fact subject to challenge, and not solely for reasons of circularity. For, "If we are to accept the ecclesiology of Vatican II that the Body of Christ embraces, in varying degrees, the whole Christian community and not the Catholic Church alone, then it follows that the Body of Christ was not adequately represented at the nineteenth century council and that such a council can be called 'ecumenical' [only] in a limited, perhaps even analogical, sense."[4] So, which ecclesiology should we embrace—the narrower, the broader, or perhaps some other?

"It seems evident," writes Avery Dulles, "that, while all Christians distinguish between the 'true' Church and its defective sociological realizations, there is no general agreement about what the true Church is or how it is to be recognized."[5] There is considerable agreement, however, that today's true church is somehow identical with the original, apostolic church. So, greater clarity may come if we inquire as follows. First, what kind of case can be made for the exclusive, pre-Vatican II sort of identity, between one specific church and the church Jesus initiated? Second, what kind of case can be made for an inclusive, post-Vatican II sort of identity, between a larger church, embracing various denominations, and the church Jesus initiated? Finally, in view of the answers to these queries, what significance do such identity questions possess? How important is it that today there exist a church, exclusive or inclusive, which not only accords with the mind of Christ but is in fact the very same church as that of the Apostles and can be recognized as such?

---

[3] McBrien, Contribution, 51. Cf. McSorley, Contribution, 105.

[4] McBrien, Contribution, 36. In *Magisterium*, 59-60, Sullivan argues that "to be consistent with the doctrine of Vatican II, one has to say that the Councils of Trent and the Vatican were ecumenical councils. For, according to *Lumen gentium*, the authority of an ecumenical council is essentially the authority of the episcopal college . . . But membership in this college requires hierarchical communion with the bishop of Rome . . . It follows that a council in which the college of bishops in communion with the bishop of Rome exercises its supreme pastoral and teaching authority is an ecumenical council." It follows, that is, if one accepts these further premises from one of the councils called in question by McBrien's reasoning.

[5] Dulles, *Models of the Church*, 128.

Exclusive Identity

With the Reformation, there commenced the war of competing "marks" or "notes" of the one true church of Christ. The Augsburg Confession cited two; Luther listed one, three, seven, ten; Bellarmine weighed in with fifteen; others went as high as a hundred; and no list agreed with any other. Even when discussion finally focused on the traditional four notes—"one, holy, catholic, and apostolic"—these received widely varied interpretations. So the situation looks disturbingly familiar. Tailor your terms, carefully select your premises, and you can prove whatever you wish. In such a confrontation, it becomes imperative to ask: What traits *define* the referent in question—what is *meant* by "the true church" or "the church of Christ"—and which traits, instead, *reveal* the referent so defined?

Two answers can be discerned to the first, definitional question. In one, "That is the true church of Christ which has all the notes promised and predicted by Christ for his church."[6] It is a church according to the mind of Christ. In the other answer, the true church is "that which Christ himself founded,"[7] or "which the apostles founded."[8] It is the church which existed then and exists now. In this latter conception, the question of the "true church" becomes a question of identity, in the sense of this inquiry.[9] "Where, what is this thing in this age," asked Newman, "which in the first age was the Catholic Church?"[10] If St. Athanasius or St. Ambrose came suddenly to life, what communion would he take to be his own?[11] What church is identical with that one? In this vein Luther wrote:

> It is just as if I asked a drunkard or a fool or someone half-asleep, "Tell me, friend, who or where is the church?" and he answered me, ten times over, nothing but, "One should listen to the church!" But how am I to listen to the church when I do not know who or where the church is? "Well," they say, "we papists have remained in the ancient and original church ever since the time of the apostles. Therefore we are the true church, for we have come from the ancient church and have remained in it; but you have fallen away from us and have become a new church opposed to us."

---

[6] Zapelena, *De ecclesia Christi*, 472.

[7] Schultes, *De ecclesia catholica*, 144; cf. San, *Tractatus*, 4; Dublanchy, "Église," 2135 ("We have the right to conclude that the Catholic Church is the only veritable church really established by Jesus Christ").

[8] "This is the nub of the whole debate, namely which of the various denominations of Christians is the church that the Apostles founded" (San, *Tractatus*, 144).

[9] Cf. Falcon, *La crédibilité du dogme catholique*, 499 (with the heading: "The identity of the Catholic Church with the Church founded by Christ"); Lash, *Change in Focus*, 87 (on Newman): "He had formerly appealed to history to justify the anglican position. If he now wishes to make such an appeal on behalf of the Roman catholic church, he must both find a flaw in the argument he had employed in the *Lectures on the Prophetical Office* and overcome what had previously seemed the crucial weakness in the Roman claims: namely, the apparent lack of identity between the Roman catholic church and primitive christianity."

[10] Newman, *Certain Difficulties*, 368.

[11] Newman, *Essay*, 97-98.

Answer: "But what if I prove that we have remained faithful to the true ancient church, indeed, that we are the true ancient church and that you have fallen away from us, that is, the ancient church, and have set up a new church against the ancient one?" Let us hear that![12]

Having made his case, Luther concluded: "Thus we have proved that we are the true, ancient church, one body and one communion of saints with the holy, universal, Christian church."[13]

Sometimes, as here, the perspective seems relatively clear. But the two perspectives—church prescribed by Christ or church founded by Christ—are easily conflated. For disputants have generally agreed that the true church is both the church Christ prescribed and the church Christ founded. The original church was not untrue to Christ's promises and prescriptions; the church Christ envisaged did not first appear in the sixteenth century. However, the two perspectives differ and call for different approaches. The apologist can attempt either to prove identity and infer fidelity, or to prove fidelity and infer identity—or perhaps to do both, without, however, confusing them.

It is understandable that emphasis fell on identity and not just on fidelity. If a tree grows and you break off a branch, the branch is not the original tree. If a human body grows and you lop off a limb, the limb is not the body. Catholics contended that the like holds for Christ's Body, the Church, and their Protestant opponents felt obliged to answer in similar terms. Like Luther, they had to address the identity question. It was incumbent on both sides not to conflate that question with the fidelity question, but that was difficult to avoid. For, what are the criteria of sameness? What are the criteria of sameness for a church? How might one establish that this or that contemporary church is identical with one many centuries earlier? Perhaps the most significant fact about the whole dispute is that these underlying questions received so little attention.

From previous chapters we can sense likely explanations for this fact. Within a pervasive essentialism, the supposition of strict identity saves the trouble of ascertaining what kind or kinds of identity obtain in any particular case, for instance between churches. Identity is identity—always strict, always the same. More specifically, an essentialistic conception of the church begets an essentialistic, unproblematic conception of ecclesial identity; and an essentialistic conception of the church has been common down to the present day. A. D. Sertillanges gave it typical expression: "The essence of a being is always the source of all its characters, be they permanent or in course of development . . . So the divine and human essence of the Church—its character of being the social embodiment of Christ, of giving God to man by the Holy Spirit in the form of man as being a member of Society, and of uniting man to God by the same spirit in the same form and with an eye to the same destinies—this essence of the Church explains everything."[14]

---

[12] Luther, *Against Hanswurst*, 194.

[13] Ibid, 199.

[14] Sertillanges, *The Church*, 53. See Perrone, *Praelectiones theologicae*, 746: "Properties are intrinsic and belong to a thing's essence, whereas notes are extrinsic,

Though accounts of the church's essence may differ, there is, writes Küng, "a constant factor in the various changing historical images of the Church, something which survives however much the history of mankind, of the Church and of theology may vary, and it is on this that we must concentrate. There are fundamental elements and perspectives in the Church which are not derived from the Church itself; there is an 'essence' which is drawn from the permanently decisive origins of the Church."[15] Thus, "It is an all-embracing *identity* which at bottom makes a Church catholic, the fact that despite all the constant and necessary changes of the times and of varying forms, and despite its blemishes and weaknesses, the Church in every place and in every age remains unchanged in its essence, whatever form it takes."[16] If same essence, then same church; the only problem, it seems, is to ascertain the essence.

That should prove difficult. The problem, again, is more one of meaning and method than of execution. What, in general, counts as the essence of a church? What counts as the essence of an individual church? When defining a class or kind, one might, for instance, take an Aristotelian approach and stipulate that the essence must be present in all and only instances of that class or kind, and necessarily so. Specifically, one might stipulate that the essence of a church is that trait or set of traits which, in fact and of necessity, all and only churches possess. But the essence that Sertillanges, Küng, and others have in mind is not an essence which the church of Christ shares with all other churches, Christian or non-Christian. So what kind of essence is it, if not Aristotelian? What is meant by an "essence" of the church?

Even if this question were clarified, and a search then revealed a trait or set of traits which answered it, the result would not automatically establish a test of identity. Criteria for being a member of a given class do not translate into criteria for being the same member of that class. For example, the conditions for being a river ("a large natural stream of water emptying into an ocean, a lake, or another body of water") do not determine the conditions for being the same river. A river may run dry for a spell, then resume, and still be the same river. What of a church? What of Christ's church? Might that run dry for a few centuries, so that no one would recognize it as a church, much less as Christ's church, then resume and become recognizable again not only as a church but as the one true church of Christ?

---

manifestations of the essence and properties and blossoming forth from the intrinsic properties . . . Thus first of all we grasp that these extrinsic notes necessarily originate from the very nature of the thing, that is, from the essential constitution of the Church as instituted by Christ, so that from them the true Church of Christ can be recognized, as though from its external appearance and physiognomy, and can be distinguished from any society that is not Christ's."

[15] Küng, *The Church*, 4.

[16] Ibid., 302 (Küng's emphasis). Cf. Walgrave, *Unfolding Revelation*, 14-15: "The ontological reality of the Church is simply suprahistorical and therefore always the same, but its expression in human forms of life and thought is entirely historical and therefore always moving with the stream of history."

Swinburne is the only author I know who has addressed these questions. His detailed discussion in *Revelation* can be summarized as follows:

1. For all societies, a later society being the same society as an earlier society is a matter of its continuity with it in two respects: aim and organization.[17]

2. If there is a clear "best candidate" for continuity with the original society, then that society is identical with it[18] and no other society is.[19]

3. If Christ founded anything like an earthly society, then he must have understood something along these lines as necessary for its sameness over time.[20]

4. In this instance, continuity of aim is dictated by continuity of doctrine; for the other aims of the Church are largely controlled by that aim.[21]

5. The second criterion, church organization, is a matter of admission procedures (e.g., baptism), kinds of worship (e.g., the eucharist), who conducts the worship (e.g., episcopally ordained priests), how officers are appointed (e.g., elected by the congregation, or appointed by the Pope) and how they are installed (e.g., whether bishops are consecrated by bishops, or by congregations), and how interpretations of doctrine are worked out and proclaimed.[22]

Swinburne notes that this twin appeal to continuity of doctrine and of organization "is in fact common to Roman Catholic, Orthodox, and quite a bit of Anglican and Protestant teaching."[23] One can therefore surmise that, even if Swinburne's careful guidelines were adopted and systematically applied, no ready verdict would emerge favoring one church or another. Having amply demonstrated how difficult in fact they are to apply, Swinburne passes his baton to the historian to show which present-day body, if any, best preserves, in its doctrine and organization, continuity with the church of the Apostles.

Swinburne's exposition invites varied reactions. Some may feel that he slights Christian life and worship, others that he assumes a too institutional picture of the early Christian *ekklesia* with which some present-day "church" is to be identified. My misgivings focus, in part, on weighting. If all indicators pointed in the same direction, or no indicators pointed in any direction but one, it would be evident which claimant was the "best candidate." However, reality may be more complex and comparisons less one-sided than apologists have often made out. And when

---

[17] Swinburne, *Revelation*, 120.

[18] Ibid., 123.

[19] Ibid., 122.

[20] Ibid.

[21] Ibid., 123.

[22] Ibid., 125.

[23] Ibid., 126.

credits and debits appear on both sides, it does not suffice simply to count their number on each side and compare. Do aim and organization count equally? Do all doctrines count equally? Does each aspect of organization count equally? Without answers to such queries as these, historians might ascertain the pertinent facts as fully as you please and still not know what to conclude from them. If, having received the baton from a philosopher, the historians then pass it to theologians, what will the theologians do with it? Will they return to arbitrary stipulations to make the answer come out right? Where, in what theological heaven, are criteria of ecclesial identity established for application in this instance?

Such worries may appear unrealistic. Even without precise, reflective criteria of identity we judge well enough what societies are identical with previous societies and which are not. The Society of Jesus was the same religious order after its restoration in 1814 as before its suppression in 1773, the church that met at the Vatican in 1962 was the same as convened at Trent in 1545, and so forth. Where is the problem? It appears, for instance, when we ask: Which of the contemporary Lutheran churches is the one that Luther founded? Which of the contemporary Franciscan orders is the one that Saint Francis founded? To my knowledge, such questions are not frequently posed or vigorously pursued; but if they were, the resulting discussions would not likely reveal consistent criteria of identity implicitly at work. Given the vested interests of the contending parties, doubtless their discussions would resemble the centuries-long debates about "the one true church of Christ."

Or the debates about fetal status. Multiple parallels suggest this comparison, but the one that interests me at the moment is the following. As many people (perhaps most) believe that the question "Is the embryo or fetus a human being?" has a correct answer regardless of how English-speakers employ the expression "human being," so many people have believed that the question "What church is the same as the one Christ founded?" has a correct answer regardless of how English-speakers have used the expression "same" or "church." How wrong-headed to equate such a question with one of semantics—and of *English* semantics, at that! To be sure; however, in reply I would suggest that the correctness or truth of statements depends on the words employed and their meanings (in whatever language) as well as on the realities described; that debates such as those about fetal status and ecclesial identity not only suggest the lack of linguistic backing for either side but also confirm it; and that, in the absence of such backing, there is no correct answer to either question. One might as well wrangle about whether a publication of forty-nine pages is or is not a "book."[24]

Swinburne recognizes that "the final result of historical investigation into all these matters might be a draw: there may be no 'closest continuer' of the Church of the apostles."[25] I am going farther. There may be no answer, not because the verdict is a draw, but because there exist no criteria which historians might apply

---

[24] On the fetal question, see Hallett, *Christian Moral Reasoning*, 92-96, and *Logic for the Labyrinth*, 165-78.

[25] Swinburne, *Revelation*, 142.

to conclude that there is or is not a draw. Given the course of this section's discussion, this appears a realistic suggestion. Prior to Swinburne, theological disputants did not attend to the issues of identity underlying their debates about identity with the church of the Apostles, much less did they settle those issues to everyone's satisfaction. Swinburne, consulting criteria for societal identity and applying them to ecclesial identity, provides descriptive but not evaluative criteria. It is not to be expected that he could. How could weightings for the aims or organizational aspects of banks or chess clubs (if such existed) furnish weightings for the aims or organizational aspects of churches? How could weightings for churches in general (if such existed) furnish appropriate weightings for the specific church in question —the one true church of Christ?

At this point a further parallel with the fetal issue comes to the fore. In that debate, people strongly resist the verdict "no correct answer." One chief reason, I believe, is their lack of linguistic reflection, hence their slight understanding of truth's relation to language. They are interested, they insist, in the facts, in reality, and not in mere words. Words are what we express our judgments with, not what determines their truth or falsehood. The only alternative, they would object, is "relativism." Another chief reason for resistance is the impression that life-and-death matters are at stake and that without an answer to the query "Is it a human being?" or "Is it a person?" no verdict for or against abortion can be given. Question the typical approach, and there seems to be no alternative one, for those who have taken that approach have never envisaged any other. It has seemed obvious that the question of fetal status—human being or not, person or not—is decisive.

Similarly, I am sure, many readers will resist my suggested verdict "no correct answer" when ecclesial contests are at all close, and will do so for much the same reasons. They will feel that I have turned an important factual question into a merely verbal question. ("It does not matter what we say! *Are* they identical?") And they will feel that there *must* be a correct answer, for otherwise matters of great moment would be left without solution. In particular, how, amid the confusion of theological positions, can we ascertain the truth save through a doctrinal authority, and where can we discover such an authority save in the one true church of Christ?

> Even if you think [writes Swinburne] that the Bible provides a totally true and perspicuous account of what Christ did and said, you need . . . some grounds for supposing that that is so, and the only remotely plausible such grounds are that it was authenticated by the Church which Christ founded. But for those grounds [to] operate, there must be a test for which society is the Church other than the fidelity of the teaching of that society to the original revelation—otherwise the argument moves in a vicious circle into which we can never break.[26]

Doubtless the moment must finally arrive when theological reflection ends in mystery, but must that moment arrive so soon, and must the mystery be so deep?

---

[26] Ibid., 120.

Various solutions suggest themselves. Perhaps adequate inquiry would reveal a clear verdict, for which even rough, indefinite criteria would suffice. As the verdict for a fetus may be doubtful, but not that for a newborn child, so the verdict between churches *x* and *y* may be doubtful, but not that between church *z* and all others. Or perhaps, instead, a solution should be sought in a less polemical, more ecumenical direction.

Inclusive Identity

More inclusive conceptions of Christ's church take various forms. Some, to start with, embrace more and more individual churches within the one true church. Thus many have agreed with Louis Bouyer that "the Orthodox Church and the Catholic Church, though dreadfully tempted by the spirit of division, remain one Church, in fact and by right, despite contrary appearances."[27] Edward Pusey and other Anglo-Catholics held that the true Church of Christ now consists not of two but of three mutually divided communions—the Roman Catholic, the Orthodox, and the Anglican.[28] Taking their cue from Vatican Council II, many Catholics now envisage a still broader extension, in agreement with McBrien's suggestion above, "that the Body of Christ embraces, in varying degrees, the whole Christian community and not the Catholic Church alone."[29] Following this path, should we conclude, unambiguously, that the church of Christ is, or consists of, not just two or three but many different Christian churches or communions?

According to Medard Kehl, the lesson of Vatican II is that "fundamentally the boundary between church and not-church cannot be defined unambiguously in definite and institutional terms; hence it is never possible to determine on theological grounds with absolute and irrevocable certainty exactly where the society of believers 'leaves off.'"[30] I view the Council's import differently. Precision is a derivative, secondary problem, dependent on what counts as the "church" and on the corresponding criteria of identity, and not vice versa. To determine the sameness over time of a river or a riverbed, we need not know precisely where either leaves off; but we do need to know which we are talking about—river or riverbed. Similarly, to determine the identity over time of an organized society or a fellowship of kindred souls, we need not know exactly where either leaves off; but we do need to know which we are talking about—organized society or structureless fellowship. In recent ecclesiology, the

---

[27] Bouyer, *The Church of God*, 512. Cf. Sullivan, *The Church We Believe In*, 62-63; Congar, *Diversity and Communion*, 74 ("Paul VI has spoken of a 'universal and holy church of Christ' which always embraces the two sister churches") and 170: "My profound conviction is that this is the same church of Christ and the apostles which exists in the Orthodox church and the Roman Catholic church. We know that the Orthodox reject this idea. For Roman Catholics it is a certainty."

[28] Dulles, *Models of the Church*, 133.

[29] Cf. ibid., 141-42.

[30] Kehl, "Ekklesiologische und christologische Überlegungen," 144.

most fundamental straddling concerns not the membership of the institutional church, but the nature of the "church" in question. Is it an institution or is it something else?

According to Article 7 of the Confession of Augsburg, the church of Christ "is the congregation of believers, where the Gospel is purely preached and the holy Sacraments offered in accordance with the Gospel."[31] Rome was therefore excluded, as a church, but individual Catholics were not. There could be true believers within the Catholic fold and false believers within the Lutheran fold. Thus, in this perspective, "The *ecclesia proprie dicta* [church in the proper sense] remains hidden till the last day within the *ecclesia large dicta* [church in the broad sense]."[32] It is not identical with any institution. The same holds in various kindred accounts. For instance, "*All* people who *believe in Jesus Christ* belong to this one society"—this single church which "has *one* Lord, *one* faith, and *one* baptism (Eph 4,5)."[33] Or, the Church is "that community of persons called by the Holy Spirit to continue Christ's saving work of reconciliation."[34] Again, "if the Church is the Body of Christ, it is where His Spirit is effective"; "no outward forms can guarantee the Church's presence."[35] Like the church-of-churches view, these conceptions, too, are inclusive. However, they cut across institutional boundaries. They do not embrace all Christian churches or denominations but rather all true Christians, to whatever church they belong in the institutional sense of the term.

Dulles favors a still more inclusive conception of the church—inclusive not only in its membership, as in the two preceding conceptions, but also in its definition. From the writings of Protestant and Catholic ecclesiologists, he sifts out five major types, or, as he prefers to call them, "models" of the church—first as institution, then as mystical communion, sacrament, herald, and servant. He discerns the most fundamental divergence between the first conception and the rest. "The institutional model identifies the true Church undialectically with a given existing body, which is said to be 'substantially' the Church of Jesus Christ. The other four models by their inner logic tend to depict the attributes of the true Church as ideals that are to a certain extent incarnated in history, thanks to the work of Jesus Christ and the presence of the Holy Spirit in the communities that accept Jesus as Lord."[36]

---

[31] Schlink, *The Coming Christ*, 119. Cf. Luther's trenchant judgment: "If the words, 'I believe that there is a holy Christian people,' had been used in the Children's Creed, all the misery connected with this meaningless and obscure word ('church') might easily have been avoided. For the words 'Christian holy people' would have brought with them, clearly and powerfully, the proper understanding and judgment of what is, and what is not, church" (*On the Councils and the Church*, 144).

[32] Schlink, *The Coming Christ*, 126.

[33] Härle, "Kirche VII," 290 (his emphasis).

[34] The "Agreed Statement on the Purpose of the Church" of the Anglican-Roman Catholic Consultation in the U.S.A., quoted in McBrien, *Catholicism*, 703.

[35] Craig, "The Church of the New Testament," 41.

[36] Dulles, *Models of the Church*, 129.

In Dulles's view, a balanced theology of the Church must find a way of incorporating the major affirmations of all five basic models.[37]

Does this signify embracing them all as a *goal* or including them all in the description of some *present reality*? Summarizing Dulles's position, McBrien writes in both the imperative mood, suggesting a goal, and in the indicative mood, suggesting a present reality. In the imperative, he observes: "The institutional model makes it clear that the Church must be a structured community, including pastoral officers bearing authority to direct and guide it, to preside over worship, to determine the limits of dissent, and to represent the community in an official way."[38] This, though, is not all that the church must be, in McBrien's view; neither is it all that the church is. Institution, mystical communion, sacrament, herald, servant—"It is all of these."[39] It *is* an institution, and it *is* also something more. The *New Delhi Report* of the World Council of Churches, likewise, speaks in the indicative: "The church is not merely an institution or organization. It is a fellowship of those who are called together by the Holy Spirit and in baptism confess Christ as Lord and Saviour."[40] The implication, however, seems clear: if the church is not merely an institution, it is at least that. So the query keeps returning, insistently: if the church is indeed an institution, what institution is it? Some particular sect or communion? The World Council of Churches? An embryonic reality not yet recognizable as the society it will one day become? An ideal entity nowhere discernible yet postulated by the needs of theology?

However developed, the more comprehensive, Dulles-type view is likely to exacerbate the problem of identity. For the institutional model, Swinburne could at least draw on societal analogs and propose criteria of identity over time. For noninstitutional models, no such criteria are available. A comprehensive model, combining the institutional and the noninstitutional, might inherit all the problems of these constitutive models and add others of its own. As weightings were needed in the institutional model, for aim and organization and their various constituents, so weightings might be needed for the disparate ideals contributed by each of Dulles's five models. The existence of such a need would depend, however, on whether any identifying or selecting remained to be done by their means. In the institutional perspective of the preceding section, church vied with church. In the inclusive perspectives I have noted and in Dulles's last four models, all such competition ceases. The church of Christ either cuts across denominational boundaries or encompasses them all. If, then, as Dulles's remarks suggest, we transcend the "undialectical" identification of the true Church with a given existing body, the identity question becomes more radical—not which present-day church is identical with the church of the Apostles but whether *any* church is. Does the whole of Christendom, divided though it is, constitute a "church"? If so, is it the same

---

[37] Ibid., 7.
[38] McBrien, *Catholicism*, 695-96 (emphasis omitted).
[39] Ibid., 695.
[40] *The New Delhi Report*, 119.

church as the early church? What happens to identity in these expanded, more ecumenical perspectives?

Identity?

The alternative to a single church of Christ, inclusive or exclusive, is a Christian family of churches—some more estranged than others, all aspiring to greater unity, or at least to greater harmony within the family circle.[41] In this alternative, a recognizable family resemblance relates each current church to the early church from which all variously derived, and the resemblance may be closer in some instances than in others; but no single church is identical with that earlier one (any more than children are identical with their mother), still less are all collectively identical with it. With the passing generations, identity has ceased. Now, is such the conclusion to which reflection on ecclesial identity leads—to identity's demise? Let us consider reasons for and against this apparently drastic conclusion.

In no familiar sense is a mere ensemble of true Christians—Anglican, Lutheran, Orthodox, Catholic, Methodist, Baptist, and so forth—a "church." In no familiar sense of the term is a collectivity of churches—Anglican, Lutheran, Orthodox, Catholic, Methodist, Baptist, and so forth—a single church. When people ask, "To what church do you belong?", they are not asking for any such identification. The answer "I'm a Christian" would only befuddle them. It would suggest that the respondent did not understand the question—did not understand what was meant by the word "church" (as distinct, for instance, from "religion"). To be sure, expressions may be extended by analogy, in keeping with CRS. However, terms may also be abused, in keeping with longstanding practice in both philosophy and theology. Facts may be forced to fit theory by means of verbal legerdemain, rather than theory be made to fit the facts as expressed in familiar terminology. If, for instance, the familiar societal use of the term "church" ("ecclesia," "Kirche," etc.) does not favor a splinter group's claim to identity with the church of the Apostles, the term can be given an "ideal," nonsocietal sense. If the familiar institutional sense of the term perpetuates past animosities, it can be given a more ecumenical sense. And so forth. Then everything comes out right. All can continue to confess, with Christians of the fourth century, their belief in "one, holy, catholic, and apostolic church," as they feel they should and must.

Why must they? Why must there still be a church, in some sense of the term "church," which is identical with the fourth-century or first-century church of

---

[41] Cf. Brosseder, "Towards What Unity," 137: "The question 'Towards what unity of the churches?' which is discussed here leads us to bid farewell to a model of organic union which has long been favoured. This model can only think of the church as a single organization and has today disappeared from the ecumenical debate . . . But the model of *koinonia/communion*/fellowship of the churches goes very well with the model of 'unity in reconciled difference,' 'the one church as a conciliar community' and the view of the other Christian churches as 'sister churches.'"

Christ? Journet's response, expressive of a long, still powerful tradition, stresses the church's apostolicity. For Journet, this signifies two things. First,

> To maintain that the true Church is apostolic is to maintain that she depends, as heat on fire, on a spiritual virtue residing in the Holy Trinity and thence descending by stages, first into the humanity of Christ, then into the two-fold power, sacramental and jurisdictional, of the apostolic body, and finally to the Christian people. Where we find this mediation, this chain of dependence, there we find the true Church (composed, it must be added, of the just who are to be saved and of sinners who are to be damned). Where this mediation is lacking there also the true Church is lacking.[42]

The mediation depends in turn on apostolic succession. Here is the second aspect of the church's apostolicity. "The apostolic body can be indefectible only in virtue of an uninterrupted succession. Suppose it had failed, and then been replaced by another institution to all appearances identical: apparently nothing would have been altered, but in point of fact everything would have been subverted; and this would quickly become apparent."[43] No longer identical with the church of the Apostles, the new church could no longer mediate the spiritual virtue received and transmitted by the Apostles. For this mediation was entrusted "not to isolated individuals but to an organic group capable of retaining a continuous personality in spite of the death of its individual members."[44] There, at the beginning, "The last link of the chain which is to bring the apostolic virtue to men, namely the apostolic or hierarchic body, was instituted by Christ Himself to endure till the end of time."[45]

In this perspective, the "apostolic virtue" transmitted is both doctrinal and sacramental. Contrary to likely first impressions, the doctrinal legacy depends on ecclesial identity more than does the sacramental. To be sure, the truth of the Christian message is not affected by its ecclesial source. What does it matter, said Paul, who does the preaching, provided Christ is proclaimed? However, neither is the efficacy of sacraments limited by their ecclesial source. In the very document in which he declared Anglican orders to be null and void, Leo XIII affirmed "the doctrine that a Sacrament is truly conferred by the ministry of one who is a heretic or unbaptised, provided the Catholic rite be employed."[46] Schism poses no barrier to sacramental grace. Thus, identity plays its most significant role with regard to authority, especially doctrinal authority. As already noted, according to Vatican Council I the pope "possesses through the divine assistance promised to him in the person of St. Peter, the infallibility with which the divine Redeemer willed his Church to be endowed in defining doctrine concerning faith or morals."[47] The promise was made to Peter as head of the church—that is, of Christ's church, the

---

42 Journet, *The Church*, 526.

43 Ibid., 527.

44 Ibid., 528.

45 Ibid.

46 Leo XIII, *Apostolicae curae*, 9, in Franklin, *Anglican Orders*, 135.

47 *The Church Teaches*, 102.

one over which Peter first presided and over which his successor still presides. Only on the understanding that the Roman church is identically Peter's church could the Council reiterate Florence's earlier claim that to the Roman Pontiff, "in the person of St. Peter, was given by our Lord Jesus Christ the full power of feeding, ruling, and governing the whole Church."[48]

At this point, our inquiry can be seen to coincide with ecumenical concerns. Today, as Christians feel the call to fuller fellowship, it is incumbent on all to re-examine whatever hinders unity. On the Catholic side, Petrine primacy, papal infallibility, and ecclesial infallibility pose the most serious problems. These very doctrines, it now appears, are the ones that depend most crucially on ecclesial identity. But when examined, such identity, between the church of Rome and the church of Peter, appears more problematic than has been supposed. Surely the essentialism that made it appear unproblematic might be questioned without being unfaithful to the gospel. So might the Platonic notion that Identity, with a capital I, has a definite nature unaffected by how anyone uses the word "identity." So might any criteria of ecclesial identity which, by redefining words, yielded a more decisive verdict than do Swinburne's criteria. When verdicts surreptitiously dictate definitions and definitions then dictate verdicts, only babel and circular question-begging result. (Compare the debate about fetal status.) Swinburne's criteria avoid any notable loading of terms and might be accepted, at least in their most general form (continuity of organization and doctrine), by most ecclesial disputants. Still, they face more problems, both epistemological and logical, than I have so far indicated.

To focus the epistemological difficulties, consider some contested doctrine—for instance, transubstantiation. Does the doctrine count for or against the church that endorses it being identical with the apostolic church? Catholics would say "for," Protestants would say "against." As we have noted, the arguments which have seemed decisive for or against the doctrine are not in fact decisive, relying as they do on SIS. If, however, the church which has taught the doctrine as revealed truth could claim identity with the church of the Apostles and from that identity could infer infallibility, the doctrine would be true and would constitute a link with the church of the Apostles. And the same might be claimed for other contested points—on the same supposition. Of course, if the church in question did thus argue its case, reasoning from ecclesial identity to infallibility to doctrinal resemblance to ecclesial identity, the argument would be circular, ending with identity because it began with identity. It is understandable, however, that so long as recourse to ecclesial authority appears crucial, the underlying assumption of identity will appear crucial. For there to be such authority, there must be such identity.

What, logically, would establish the identity of a present-day church with that of the Apostles? Of Newman's thinking, Owen Chadwick has written: "The argument is that though history shows none of the modern churches to be identical with the ancient Church, history also shows one of the modern churches to be more nearly

---

[48] Ibid., 100.

identical than any other."[49] The phrase "more nearly identical" poses problems. Though identity permits much variation over time, it does not clearly admit degrees. A child, for instance, does not grow into an adult that is simply "more nearly identical to the child" than any other adult. So it might have been better for Chadwick to say: "Though history shows none of the modern churches to *perfectly resemble* the ancient church, it also shows one of the modern churches to *resemble* it more closely than any other does." However, his wording, in terms of identity, alerts us to the fact that the best candidate for identity need not be a successful candidate. As one of the corporations into which Standard Oil split might resemble that corporation more closely than does any rival and still not be identical with it, so one church might resemble the church of the Apostles more closely than does any other and still not be identical with it.

So saying, I may appear to have forgotten about CRS—the Criterion of Relative Similarity. However, the choice here is not between "church" and "club," "corporation," and various other rival expressions (as it was earlier, for example, between "chess" and "poker," "checkers," "badminton," and the like) but simply between "same" and "different," or "identical" and "not identical." And as greater similarity between one successor company and Standard Oil does not automatically satisfy the criteria for sameness between companies, so greater similarity between one successor church and the earlier church may not satisfy the criteria for sameness between churches—whatever the criteria may be. CRS speaks of closer similarity to established word-uses, and there is no established, relatively uncontested use of the word "same" with respect to churches as there is with respect to companies. People agree about the sameness or difference of the companies. They do not agree about the sameness of the various Christian churches with the church of the Apostles. They have not agreed even about whether to call them all churches.

Swinburne indicates criteria of identity, but he does not indicate what more, besides coming closer than any rival candidate, would be required in order to satisfy the criteria. If one assumes, as many have, that there is and must be a successful candidate, then doubtless the strongest candidate is a successful candidate. But our present question is, why assume that there is and must be a successful candidate? Why assume that among contemporary churches, some one communion must be identical with the church of the Apostles?

Some might answer this question with a counterquestion: If at some moment the church of the Apostles did cease to exist, when was that? In the first century, when the first heresies and sects sprang up? At the time of the Arian heresy, or the split between East and West, or the Protestant Reformation? If no answer can be given to this question, does the hypothesis of identity's demise make sense? Yes, it may. Think of a seed that sprouts as a sprig, then divides, branches, and becomes a tree. Clearly, the tree is not a mere sprig and the sprig is not a mere seed, but no criteria exist which allow us to discern the moment at which the seed becomes a sprig or the sprig becomes a tree. Similarly, no criteria exist which allow us to determine at what moment a single church becomes two churches, three churches, or a family of

---

[49] Chadwick, *From Bossuet to Newman*, 143.

churches. The substantive, really important question, it seems, is the one Journet stressed: does the sprig derive life from the seed and the tree derive life from the sprig? Clearly it does, and the like may be asserted of the family of Christian churches. These churches do live, and they do derive their life from the apostolic church, as that derived its life from the risen Lord.

> In Christ we are already united [writes Küng]—in spite of the conflicting multiplicity of Churches. We know this by faith; the unity of the Church is a unity in faith. In him all Churches, whatever their disagreements among themselves, acknowledge the *one* Lord and at the same time in the *one* Spirit, his Spirit, the *one* Father, his Father. In him all Churches possess the one Gospel, his good news, however differently they may interpret it. And if these Churches baptize validly in his name—which is not in dispute—in which ecclesia are the baptized incorporated if not in his, the one ecclesia, of which body are they members if not the one body of Christ? And if these Churches also validly celebrate the Lord's Supper—which is only disputed in a few cases (with justice?)—what body do they receive and in what body are they united, if not in his, the one body?[50]

What, then, of Journet's fears? In this ecumenical perspective, has everything been subverted, and have the gates of hell prevailed? This at least can be said, that the facts—the differences and disagreements which remain among Christians—are not mitigated by recognizing some one Christian church as alone the church Jesus founded and rejoicing in its more perfect unity.[51] (In this connection I am reminded of my grandmother, who discerned God's loving providence in the fact that lightning struck the neighbors' house and not hers.) Neither are the unfortunate facts of division altered by identifying many churches as together forming the one true church of Christ. Matthew 16:18 or Matthew 28:20 might foster a more triumphalistic perspective, but experience teaches us to question our too-certain expectations. "My thoughts are not your thoughts, nor are your ways my ways, says the Lord" (Is 55:8).

Mystery

Recognizing our limits means recognizing mystery, and that can be painful. It goes counter to our desire to search God's judgments and scrutinize God's ways. It goes counter to common conceptions of revelation and doctrinal development and therefore begets "withdrawal symptoms." To mitigate them, both with regard to the church and more generally, it may be helpful to recognize a model of doctrinal identity widely implicit in current theological discussion yet seldom made explicit

---

[50] Küng, *The Church*, 285 (Küng's emphasis).

[51] Cf. Joyce, "Church," 759: "If a diversity of creeds could be found in His Church, this could only be because the truth He revealed had been lost in the quagmire of human error. It would signify that His work was frustrated, that His Church was no longer the pillar and ground of the truth."

in treatments of doctrinal development. Besides logical identity, mixed-truth identity, and their variants, considered in the last chapter, we can also envisage a further kind—what might be termed "identity of dialectical return."

To grasp the label's sense, recall Jesus' penchant for parables. Mark goes so far as to say, "he did not speak to them except in parables" (Mk 4:34). Yet in Mark and the other synoptics we notice already the tendency to treat Jesus' parables as point-by-point allegories (the seed means this, the sower means that, and so forth). In the Fathers, allegorical interpretations proliferated, but the readings which the gospels attributed to Jesus became fixed as definitive. Nowadays, exegetes view Jesus' parables differently. Parables are not veiled allegories. Neither are they concrete, imaginative renderings of abstract generalities. "At its simplest," writes C. H. Dodd, "the parable is a metaphor or simile drawn from nature or common life, arresting the hearer by its vividness or strangeness, and leaving the mind in sufficient doubt about its precise application to tease it into active thought."[52] For example:

There is one of [Jesus'] parabolic sayings which runs: "I have come to set fire to the earth, and how I wish it were already kindled!" Few parables are more difficult to interpret with precision; none perhaps is clearer in its main purport. Indeed any attempt to paraphrase its meaning is both less clear and less forcible than the saying as it stands. It is exactly the phrase we need to describe the volcanic energy of the meteoric career depicted in the Gospels. The teaching of Jesus is not the leisurely and patient exposition of a system by the founder of a school.[53]

Parables vary, as do doctrines, but these indications suffice to suggest, by comparison, the meaning of the phrase "identity of dialectical return." Exegetes have returned to the parables themselves, as parables: there is the identity. They have done so dialectically, returning to the parables themselves but bringing with them new, reflective understanding of Jesus' innovative form of teaching: there is the difference. With this understanding, they can more surely intuit the parables' intended message, yet are slow to propose any precise reading as the one Jesus certainly had in mind and meant to convey.

With this possible parallel in view, we can ask: Did Jesus sometimes teach in allusive, parable form and sometimes much more definitely? For example, the words "This is my body" are powerfully suggestive and invite interpretation, but how definite can the interpretation become, and how exclusive, without losing touch with the original saying and its form? Metaphysical readings of the text, some as detailed as any allegory, have aimed at logical identity with Jesus' words, but how can the definite be logically identical with the indefinite? To this query, theologians have replied as have allegorists: the explicit rendering, they have held, may be identical with the implicit content. In one instance the implicit meaning is spelled out as allegory, in the other as dogma. With our present understanding of parables, such a parallel elicits misgivings. Along the spectrum from parable to

---

[52] Dodd, *The Parables of the Kingdom*, 5.

[53] Ibid., 13.

conciliar definition, where do the words of institution fall? Indeed, do they fall anywhere within such a spectrum, or is their function more performative than didactic? What type of utterance do they exemplify?

Similar queries arise for a saying such as Matthew 16:18: "And I tell you, you are Peter, and on this rock I will build my church, and the gates of Hades will not prevail against it." How much lies implicit in these words? An institutional church, successors of Peter, papal infallibility, and the rest are possible renderings of the words' sense, as various allegorical accounts (e.g., of sower, seed, birds, briars, path) are possible renderings of the parables. However, these are not the only ways to understand the words. As Pheme Perkins notes, with historical examples in mind:

> An author may focus on the christological significance of Christ as the rock, on Peter as the model for the believer, or on the security of apostolic faith. Matthew 16:17-19 applies to episcopal authority only in instances where that authority needs to be strengthened. The suggestions that it also implied Roman primacy were clearly resisted by Tertullian and Cyprian. The emergence of Roman primacy as the primary meaning of the passage for Catholic theologians resulted from the schism that has permanently divided Western Christendom, the Protestant Reformation.[54]

Perkins remarks that the varied readings she cites may not exclude one another. As for many a parable, the interpretation of such a passage is "inherently polyvalent." However, a distinct question, of more interest for doctrinal identity, is whether any one reading, whether unique or not, can be said to lie "implicit" in the text. For instance, can papal primacy?

Implicitness or nonimplicitness, identity or nonidentitythese depend largely on context: who uttered the words, when, in what circumstances? So exegetes studying Petrine or other texts focus on the context as best they can—and come up with varying interpretations. For the context—scriptural, cultural, and other—is now imperfectly known to us. Here, three possibilities can be distinguished: a once-definite meaning in a context imperfectly known, an indefinite meaning in a context imperfectly known, and an indefinite meaning in a context better known. But the upshot for all three is the same: indefinite understanding, a degree of mystery. What is more, it may be difficult or impossible to determine which of these three alternatives confronts us in any instance. For example, if the context is imperfectly known to us, the definiteness or indefiniteness of the meaning in that context may be difficult to discern. Doubtless Dodd is right about "I have come to cast fire on the earth": the meaning never was sharp. But what about "On this rock I will build my church" or "This is my body"? Do we know enough to discern that the meaning was once precise, let alone to discern what the precise meaning was?

These queries are intended, not to invite agnosticism, but to fill out what might be meant by "identity of dialectical return." Returning to scriptural data, we might recognize their indefiniteness. Going beyond the data, we might nonetheless suggest precise interpretations, and these interpretations might coincide with an

---

[54] Perkins, *Peter*, 178.

objective meaning which the interpreted saying once had. However, whatever the merits of our interpretations, so long as we recognized the initial indefiniteness, we would return not merely to the data (allegorists did that) but to the data as they are: imprecise, indefinite. This understanding of the data would determine how strongly and surely we advanced our interpretations and how open we were to alternative understandings.

Küng might intervene at this point. "The Churches," he warns, "cannot be unified satisfactorily on the basis of indifferentist faith and half-hearted allegiances. Diplomatic settlements and compromises in dogma are not the right way. We must be mistrustful of formulas or forms of unity which conceal our differences rather than overcoming them. If unity is to be genuine, dogmatic differences must be settled theologically."[55] For that to be possible, a balance must somehow be struck between half-hearted allegiance on the one hand and dogmatic rigidity on the other.

The comparison with parables can illustrate this possibility. Most scriptural scholars would agree with Dodd that the parable of the sower, for example, was not originally an allegory; many would agree that in its original context it conveyed some single message; but not all would agree with Dodd's reading of that message:

> Jesus, I have suggested, in the parable of the Seed growing Secretly, pointed his hearers to the facts of past and present history as showing that the time has come when the gains of the whole process may be realized. The crop is ripe; it is time to reap. But, they might have objected, even the work of John the Baptist has not brought about that complete "restoration of all things" (Mk. ix. 12) which was anticipated as the immediate prelude to the day of the Lord. Much of his work, as of the work of all the prophets, has been a failure. True, says Jesus; but no farmer yet delayed to reap a good crop because there were bare patches in the field. In spite of all, the harvest is plentiful: it is only the labourers that are lacking. "Pray the Lord of the harvest to send labourers into His harvest."[56]

It would be misleading to say that Dodd gives this line of interpretation "half-hearted allegiance." He finds it persuasive. He will stand by it until some other reading is shown to be preferable or at least equally persuasive. Still, he is open to that possibility. And far from manifesting indifference, this openness is a measure of the seriousness with which he takes the parable and its interpretation. Such an attitude we now find natural and admirable, but it was not always so. And a similarly balanced attitude with regard to doctrinal matters has not achieved equally widespread acceptance. Only recently has theological discussion reached a point where, with regard to such questions as the Eucharist and the church, identity of dialectical return may be proposed and be taken seriously by Catholic,

---

[55] Küng, *The Church*, 289.

[56] Dodd, *The Parables of the Kingdom*, 146-47. Cf. Jeremias, *The Parables of Jesus*, 150-51.

Orthodox, and Protestant alike as an alternative to logical, organic, or other favored forms of doctrinal identity.

Chapter 8

Resurrection

One major theme remains to be addressed: resurrection, afterlife. Here, too, issues of identity figure prominently; and here, too, connections criss-cross with other themes of Christian faith. While previous chapters linked Incarnation with Trinity and Eucharist, Eucharist with Word, and Word with Church, they also noted how, for example, Jesus' resurrection has been viewed as an indication of his divinity or as an obstacle to belief in his real presence in the Eucharist. ("The very body of Christ," we have seen Zwingli object, "is the body which is seated at the right hand of God.") However, such connections cast little light on the issues of identity raised by the life to come; so they need not detain us. Let us go directly to the heart of the matter.

Some years ago, studies conducted by the National Opinion Research Center and the International Social Survey Program indicated that people believed in life after death primarily because they believed that they were loved.[1] This inference is no mere quirk of popular piety. The New Testament conveys nothing more clearly than God's love, nothing more firmly than life to come; and the link between the love and the life is equally clear. "For I am convinced," writes Paul, "that neither death, nor life, nor angels, nor rulers, nor things present, nor things to come, nor powers, nor height, nor depth, nor anything else in all creation, will be able to separate us from the love of God in Christ Jesus our Lord" (Rom 8:38-39). And yet, what angelic and cosmic forces cannot achieve, sheer logic might. If resurrection or life after death involves a contradiction, then Jesus did not rise and we shall not rise with him.

To be sure, there is no contradiction in life following death or person following person, but, as a dying woman puts it in John Perry's "Dialogue on Personal Identity and Immortality": "In a few days *I* will quit breathing, *I* will be put into a coffin, *I* will be buried. And in a few months or a few years *I* will be reduced to so much humus."[2] This she takes as obvious, as given. So what sense does it make to suggest that *she* will survive? And yet, according to Christian belief the Father's love for Jesus is shown by raising Jesus, not some other; and God's love for those whose very hairs are numbered is shown by raising those people, not others. Thus:

> the Christian does not merely hold that there shall be people living a blessed life in the world to come, nor even that such people will in some way or other be very much like some people who have lived here. He believes that it is these very people

---

[1] Zaleski, *Life*, 37.
[2] J. Perry, "A Dialogue," 321 (Perry's emphasis).

themselves, the people who have begun their careers in this world and here suffered the agony of death, who will share that blessed life. And when he believes in or hopes for that destiny for himself it is indeed *for himself*.[3]

For so it was, exemplarily, in Jesus' case. In Luke, as O'Collins remarks, the risen Lord "does not say, 'I was Jesus,' still less, 'I come in place of Jesus,' but he announces, 'It is I myself' (24:39)."[4] Hence a crucial problem for afterlife is that of identity: Can personal sameness persist beyond this present life?

The problem interests faith seeking understanding as well as faith seeking validation, for it may restrict available readings of Scripture's indefinite sayings. Viewed one way, resurrection may look possible; viewed another way, it may not. Actually, no interpretation that retains Christian belief in bodily survival is entirely free of difficulties. Three alternative conceptions, each with its own perplexities, can be ordered dialectically as follows:

1. Simple Resuscitation. In this conception, which some New Testament texts suggest, Jesus' soul left his body on Good Friday and returned to the same body on Easter morning. Similarly, it is thought, our souls leave our bodies at death and will return to the same bodies at the resurrection of the dead. "We do not believe," declared the Eleventh Council of Toledo, "that we shall rise in an ethereal body or in any other body, as some foolishly imagine, but in this very body in which we live and are and move."[5] For resurrection so conceived, questions arise both about the interim period (e.g., how does the person survive if only the soul survives?) and about the subsequent reunion of soul and body (e.g., how can the soul be reunited to a body that has been recycled through several bodies or scattered to the winds?). These problems disappear in a second, antithetical conception:

2. Replication. The alternative popularized by John Hick involves "the divine creation in another space of an exact psycho-physical 'replica' of the deceased person."[6] Here, no problems arise concerning the identification of a disembodied spirit with the deceased person, or concerning the survival of the identical former body, but other problems replace them. In particular, does mere similarity, however close, suffice to identify the newly created person with the deceased? Is a replica of a person the same person?[7]

3. Glorification. Rejecting simple resuscitation on one hand and simple replication on the other, contemporary accounts commonly favor those New Testament texts which accentuate transformation. "What is sown is perishable, what is raised is

---

[3] Mavrodes, "The Life Everlasting," 30 (Mavrodes's italics).

[4] O'Collins, *The Resurrection*, 115.

[5] Neuner and Dupuis, *The Christian Faith*, 621.

[6] Hick, *Death and Eternal Life*, 279.

[7] In "Persons and Replicas," Gerard Loughlin summarizes, then continues, the debate on Hick's replica hypothesis. "Copies may be perfect," he argues with Flew and others, "but they are not the same as their originals" (305).

imperishable. It is sown in dishonor, it is raised in glory. It is sown in honor, it is raised in glory. It is sown in weakness, it is raised in power. It is sown a physical body, it is raised a spiritual body" (1 Cor 15:42-44). So it was for Jesus, so it will be for us. And yet, "The one who is alive and active in the world is identical with the pre-resurrection Jesus; he lives in a radically new mode of existence, to be sure, but the substance of the risen Lord's reality is the earthly one as uniquely confirmed by his God."[8] How, though, if the mode of existence is radically new, is identity preserved? By bodily identity? Then problems of the first kind return, from cremation, cannibalism, and the like. By bodily replication? Then problems of the second kind return, intensified. "The person at death," writes Donald Goergen, "does not become disembodied (a soul) or naked but is rather newly clothed or re-embodied with a spiritual body and glory, and the materiality of the corpse is matter unnecessary to the new mode of embodiment."[9] Hick at least preserved close similarity; here even that disappears. The replica is not even a replica. So how is this new body my body? How is this new person me?

Responses to these and other difficulties[10] can take any one of three directions:

1. Transcendence. "'Resurrection,'" writes Küng, "means a life that bursts through the dimensions of space and time in God's invisible, imperishable, incomprehensible domain."[11] In that transcendent realm, "By losing himself into the reality of God, man gains himself. By *entering into the infinite, the finite person* loses his limits, so that the present contrast of personal and impersonal is transcended and transformed into the *transpersonal.*"[12] Our familiar categories, it seems, no longer apply. If so, the problem of identity may be transcended, for the one transformed is no longer a person and no longer the same person, but something different, higher, ineffable. Who, without having observed such a thing, would imagine a butterfly emerging from a chrysalis? Who, knowing only caterpillars, would have the right words for butterflies? One wonders, though, how in this account a person can be said to have gained "himself." Do personal pronouns still apply? Was Paul

---

[8] McDermott, "Roman Catholic Christology," 351 (on Küng). Cf. ibid., 345: "the pre-Easter Jesus is the one who died and was raised. This apparently simple proposition acquires significance to the degree that systematic theology appreciates the theological role of the Resurrection. Besides providing the divine vindication of Jesus' claim and message, the Resurrection is the consummation, the coming to totality, of the life of Jesus. *Who* was raised is as important as the fact *that* he was raised."

[9] Goergen, *The Death and Resurrection of Jesus*, 146.

[10] Clearly, the problems for identity are not lessened in the view John Cooper cites, "that humans pass out of existence at death and remain nonexistent until the resurrection, when they are completely recreated by God" (*Body, Soul, and Life Everlasting*, 117).

[11] Küng, *Does God Exist?*, 678 (Küng's italics omitted). Cf. Rahner, *Foundations of Christian Faith*, 271-73 ("the final and time-conquering state of man's existence which has been actualized in spirit and in freedom has to be taken out of time").

[12] Küng, *Eternal Life?*, 112 (Küng's italics).

mistaken, or at least incautious, in saying that *we* shall rise? The problem of identity will not go away.

2. Reductive Reinterpretation. In sufficiently reductive readings of "resurrection," the identity problem does disappear. It does not arise, for example, if Jesus' resurrection consists in his ongoing influence (Barnes),[13] the survival of what he stood for (Marxsen),[14] the disciples' "encounter with grace" (Schillebeeckx),[15] the continued presence of Jesus' Spirit (Carnley),[16] or "the Eschatological Event which is present in the Word of preaching at any given time" (Bultmann).[17] The New Testament does not suggest such readings;[18] a reductive naturalism does. So too, no doubt, do logical difficulties of the kinds just cited. If Jesus' resurrection is not possible, it did not occur. If our resurrection is not possible even for God, then that belief, too, must be abandoned or reinterpreted. At best, we may have to settle for purely spiritual survival—for "resurrection as 'the resurrection of human personality' of which 'Jesus is the first fruits.'"[19] But is bodily resurrection impossible?

3. Closer Scrutiny. A mere sampling of conceptions and their respective problems, as above, permits no verdict. On closer examination, how strong are the objections? What alternative conceptions perhaps mitigate or resolve them? Eventually, I shall review the alternatives one by one. First, though, it will be helpful to examine three major sources of perplexity concerning afterlife identity. How and why do puzzles arise for whatever position one considers?

Borderline Mystery

If, using other atoms, God formed a perfect replica of a person at the moment of death, would that replica be the same person? If, instead, God formed a perfect replica of the person as the person was at an earlier stage of life, would that more youthful replica be the same person? If God performed the replication some time

---

[13] Fuller and Perkins, *Who Is This Christ?*, 34.

[14] Marxsen, *The Resurrection*, 138-48. Cf. O'Collins, *Jesus Risen*, 63.

[15] Schillebeeckx, *Jesus*, 394. "Schillebeeckx is at pains to distinguish his position from that of Marxsen, but at times he seems to equate the statement 'God raised Jesus from the dead' with the statement that the offer of salvation made in Jesus' earthly life is renewed after Easter" (Fuller and Perkins, *Who Is This Christ?*, 35).

[16] Carnley, *The Structure of Resurrection Belief*, 325-26.

[17] Bultmann, *Essays Philosophical and Theological*, 288. "Rudolf Bultmann, whose theology of the Word was very different from the liberal Protestantism of Bishop Barnes, once accepted the statement 'Jesus rose into the kerygma' as an adequate expression of what he understood by the resurrection" (Fuller and Perkins, *Who Is This Christ?*, 34-35).

[18] O'Collins, *What Are They Saying about the Resurrection?*, 44-45.

[19] Badham, *Christian Beliefs*, 41 (quoting Bishop Montefiore's view, which Badham endorses). The following discussion leaves open this alternative, but does not focus on it.

after the person's death, leaving an existential gap, would the result be the same person? To numerous queries such as these, and to more refined variants, some theorists answer yes and some answer no. "Intuitions" diverge. More basically, opinions differ as to whether there must be a correct reply to each such question. Suppose that a perfect replica preserved identity but a notably imperfect replica did not: along the continuum between these two extremes would the verdict switch suddenly at some precise point, or could borderline cases be imagined for which there was no verdict? Or suppose two perfect replicas were fashioned and not just one: would one or the other be the same person, or would neither? Is there always a correct yes or no answer to all such questions of personal identity?

For reasons of a kind already suggested, I favor a negative reply. Round about each term of a natural language an indefinite borderline extends, where usage offers no backing for either "Yes" or "No" and rival expressions make equal, undecidable CRS claims to descriptive aptness. So it is for the "personhood" of fetuses and so it is for the "sameness" of replica people, duplicate people, split people, and the like. Arguments can be constructed by focusing on similarities so as to reach an affirmative verdict or on dissimilarities so as to reach a negative verdict, but such arguments are worthless. Statements are not made true by facts alone but also by the words employed and their meanings, and if neither usage nor stipulation has sharpened the meanings in anticipation of philosophers' far-fetched imaginings, then, as Terence Penelhum puts it, in borderline instances philosophers will simply have to decide for or against application of the term.[20] Or rather, since there is generally no need to decide one way or the other, they can simply acknowledge that where language permits no answer there is no answer.

To such reasoning, Derek Parfit retorts:

> This criticism might be justified if, when considering such imagined cases, we had no reactions. But these cases arouse in most of us strong beliefs. And these are beliefs, not about our words, but about ourselves. By considering these cases, we discover what we believe to be involved in our own continued existence, or what it is that makes us now and ourselves next year the same people. We discover our beliefs about the nature of personal identity over time.[21]

Most fundamentally, we discover our belief "that our identity must be determinate."[22] That is, we believe that, even in borderline cases, "the question 'Am I about to die?' must have an answer. And, as Williams claims, we believe that the answer must be either, and quite simply, Yes or No. If someone will be alive, and

---

[20] "An answer to our question is not a mere matter of making explicit a decision we have already made implicitly, but of making a new one. In making it, however, we have to try to stay as close as possible to the conceptual conventions we already follow, if we are to avoid inconsistencies" (Penelhum, *Survival and Disembodied Existence*, 81).

[21] Parfit, *Reasons and Persons*, 200.

[22] Ibid., 214.

will be suffering agony, this person either will or will not be me. One of these must be true."[23]

How should we assess such a "deep" conviction? Can it establish "a strong presumption" one way or the other (as Peter Unger suggests)?[24] Consider the parallel remarks that might be made about the status of zygotes, embryos, or fetuses. These cases, too, "arouse in most of us strong beliefs." These beliefs, too, "are not about words" but about zygotes, embryos, or fetuses. Concerning them, too, verdicts diverge. Yet despite this divergence, most people suppose that there must be a definite answer. As the split person, duplicated person, or replicated person is or is not the same person, so the zygote, embryo, or fetus is or is not a person, a human being. Such is the common reaction. But that is all it is, a reaction, not a conceptual "intuition."[25] And in this case as in the other, the reaction is readily accounted for.

One major explanation goes as follows:

1. Conceptual borders are blurred; no term in any language differentiates so precisely between instances and noninstances that in-between cases, conceivable or actual, are excluded.

2. Borderline cases are not only conceivable, but exist for many concepts. Actual items fall between purple and blue, rain and sleet, bushes and trees, desks and chairs.

3. However, the vast majority of the things we identify fall clearly within or without the conceptual borders drawn loosely but effectively by usage. The rain clearly is rain; the plane clearly is a plane; the prediction clearly is a prediction; the person clearly is a person; and so forth.

4. This fact begets in those who do not reflect on language—thus, in most people—the assumption that answers exist for all such questions. If we cannot tell whether something is rain, a plane, a prediction, or a person, the fault must lie in us and not in the language we speak.

5. Accordingly, when discussion does focus on a borderline case, we assume that an answer exists.[26]

---

[23] Ibid., 233.

[24] Unger, *Identity, Consciousness and Value*, 29.

[25] Jonathan Cohen characterizes "intuition," in a common contemporary sense, as "an inclination of mind that is taken to originate from the existence of a system of tacitly acknowledged rules for making judgements about relevant topics" (*The Dialogue of Reason*, 76). I here suggest a likelier origin for Parfit's and Williams's reaction than a tacit semantic rule extending, like a rail laid to infinity, beyond familiar instances of identity or nonidentity. (Cf. Wittgenstein, *Philosophical Investigations*, §§ 80, 142, 218-21.)

[26] A second explanation connects with this one. Influenced by common paradigms, we too readily suppose that, since expressions of degree (e.g., "crueler") correlate

If, in addition, the answer looks important (as it does for fetuses and personal identity), we seek it, give it, argue for or against it. So doing, we largely ignore words and their meanings, and make no effort to work out their relevance, via some such formula as CRS. For, after all, the unborn are what interest us, or persons and their identity, and not mere vagaries of linguistic usage. As Humpty Dumpty might put it, who is to be master here—we or our language? This way lies darkness, a darkness that accounts for much of the mystery that envelops personal identity and personal survival.

The darkness is deepened, and futile debate perpetuated, by the impression that an account such as the one I have just given cannot be correct. How can even borderline verdicts on identity have slight significance if identity has great significance? "A matter of great cosmic moment seems to hinge on a linguistic decision."[27] Parfit replies by denying that personal identity is what matters in survival. Most of what matters, he suggests, "are two other relations: the psychological continuity and connectedness that, in ordinary cases, hold between the different parts of a person's life."[28] The parallel with fetal status suggests a more balanced response, between "decisive importance" and "no importance." As paradigm personhood clearly is important, so too, for reasons such as Parfit singles out, is paradigm identity of the kind we daily experience. It does not follow, though, that nonparadigm forms of personhood or identity are equally important, or that the shift from borderline personhood to borderline nonpersonhood is as momentous as the shift from paradigm personhood to paradigm nonpersonhood, or that the shift from borderline identity to borderline nonidentity is as momentous as the shift from paradigm identity to paradigm nonidentity. In one case the difference may be slight, in the other it is great. And the difference between adjoining instances within the fuzzy borderline may be still slighter. If, however, we regard personhood or identity as invariant, then we will wonder how verdicts on even far-fetched, borderline cases can fail to be momentous. If, on the contrary, we regard identity less essentialistically, our puzzlement subsides.[29]

And yet, this greater conceptual clarity brings greater *value* unclarity. If identity no longer looks simple, neither does its importance look simple. Precisely

---

with indefinite borderlines (e.g., the border between "cruel" and "kind"), the absence of such expressions (e.g., "more identical" or "more a person") signals a sharp borderline (e.g., between identity and nonidentity or between persons and nonpersons). A third explanation is our tendency to suppose simple, all-or-nothing essences, even for such relatively perspicuous concepts as those of color. "*All* the shades we *see*," wrote G. E. Moore, "occupy some position in the colour octahedron; but 'blue,' in the sense in which many of the shades in the octahedron are 'blue,' occupies *no* position in it; therefore it is not seen" (*Commonplace Book*, 21). Accordingly, it makes no sense to speak of objects being more or less blue; all shades of blue share the common, invariant essence. To perceive the relevance of these remarks, see, e.g., Coburn, "Personal Identity Revisited," 391.

[27] Penelhum, *Survival and Disembodied Existence*, 98-99.

[28] Parfit, "The Unimportance of Identity," 29. Cf. Lewis, "Survival and Identity," 55 ("*what matters in survival is mental continuity and connectedness*").

[29] Compare Hallett, *Essentialism*, 37-38.

where—in which of identity's varying aspects, physical, mental, or both combined—does its importance reside? No clear answer is likely to emerge without greater clarity about persons and their identity, and in particular about the everyday, paradigm persons and the everyday, paradigm identity which ground our desire that we and others may survive.

Semantic Mystery

Talk of "borderline cases" evokes the image of a firm conceptual core surrounded by a fuzzy border: the indefiniteness is only peripheral. On the contrary, with regard to persons and their identity the core itself is shrouded in semantic mystery. For at its heart lies the pronoun "I" (with variants and equivalents), and that does not function as a precise descriptive term. Indeed, it has been said, "the first person is unanalyzable. What it is for an experience to be mine cannot be analyzed into something of the form 'being an experience satisfying some specified description.'"[30] It would seem to follow that personal identity is equally unanalyzable—that (as Butler, Reid, Chisholm, Swinburne, and others have held) "personal identity is something ultimate, unanalysable in terms of such observable and experienceable phenomena as bodily continuity and continuity of memory."[31] This, in turn, might suggest that personal identity is something simple, something distinct from all such phenomena. (The artichoke, which might lose any one of its leaves and still remain, must therefore be distinct from all its leaves.)

Reflection on the pronoun "I" may take us some distance along this path, if not to the final, essentialistic conclusion. Thus consider an expressive utterance such as, "I hope you'll come back soon!" The speaker has not observed an inner act, identified it as an act of hope with the stated content ("you'll come back soon"), then reported this inner occurrence. That is why it makes so little sense to suppose that the speaker mistakenly identified the act or its content. Similarly, and for a similar reason, it makes no sense to suppose that the speaker has misidentified the subject of the hoping; for the speaker has not observed the agent of some inner act of hope, identified the agent by tell-tale clues ("It looks like me"), then included this further information in the report. Rather, it is as Wittgenstein observed: "there is a great variety of criteria for personal '*identity*'. Now which of them determines

---

[30] Madell, "Personal Identity," 29. "Thomas Nagel has recently pointed out, in effect, that there is no description at all which is free of token-reflexive expressions and which can be substituted for 'I'; no matter how detailed a token-reflexive-free description of a person is, and whether or not it is couched in physicalistic terms, it cannot possibly entail that *I* am that person" (Shoemaker, "Self-Reference and Self-Awareness," 560). Cf. Nagel, "Physicalism," 353-55, and Evans, *The Varieties of Reference*, 206.

[31] Swinburne, in Shoemaker and Swinburne, *Personal Identity*, 26. Cf. Swinburne, "Personal Identity," 235-40, and "Persons and Personal Identity," 227-28.

my saying that '*I*' am in pain? None."[32] The like holds, typically, for "I hope," "I regret," "I believe," "I remember," and so forth.

As Wittgenstein observed, with such instances in mind, "My own relation to my words is wholly different from other people's."[33] The speaker does not observe the mouth that says "I hope" or "I'm in pain" and thereby discern who it is that has the hope or the pain, but hearers do.[34] The speaker does not observe what predicate is uttered and thereby discern what state he or she is in, but hearers do. And they base their reports on what they have observed. This linguistic bipolarity between first-person speaker and third-person hearer constitutes a further major source of perplexity concerning persons and their identity. From the first-person perspective it appears that there are no criteria. From the third-person perspective it appears that there are only external criteria. And yet there is more to pain than a cry, grimace, or verbal utterance of pain; there is more to hope than the words "I hope" or other behavioral indications. The expressive use of the first-person pronoun adds a further, inner dimension. Similarly, if there is more to a person than a body, that more may be indicated by the term "person" and by personal pronouns. For they all connect with the personal pronoun "I," and that sets no limits. It rises from and gives expression to whatever depths the person possesses.

Similar remarks apply to diachronic personal identity. As speakers do not use criteria to identify themselves as the ones who hope or believe when they say, in the present tense, "I hope" or "I believe," so they do not use criteria to verify their continuing identity when, for instance, they say "I hoped for better things" or "I believed the report." If they have no doubts about who did the hoping or believing, it is not because they observed the person so engaged and spotted sure clues (fingerprints, birthmarks, DNA?) that the person was themselves. Again, as third-person uses of "hope" and "believe" do not define hope or belief more tightly than do the first-person uses with which they form the single concept "hope" or "believe," so third-person ascriptions of identity do not define personal identity more tightly than do the first-person ascriptions. The third-person uses suggest an indefinite conceptual border; the first-person uses smudge even that.

To be sure, for both psychological assertions and identity assertions, there are limits. But the Criterion of Relative Similarity (CRS) loosens the restrictions often imposed.[35] In an embodied afterlife, speakers might speak aptly of having done this or that in the present life, provided that their utterances ("I remember being there," "I regret what I did to her," etc.) conformed to CRS. Of a disembodied (hence speechless) person we might say aptly that he or she remembered where she had lived, regretted what she had done, and so forth, provided that these utterances

---

[32] Wittgenstein, *Philosophical Investigations*, §404 (original emphasis; paragraph break omitted).

[33] Ibid., 192.

[34] Wittgenstein, *The Blue and Brown Books*, 68.

[35] E.g., "'Souls' can afford no principle of identity. And so they cannot be used to bridge the gulf between my existence now and my existence in the hereafter" (Perry, "Dialogue," 326).

of ours conformed to CRS. Disembodiment would not automatically preclude being a person or being the same person as the embodied individual who lived in the remembered place, did the regretted deed, and so forth. (Think again of computers playing chess without boards or pieces.)

A type of reasoning often employed to exclude any form of disembodied survival illustrates CRS's significance. If a person survives, it is commonly supposed, then whatever survives is identical with that person and has been so from the start. If, for example, the person survives as a soul, the person never was anything but a soul; the body was a mere appendage.[36] ("If I am with Christ, then I—my essential selfhood or core personhood—must survive physical death. The being or entity who I am must continue to exist . . . Otherwise it would not be I but someone or something else that is with Christ."[37]) Objections to such reasoning and to the split it infers in the presently existing self beget objections to dualism generally and to any form of disembodied existence. It is therefore important to note that the possibility of disembodied existence carries no such implications—any more than the possibility of handless, noseless, limbless, or heartless existence (e.g., during heart surgery) implies a split between an essential me and my nonessential appurtenances: hands, nose, ears, eyes, limbs, heart, kidneys, spleen, and the rest. These, too, constitute who and what I currently am.

An "essential me" might, of course, be understood differently, as simply that which is minimally required for my survival and without any suggestion that this minimal core is coextensive with me. Thus Swinburne remarks,

> The crucial point that Descartes and others were presumably trying to make is not that (in the case of men) the living body is not part of the person, but that it is not essentially, only contingently, part of the person. The body is separable from the person and the person can continue even if the body is destroyed. Just as I continue to exist wholly and completely if you cut off my hair, so, the dualist holds, it is possible that I continue to exist if you destroy my body. The soul, by contrast, is the necessary core which must continue if I am to continue; it is the part of the person which is necessary for his continuing existence.[38]

---

[36] Cf. Flew, "'Personal Identity and Imagination,'" 123-24; Badham, *Christian Beliefs*, 100-101; Badham and Badham, *Immortality or Extinction?*, 27 ("I suggest that it can therefore be regarded as an intelligible possibility provided we are satisfied on two counts: first that our selfhood can be legitimately identified with our 'inner life'"); Olson, "Is Psychology Relevant?," 174 ("If we can outlive, or be outlived by, 'our' organisms, we cannot *be* those organisms, for a thing cannot outlive itself"); Vardy, "A Christian Approach," 15: "However, either the soul is in purgatory and the soul is me or else I am not in purgatory. Aquinas attempts to circumvent this problem by claiming that the soul is not fully the person, but this is problematic. Either I will or I will not go to purgatory and this must mean that either I am or am not my soul."

[37] Cooper, *Body, Soul, and Life Everlasting*, 177. Cf. Badham, *Christian Beliefs*, 40, and John Perry, "A Dialogue," 322-23.

[38] Swinburne, *The Evolution of the Soul*, 146.

But the single, invariant part? Can there be no nonphysical analogy with losing a lung *or* a limb *or* a kidney and still remaining the same person (say, losing memory *or* feelings *or* imagination)? CRS counters essentialism of any kind, at any level.

Thus, it also counters the common allegation, found in Geach, Penelhum, and others, that a surviving person would have to satisfy this or that familiar criterion of identity in order to qualify as the same person. In terms of Wittgenstein's comparison, no one artichoke leaf is more essential than another; none, singly, is required for the continuing existence of the artichoke.[39] However, strip off too many leaves and the remainder may no longer qualify as an artichoke, nor the same artichoke, even by CRS's standards. Further, the more leaves the artichoke loses, the less culinary, commercial, or other interest it retains, even if it still manages to qualify as an artichoke and the same artichoke. What this comparison suggests is that, despite its semantic interest, CRS possesses slight ontological or existential import. It does not ensure the existence of any such enduring core as might assure personal identity after bodily death. Neither does it ensure that such a core would retain the kind of interest that people attach to their own or others' survival. These questions go deeper.

Before addressing them, I should note a further dimension of semantic mystery. CRS itself is wreathed in mystery or at least in great indefiniteness. Paraphrasing Robert Nozick, I might say: CRS helps us to sort out and structure the issues; it does not, however, by itself, answer any questions of identity. For it does not, by itself, tell which dimension or weighted sum of dimensions determines closeness of resemblance; rather, it is a schema into which such details can be filled.[40] Thus, even if we knew all there was to know about the persons we experience, when it came to deciding the personhood of some very different individual, what list of pertinent characteristics would we draw up to determine whether "person" came closer than any rival expression, and how would we weight the characteristics in such a list? (Would having hair count equally with having consciousness?) Again, even if we knew all there was to know about the continuing identity of the persons we experience, when it came to deciding whether some very different individual was the "same" person as an earlier one, what aspects of continuity should we list, and how should we weight them, to determine whether "same" won out over any rival expression (e.g., "different")? (Would a persisting preference for vanilla count equally with persistence in space, or would persistence in the same country count equally with persistence in the same spot?) Even if we could ignore context in answering such queries,[41] we still could not respond to them, if only for the evident reason that we do not know all there is to know about persons or about

---

[39] Compare Nozick: "Notice that on the closest continuer view, a property may be a factor in identity without being a necessary condition for it. If persons conceivably can transfer from one body to another, still, bodily continuity can be an important component of identity, even (in some cases) its sole determinant. The dimension of bodily continuity can receive significant weight in the overall measure of closeness for persons" (*Philosophical Explanations*, 35).

[40] Ibid., 33.

[41] Cf. Borowski, "Identity and Personal Identity," 498.

their temporal persistence. Attempting to apply CRS, we encounter the mystery not solely of our language but of ourselves.

Ontological Mystery

In this scientific age, many share thoughts like Russell's: "All the evidence goes to show that what we regard as our mental life is bound up with brain structure and organized bodily energy. Therefore it is rational to suppose that mental life ceases when bodily life ceases."[42] Death is the end. Of the three versions of survival I have cited, one (Hick's) responds to Russell's challenge by straightway providing a new body to continue mental life, but it thereby prompts doubts about the sameness of the person whose mental life it is. Whether the remaining accounts meet Russell's challenge depends on what, precisely, "all the evidence" goes to show about the relation between the mental and the physical. In what sense is mental life "bound up" with bodily life?

Many once answered as did, for instance, J. J. C. Smart. The mental simply *is* the physical. Sensations, for example, simply are brain processes, pains simply are c-fiber firings, and so for daydreams, sudden insights, pangs of regret, mental calculations, introspective observation, and all the varied aspects of our conscious mental life: all can be identified with physical occurrences. This view occasioned puzzlement. "My first inclination, when I began to think on this topic," wrote Norman Malcolm, "was to believe that Smart's view is false—that a sudden thought certainly is not a brain process. But now I think that I do not know what it *means* to say that a sudden thought is a brain process."[43] Subsequently, various refinements have clarified and sharpened the mind-body identity thesis. A shift has occurred, for example, from type-type identities (e.g., of pains in general with c-fiber firings) to token-token identities (e.g., of this pain with this c-fiber firing). Still, problems of meaning remain. "It is here," writes John Foster, "that we encounter the most fundamental issue. Can we really make sense of the psychophysical identities which the theorist is postulating?"[44] Many, myself included, are inclined to answer with E. J. Lowe: "Unless . . . mental typology and physiological typology can be shown to be capable of being appropriately matched, the proposal that one might ('barely,' as it were) *identify* particulars of the relevant types (mental and physical) is devoid of determinate sense; and in the absence of the required arguments, such an 'identity theory' of mind and brain amounts to nothing more than an empty gesture, which may give emotional satisfaction to the committed materialist but has no intellectual substance to it."[45]

---

[42] Russell, *Why I Am Not a Christian*, 51.

[43] Malcolm, "Scientific Materialism," 171-72 (Malcolm's emphasis).

[44] Foster, "The Token-Identity Thesis," 300.

[45] Lowe, *Kinds of Being*, 114. Cf. Margolis, "Difficulties," 217; Nagel, "What Is It Like?," 166 ("we have at present no conception of what an explanation of the physical nature of a mental phenomenon would be"); C. J. F. Williams, *What Is Identity?*, viii

By way of comparison, what would it mean to say that love and truth are identical, as one writer has suggested?[46] The terms "love" and "truth" are not synonymous. Not all instances of love appear to be instances of truth or vice versa. If, nonetheless, the claim were advanced that all instances of the one are in fact instances of the other since, deep down, love and truth are identical, the chief problem for the theory would be one not of verification but of meaning. "But surely," the identity theorist might object, "you know what is meant by saying that the Morning Star is identical with the Evening Star, or that George W. Bush is identical with the President of the United States. Well, just the same relationship is being asserted here." That answer works no better for mind and body than it does for love and truth. The most one might say for the asserted identity is that it involves no evident contradiction. However, neither is its freedom from hidden contradiction at all evident. We know that a star which appears in the morning may be the same star as one which appears in the evening. We know that a person named Bush may be the same person as the person elected president. But we have no assurance that the strict identity of mind and body, or of mental events with bodily events, is a genuine possibility. And if the identity is not strict—if it is not the identity of one thing with itself but of one thing with another—what relevance does it have for the question of survival?

Some philosophers have found in psychophysical "supervenience" an attractive alternative to the reductionism of identity theories. In this alternate view, the physical is not identical with the mental but it does fully determine the mental. "Such supervenience," Donald Davidson suggests, "might be taken to mean that there cannot be two events alike in all physical respects but differing in some mental respect, or that an object cannot alter in some mental respect without altering in some physical respect."[47] One might add that in this view, when the physical alters radically the mental also alters radically. If the body disintegrates at death, so too does the person. The implications for survival look as negative as in identity theories.[48]

To assess this new challenge, let us consider with Jaegwon Kim the "strong supervenience" which he formulates as follows:

Mental properties *supervene* on physical properties, in that necessarily, for any mental property M, if anything has M at time t, there exists a physical base (or subvenient)

another chapter which argues that the attempts of certain philosophers of mind to assert identity between mental events and physical events in the brain fail, not merely to attain truth, but to be intelligible").

[46] Cf. Ebeling, *Introduction*, 179-80.

[47] Davidson, *Essays on Actions and Events*, 214.

[48] The same implications are equally clear for the type of "holism" David Myers proposes which, like supervenience, strikes a middle position between dualism and reductionism: "There is a third approach which respects the integrity of both physical and mental explanations without presuming these refer to separate events. By this holistic view, there are two ways of talking about a single event: brain-talk and mind-talk" (*The Human Puzzle*, 67).

property *P* such that it has *P* at *t*, and necessarily anything that has *P* at a time has *M* at that time.[49]

"For example," Kim explains, "if a person experiences pain, it must be the case that that person instantiates some physical property (presumably, a complex neural property) such that whenever anyone instantiates this physical property, she must experience pain." As Kim recognizes, the key question here concerns the nature of this "must." In his strong-supervenience formula, how should the recurring term "necessarily" be understood?

Kim replies noncommittally: "The modal force of necessity involved is a parameter to be fixed to suit one's view of the mind-body relation; some may go for metaphysical or even logical/conceptual necessity, while others will settle for nomological necessity."[50] Of these three alternatives, logical/conceptual necessity seems the least plausible: pain, for example, is not tied by definition to this or that configuration of neurons. It is not contradictory to suppose that the pain might exist without the configuration. Nomological necessity, amounting to constant covariance of the physical and the mental, is more plausible but poses little problem for survival: what holds, contingently, in this world need not hold in another. As the moon's movements might continue without correlated movements of Earth's tides (the oceans, for example, having dried up), so mental life might continue without correlated neural events (the body, for example, having disintegrated). The nature of the third possibility—"metaphysical" necessity, distinct from the conceptual and nomological—is seldom made clear. Here it looks like a mere stab in the dark: as mathematicians, say, established mathematically that an angle cannot be trisected using only ruler and compass, so metaphysicians might establish metaphysically (that is, in some other, unspecified manner besides the logical, conceptual, mathematical, or scientific) that the mental cannot exist apart from the physical. In post-Kantian, post-Wittgensteinian times, the prospects of such a demonstration appear slim, and no one has in fact come close to pulling it off. We are still far from having established correlations precise and complete enough to provide the physical term for any such necessity relation. And we have no idea how, if we uncovered such de facto correlations, we could go farther and demonstrate their more-than-natural necessity. As Hume sufficiently demonstrated, we cannot do that for any temporal correlations, however precise or familiar. Indeed, we have no idea how we might even try.

And yet, as CRS allows leeway for survival surmises, so it also allows leeway for opposed metaphysical surmises. Without having demonstrated the more-than-conceptual, more-than-nomological impossibility of trisecting the angle, or knowing what such a demonstration might look like, mathematicians could meaningfully envisage such an impossibility. Similarly, without having demonstrated a more-than-conceptual, more-than-nomological bond between the mental and the physical, or knowing what such a demonstration might look like, metaphysicians may

---

[49] Kim, *Mind in a Physical World*, 9.

[50] Ibid., 10.

meaningfully envisage such a bond. Thus, at the point now reached, mystery meets mystery and the two converge. How, in reality, might a person conceivably survive the death of the body? What, in reality, might render personal survival impossible even for God to accomplish? The answers to these queries lie concealed within the same human depths, and nothing better reveals the mystery of those depths than the effort to answer these two questions.

According to Charles Taliaferro, the mystery does not lie as deep on one side as the other. Spiritual survival, he argues, is not conceivable merely in the weak sense that we spot no contradiction in the hypothesis, but in a stronger sense. Thus, as "I can strongly conceive of certain states of affairs like there being a hundred blue balls on a beach,"[51] so:

> In the dualist modal thought experiment I imagine existing disembodied or switching bodies, and this involves imagining that something is present and that something is absent. I am present and my former body is not, or at least it has ceased being my body and has become a corpse, for example. . . . To imagine such a state of affairs is to imagine something positive, clear, and determinate, and one which we can specify in terms that exclude the presence of my former body.[52]

Yes, and to imagine (with Richard Gale) a machine that will "wash, dry, and iron clothes without the need for either water or any power source"[53] is to imagine something still more "positive, clear, and determinate," yet such definiteness says nothing for the genuine possibility of such a contrivance. Of itself, definiteness tells neither for nor against possibility.

To resolve the impasse brought on by our ignorance, reductionists such as Smart cite the principle of economy: what we need not postulate, we should not postulate; so we should not suppose that the mental adds anything to the physical. To counter this argument, anti-reductionists might note where the same principle would lead if applied, for example, to the equally deep mystery of the relation between sensations and physical objects. There, too, close correlation and dependence seem evident, and theories cover an equally wide range, from naive realism at one extreme to phenomenalism and Berkeleyan idealism at the other. Why complicate reality and suppose physical objects in addition to sensory experience? Or, to sharpen the objection, consider love and truth: does the principle of economy demand or justify their identification, on the ground that, regardless of contrary appearances, whenever multiplicity is not logically required it should be denied? Surely not. But mind-body identity conflicts as strongly with appearances as does love-truth identity—so strongly that we can give no intelligible content to the

---

[51] Taliaferro, *Consciousness*, 137.

[52] Ibid., 213.

[53] Gale, "Some Difficulties," 211. The viewpoint I am critiquing here, as earlier, surfaces clearly in Gale's comments on this far-fetched hypothesis. Of a man who confesses his ignorance as to how such a machine might be designed, he remarks: "His only problem is that he is not omnipotent" (ibid.). If we see no contradiction in the proposal, how can God have any difficulty with it?

hypothesis. In both instances, the best that might be said for Ockamist reduction is that no evident contradiction clearly precludes it. As a further argument against mind-body reduction, Christians and others might cite religious reasons for believing in an afterlife—provided that, as it seems, that belief does require some sort of real distinction between the mental and the physical.

Nowadays, believers in an afterlife are likely also to cite empirical evidence of various kinds suggesting the independence of the mental from the physical and hence their real distinction. Hick, for instance, has written: "The proper conclusion would seem to be that it is extremely probable that telepathy is psychologically rather than physically based, and involves a direct connection of some kind between mind and mind. If so, it is incompatible with those theories which regard the mind as epiphenomenal to the functioning of the brain."[54] Many near-death experiences beget a similar impression. Of these, John Cooper distinguishes two varieties: "those which involve perception of this world from a location other than the body; and those which claim experience of something trans-worldly."[55] Of the latter he writes:

> I recently learned of a case in which a man who had a near-fatal heart attack not only underwent the standard experience but was greeted by an acquaintance of his who appeared in bodily form, wearing clothing. After this brief meeting he was told he must return and was drawn back into his body. Later he regained normal consciousness and related his experience. What is so striking about this case is that the acquaintance whom he met had died twenty-four hours previously over two thousand miles away. His death was unknown to the heart-attack victim until two months later. Many other accounts similarly report meeting persons whose deaths were unknown to the reporter. On the other hand, subjects do not report meeting people in this sort of experience who have not died.[56]

Cooper illustrates the other type of experience (out-of-body perception) with an equally striking example:

> I know of a case in which a person in a coma near death experienced himself as leaving his body and moving to another room in the hospital where he observed several relatives in prayer for him. Later he emerged from the coma and reported that experience to those relatives with great detail and accuracy, including the wording of the prayers and the arrival of the pastor. This case is typical of many in the literature.[57]

Often, the "out-of-body" experience focuses on the person's own body and its surroundings. For example, it is reported that a woman who had been blind for 50 years was able to describe the instruments that were used in her resuscitation

---

[54] Hick, *Death and Eternal Life*, 126. See Badham, *Christian Beliefs*, 113-22.

[55] Cooper, *Body, Soul, and Life Everlasting*, 232.

[56] Ibid., 234.

[57] Ibid., 232-33.

following a heart attack—right down to their colors.[58] Michael Sabom has studied a number of similar accounts, carefully and systematically, and found them to be far more accurate and specific than prior acquaintance with pertinent CPR procedures could account for.[59]

The evidence, then, is substantial, but what does it indicate? "If it is possible," writes Paul Badham, "to present good grounds for believing that consciousness can function apart from the body before death, then it is intelligible to argue that consciousness might function apart from the body after death."[60] In support of the premise and conclusion of this argument, one might ask: How, with eyes closed, no heartbeat, and sometimes perhaps not even brain activity, could the body have any part in veridical perceptions such as those Sabom and others report? However, an equally good question would be: How might an out-of-the-body observer, deprived of sensory input, perceive people, places, and the rest? What would the light waves strike? How would their input be processed? To none of these questions, on either side, do we have any response. We are plunged once more into mystery.

And yet, such experiences have significance, if only for their effect on our vision. Subtly, profoundly, the spectacles through which we view reality—the methods, the questions, the preoccupations, the foci of inquiry—shape our conception of reality.[61] For those immersed in a scientific culture, an afterlife not subject to the laws of science may therefore appear unreal, far-fetched, out of the question. For those who have had out-of-body experiences or who have learned about them, such an afterlife is not out of the question. They sense that there is much that science cannot at present explain and that it is not likely to explain any time soon. And with this realization, their cognitive, cultural spectacles cease to be cognitive blinders.

In addition, near-death experiences have relevance for the existential question which I have postponed until related semantic and ontological issues were addressed. Semantically, CRS allows much stretching; but the more stretching it allows, the less relevant it may appear for real-life concerns. If, for instance, a replica is made of me after my decease, then CRS may possibly countenance calling that replica me—provided no second or third replica of equal perfection is made of me. But if that is all "my" survival amounts to, how does it concern me? A dying person asks:

> If I am told that tomorrow though I will be dead, someone else that looks and sounds and thinks just like me will be alive, would that be comforting? Could I correctly *anticipate* having her experiences? Would it make sense for me to fear her pains and

---

[58] P. Perry, "Brushes with Death," 17. Cf. Badham and Badham, *Immortality or Extinction?*, 74-75, for other striking examples.

[59] Sabom, *Recollections of Death*, 113-14. For a more comprehensive survey of such evidence, see Wilson, *The After Death Experience*, chapters nine and ten.

[60] Badham and Badham, *Immortality or Extinction?*, 14.

[61] Hallett, *A Middle Way to God*, 30-34.

look forward to her pleasures? Would it be right for her to feel remorse at the harsh way I am treating you?[62]

Again, ontologically there may be depths to my being which neither identity nor supervenience nor variant theories capture; but if the certain something not reducible to my body is not the whole of me, and if, furthermore, its nature remains mysterious, what relevance does it have for meaningful survival? Now, near-death experiences, if accepted as veridical, tend to allay such misgivings. Here are actual experiences, of the same "I" as the one who reports them in the first person and often of a kind the person might willingly continue or resume. If such things are possible after death, meaningful life after death is possible. But nothing demonstrates their impossibility—certainly not surmises that perhaps, in some unimaginable manner, the inert body observed in autoscopic experience might be the necessary, irreplaceable instrument of such observation as well as its object.

Dimensions of Mystery

The preceding review illustrates again my intention, stated in Chapter 1, more to locate mystery than to clarify it. We should not expect to discover yes or no answers to borderline instances of personal identity. We should not expect to discern any essence expressed by the pronoun "I." We should not expect to establish any exact, binding relationship between mind and body. All such efforts are doomed to failure. Does it follow, then, that a priori reflection imposes no limits on the reading of Scripture? Are all three of the conceptions of resurrection cited at the start equally available from a philosophical point of view, and must careful exegesis alone decide between them (if it can)? Let us review these conceptions in light of the foregoing discussions.

Simple Resuscitation. Concerning this notion I suggested that problems arise both about the interim period before the soul rejoins the body and about the subsequent reunion of the soul with the "same" body. How, I first inquired, does the person survive if only the soul survives before its reunion with the body? I have now suggested that neither semantics nor ontology precludes the meaningful survival of a nonphysical subject not identical with my whole present self yet not situated beyond the extended, CRS reach of the personal pronoun "I." Such a subject (which near-death and kindred experiences stimulate us to imagine and our ontological ignorance permits us to surmise) CRS might permit us to label the "same person." Call this interim reality the "soul" and no harm need be done, provided that the term is understood with its early indefiniteness and not, for example, as constituting the whole self or in specifically hylomorphic fashion. What, however, of the risen body with which the soul reunites? In Jesus' case, a two- or three-day interval might cause no serious problems for the body's sameness, but what about us? CRS would not endorse calling a replica body the

---

[62] J. Perry, "A Dialogue," 322.

"same body" (established word-usage would give the nod to "different" over "same"), yet short of a replica body it is difficult to conceive, realistically, what the body's sameness might consist in.

Still, let us try. At the general resurrection, we can hypothesize, God gathers all and only those atoms or subatomic particles which constituted a given human body at the moment of the soul's departure and reconstitutes the person as existing at that moment. Some atoms may have disintegrated or may have passed through successive individuals, but if the majority are recovered and relatively few are replaced, the resulting body may be as identical with the earlier body as that body was with the same person's body a day, a month, or a year before the person's death. Save for continuity. Yes, there may be the rub. If I disassemble a car or a bike, then put it back together again, it is the same car or bike, reassembled. But if a plant died and a hundred years later I tracked down the particles that composed it and somehow reassembled them as a perfectly similar plant, would that be the same plant? To this question, our conventions, even aided by CRS, furnish no clear reply. And the like holds for human bodies. Once, however, we indulge such far-fetched imaginings, we realize that atom-by-atom or particle-by-particle identity really does not concern us. We do not know and do not care what particular items compose us at any given moment or will in the future. One hydrogen atom, one proton or electron or quark, is as good as another. Clearly, the Council of Toledo envisaged no such identity when it insisted that we shall rise "in this very body in which we live and are and move."

Neither, naturally, did earlier generations consider where—in what heaven or distant galaxy—the identical physical particles might be transported and still retain their identity. A transfer of a few miles, up above the clouds, would raise no evident problems, but that nearby heaven is no longer available. Locate heaven in some distant galaxy, and eons of space travel might be needed to preserve the particles' continuity and thereby their identity. Locate heaven in some other universe, discontinuous with this one, and eons of travel could not reach it, and the discontinuity of the universes would assure the discontinuity of the particles present in one then in the other. The ones in the other universe could at best replicate those in this universe. Or so it seems.

Actually, such speculation takes us beyond our depth. To illustrate our inca-pacity, imagine that somewhere on earth there existed what might be a termed an "umbilical point" between this world and another. Once we discovered it, we would find that whoever stood on that spot disappeared in this world and appeared in another: such would be the person's experience and the experience of those who witnessed the person's disappearance here and appearance there. If that other world had a similar spot, travel back and forth would be feasible and people would take for granted the possibility of existing in both worlds with the "same body." To be sure, these suggestions sound absurd, fantastic, and contrary to all the laws of nature. However, the "laws of nature" are mere regularities for which we have no ultimate explanation, and the situation I have suggested would be equally regular. So would countless variants. We are not equipped to dictate how things must be in this or any other universe. Let us pass on, then, without entirely excluding some form of resuscitation—at least not on philosophical (much less scientific) grounds.

Replication. As Badham observes, "The doctrine of man on which Hick's theory is based is not the old patristic one that a man is his present component particles [plus his soul] but on more sophisticated theories of what it means to be a person, such as theories of 'somatic identity,' 'form,' 'substance,' 'organising principle' or 'pattern capable of being coded.'"[63] However, the term "replica" is well chosen for Hick's conception, and a replica is not identical with the thing it replicates—not in familiar parlance. So it is doubtful that CRS countenances calling a replica person the same person. Even if it did, such semantic stretching would do little to reassure us concerning the reality of our own and others' survival. An adequate response to both semantic and existential worries, it seems, would be to postulate bodily replication but mental or spiritual continuity. Many accounts of near-death experiences suggest something of the sort. In them, people recount what they experienced, without psychological break, in another world before returning to their earthly body. And they freely employ the pronoun "I" for all they have experienced, with no more concern for criteria of identity than in their everyday employment of the same term ("I hope," "I remember," "I see," etc.). Yet they say little about their other-world body. Sometimes they report "walking," "standing," or "sitting,"[64] but what sort of body did the walking, standing, or sitting—whether a perfect replica or glorified surrogate—they do not specify. Thus the same comparison with near-death experiences might apply equally well, or better, to the third conception of resurrection.

Glorification. This third perspective usually takes spiritual continuity for granted and focuses on the resurrection of the body. It envisages the body as the same but glorified—so glorified that its sameness appears problematic. Replication would not yield a "spiritual," "imperishable" body such as Paul describes. Neither would retention of the identical atomic or subatomic particles, subject to the laws of terrestrial physics. As a solution we might suggest that the sameness of the body comes from the sameness of the person, and the sameness of the person from spiritual continuity. Or we might simply ignore whether the body is the same, provided it is ours and is as described. True, when Paul writes, "It is sown a physical body, it is raised a spiritual body," the pronoun's referent does not alter from one clause to the other. The same body is first physical then spiritual. However, Paul also writes, "We will not all die, but we will all be changed . . . . For the trumpet will sound, and the dead will be raised imperishable, and we will be changed. For this perishable body must put on imperishability, and this mortal body must put on immortality" (1 Cor: 51-52). The ease with which Paul shifts

---

[63] Badham, *Christian Beliefs*, 76.

[64] Sabom, *Recollections of Death*, 40 ("I was walking up some steps"), 45 ("I was standing on something high"), 48 ("I was sitting up there").

from the "body" to "we," "the dead," and back again suggests that we should not read too precise a metaphysics into his visionary sayings.

As for my own metaphysics, in treating all three alternatives I have relied explicitly or implicitly on the sort of "holistic dualism" sketched above: dualistic because it recognizes something besides the body, holistic because it does not equate that something with the whole presently existing individual.[65] I have not established such a position philosophically nor defined it more precisely. I have not, for example, furnished criteria of identity for the nonbodily aspect of a person or for a person so constituted, but have relied on CRS to establish both personhood and identity (while questioning the existential significance of such verbal determinations). Instead, I have merely argued the availability of such a perspective: if it is needed to make sense of Christian belief in life to come, then Scripture and Christian tradition back it, theologically. That it is thus needed, or indispensable, I shall not attempt to demonstrate. The human mystery is too profound and the pertinent terms are too flexible for that to be feasible. But this at least can be said: all three conceptions of resurrected life face fewer difficulties with such dualism than without it.

Cooper has also argued, persuasively, that some form of holistic dualism is most consistent with biblical anthropology. On the one hand, he observes, a radical split between soul and body is not to be found in the Old Testament or the New. On the other hand, nonbodily survival appears in both. It seems clear, for example, that Paul did not envisage his immediate resurrection when he expressed his desire to depart and be with Christ (Phil. 1:21-24). And, "In spite of variations of language and detail . . ., Paul teaches the same general personal eschatology as the rest of the New Testament. There is fellowship with Christ during the interval between bodily death and the general future resurrection."[66] For Cooper, "The implication of this result for the monism-dualism debate about biblical anthropology is decisive . . . If the biblical view of the afterlife includes personal existence apart from the body . . . then some sort of anthropological dichotomy or dualism is entailed."[67]

Holistic dualism can take varied forms and is compatible with varied conceptions of resurrection. Here, I have not attempted to analyze "what no eye has seen, nor ear heard, nor the human heart conceived, what God has prepared for those who love him" (1 Cor 2:9). As I opted for no single, precise analysis of the hypostatic union, the Trinity, Eucharistic presence, doctrinal identity, or ecclesial identity, so I have proposed no single, precise analysis of risen life. For, with respect to themes of faith such as those here reviewed, my attitude resembles Henri

---

[65] It therefore differs from the sort of "integrative dualism" which views "the *person* and body as profoundly unified, while still remaining metaphysically distinct" (Taliaferro, *Consciousness*, 115, emphasis added) or the "radical dualism" which "holds that the mind is an autonomous entity in nature which uses the brain both to gain knowledge of the external world and to execute its intentions" (Beloff, "Dualism," 167).

[66] Cooper, *Body, Soul, and Life Everlasting*, 171-72.

[67] Ibid., 172, 173.

Bouillard's: "To suppose that theology's role is to convert confused notions into distinct ones is, whatever the intention, to subordinate revelation to theology, for it makes the word of God a confused knowledge that theology has to clarify."[68] A bright glow illumining existence: such is the light of faith. A flickering candle in the dark: such is the mind that seeks to grasp, define, or articulate the mysteries of faith. A Cartesian, enamored of clear, distinct ideas, might have problems with this contrast. And yet, as Wittgenstein remarked, we should not suppose that the light a lamp casts is no real light at all because it has no sharp boundary.[69]

Rahner has characterized theology as "the conscious and methodical explanation and explication of the divine revelation received and grasped in faith."[70] Not just explanation, not just explication, but explanation *and* explication—thorough, systematic, profound. Reading Rahner's words, I am reminded of a diverting passage in Kierkegaard's *Concluding Unscientific Postscript*.[71] The pseudonymous author, Johannes Climacus, is lounging in the Frederiksberg Garden, wondering how any-thing can be made easier than the systematizers of thought have already made it. Then the inspiration comes to him: he will make things harder! Now, such has not been precisely my intention here, and yet, chapter by chapter, theme by theme, I have found that questions of identity have led straightway into mystery. In what sense is Jesus identical with God or with the Second Person of the Trinity? In what sense, if any, can each divine Person be identified as God? In what sense is the Eucharist the body and blood of Christ? In what sense is Trent's eucharistic teaching, for example, identical with that of the Apostles? What contemporary church or constellation of churches is identical, in what sense, with the church of the Apostles? How is the risen Christ identical with the crucified Christ, and how, in their turn, are citizens of heaven identical with antecedent citizens of earth? Such queries, as here pursued, have highlighted the limits of theology as "conscious and methodical explanation and explication." Perhaps different questions, differently pursued, would permit deeper penetration into these same mysteries. Yet how might that happen if this study's queries, framed in terms of identity, are as legitimate and pertinent as they appear to be—if here too, as in the realms Wittgenstein explored, identity "hangs directly together with the most important questions"?

---

[68] Bouillard, "Notions conciliaires," 266. My attitude differs with regard to moral matters—for example, the general norm of Christian objective morality (Hallett, *Greater Good*) or Christian priorities relating self and others (Hallett, *Christian Neighbor-Love*) or relating various classes of others (Hallett, *Priorities and Christian Ethics*).

[69] Wittgenstein, *The Blue and Brown Books*, 27.

[70] Quoted in O'Collins, *Fundamental Theology*, 1, without reference.

[71] Kierkegaard, *Concluding Unscientific Postscript*, 164-66.

References

Abbott, Walter M., ed. *The Documents of Vatican II*. New York: Guild Press, America Press, and Association Press, 1966.

Adelman of Liège. *De eucharistiae sacramento ad Berengarium epistola*. PL 143: 1289-96.

Alger of Liège. *De sacramentis coproris et sanguinis dominici*. PL 180: 739-854.

Anderson, Norman. *The Mystery of the Incarnation*. Downers Grove, Ill.: Inter-Varsity, 1978.

Ante-Nicene Fathers: The Writings of the Fathers down to A.D. 325. Ed. Alexander Roberts and James Donaldson. 1885-87. 10 vol.s. Peabody, Mass.: Hendrickson, 1994.

The Apostolic Fathers. Vol. 1. Trans. Kirsopp Lake. Loeb Classical Library. Cambridge, Mass.: Harvard University Press; London: Heinemann, 1975.

Baciocchi, J. de. "Le mystère eucharistique dans les perspectives de la Bible." *Nouvelle Revue Théologique* 77 (1955): 561-80.

Baciocchi, J. de. "Présence eucharistique et transsubstantiation." *Irenikon* 32 (1959): 139-61.

Badham, Paul. *Christian Beliefs about Life after Death*. New York: Harper & Row; London: Macmillan, 1976.

Badham, Paul. "The Meaning of the Doctrine of the Incarnation in Christian Thought." In *Christology: The Center and the Periphery*. Ed. Frank K. Flinn. New York: Paragon, 1989. 85-97.

Badham, Paul, and Linda Badham. *Immortality or Extinction?* Totowa, N.J.: Barnes & Noble, 1982.

Baillie, James. "Identity, Survival, and Sortal Concepts." *Philosophical Quarterly* 40 (1990): 183-94.

Bartel, Timothy W. "The Plight of the Relative Trinitarian." *Religious Studies* 24 (1988): 129-55.

Barth, Karl. *Church Dogmatics*. Vol. 1, pt. 1: *The Doctrine of the Word of God*. Trans. G. W. Bromiley. Edinburgh: T. & T. Clark, 1975.

Batiffol, Pierre. *L'Eucharistie: la présence réelle et la transsubstantiation*. 6th edn. Paris: Victor Lecoffre, 1913.

Baum, Gregory. Untitled contribution in Kirvan, *The Infallibility Debate*, 1-65.

Bellarmine, Robert. *De sacramento eucharistiae*. In Bellarmine, *Opera omnia*, vol. 3. Naples: J. Giuliano, 1857. 235-467.

Beloff, John. "Dualism: A Parapsychological Perspective." In Smythies and Beloff, *The Case for Dualism*, 167-85.

Berengar of Tours. *Purgatoria epistola contra Almannum*. In Montclos, *Lanfranc et Bérenger*, 531-38.

Berengar of Tours. *Rescriptum contra Lanfrannum*. Corpus Christianorum. Continuatio Mediaevalis, 84. Turnhout: Brepols, 1988.

Bethune-Baker, J. F. *Nestorius and His Teaching: A Fresh Examination of the Evidence*. Cambridge, UK: Cambridge University Press, 1908.

Bettenson, Henry, ed. *Documents of the Christian Church*. 2nd edn. London: Oxford University Press, 1967.

Betz, Johannes. *Die Eucharistie in der Zeit der griechischen Väter.* Vol. 2/1. Freiburg: Herder, 1964.

Bindley, T. Herbert. *The Oecumenical Documents of the Faith.* 4th edn. Revised by F. W. Green. Westport, Conn.: Greenwood, 1980.

Blackwell, Richard J. *Galileo, Bellarmine, and the Bible.* Notre Dame, Ind.: University of Notre Dame Press, 1991.

Bobrinskoy, Boris. *The Mystery of the Trinity: Trinitarian Experience and Vision in the Biblical and Patristic Tradition.* Crestwood, N.Y.: St. Vladimir's Seminary Press, 1999.

Boff, Leonardo. *Trinity and Society.* Trans. Paul Burns. Maryknoll, N.Y.: Orbis, 1988.

Boismard, M. E. *St. John's Prologue.* Trans. Carisbrooke Dominicans. Westminster, Md.: Newman, 1957.

Bonhoeffer, Dietrich. *Christ the Center.* Trans. Edwin H. Robertson. New York: Harper & Row, 1978.

Bordoni, Marcello. *Gesù di Nazaret: Signore e Cristo.* Vol. 3: *Il Cristo annunciato dalla Chiesa.* Rome: Herder and Università Lateranense, 1986.

Borowski, E. J. "Identity and Personal Identity." *Mind* 85 (1976): 481-502.

Bouillard, Henri. "Notions conciliaires et analogie de la vérité." *Recherches de science religieuse* 35 (1948): 251-71.

Bouyer, Louis. "Réflexions sur le rétablissement possible de la communion entre les Églises orthodoxe et catholique: Perspectives actuelles." *Istina* 20 (1975): 112-15.

Bouyer, Louis. *The Church of God: Body of Christ and Temple of the Spirit.* Trans. Charles Underhill Quinn. Chicago: Franciscan Herald Press, 1982.

Bracken, Joseph A. "The Holy Trinity as a Community of Persons," I and II. *Heythrop Journal* 15 (1974): 166-82, 257-70.

Bracken, Joseph A. *The Triune Symbol: Persons, Process and Community.* Lanham, Md.: University Press of America, 1985.

Brodie, Thomas L. *The Gospel according to John: A Literary and Theological Commentary.* New York: Oxford University Press, 1993.

Brosseder, Johannes. "Towards What Unity of the Churches?" Trans. John Bowden. In *The Church in Fragments: Towards What Kind of Unity?* Ed. Giuseppe Ruggieri and Miklós Tomka. Maryknoll: Orbis; London: SCM, 1997. 130-38.

Brown, David. *The Divine Trinity.* La Salle, Ill.: Open Court; London: Duckworth, 1985.

Brown, David. "Wittgenstein against the 'Wittgensteinians': A Reply to Kenneth Surin on *The Divine Trinity.*" *Modern Theology* 2 (1985-1986): 257-76.

Brown, David. "Trinitarian Personhood and Individuality." In Feenstra and Plantinga, *Trinity, Incarnation, and Atonement,* 48-78.

Brown, Harold O. J. *Heresies: The Image of Christ in the Mirror of Heresy and Orthodoxy from the Apostles to the Present.* Garden City, N.Y.: Doubleday, 1984.

Brown, Raymond E. "Does the New Testament Call Jesus God?" *Theological Studies* 26 (1965): 545-73.

Brown, Raymond E. *The Gospel According to John.* 2 vols. Garden City, N.Y.: Doubleday, 1966.

Brown, Raymond E. *Jesus God and Man: Modern Biblical Reflections.* Milwaukee: Bruce, 1967.

Brown, Raymond E. *An Introduction to New Testament Christology.* New York: Paulist, 1994.

Bruner, Frederick Dale. *Matthew.* 2 vols. Dallas: Word, 1987, 1990.

Brunner, Emil. *The Christian Doctrine of God. Dogmatics.* Vol. 1. Trans. Olive Wyon. London: Lutterworth, 1949.

Bultmann, Rudolf. *Essays Philosophical and Theological.* Trans. James C. G. Greig. New York: Macmillan; London: SCM, 1955.

Cain, James. "The Doctrine of the Trinity and the Logic of Relative Identity." *Religious Studies* 25 (1989): 141-52.

Carson, D. A. *The Gospel according to John.* Grand Rapids, Mich.: W. B. Eerdmans; Leicester, England: Inter-Varsity, 1991

Carnap, Rudolf. *The Logical Structure of the World: Pseudoproblems in Philosophy.* Trans. Rolf A. George. Berkeley: University of California Press, 1967.

Carnley, Peter. *The Structure of Resurrection Belief.* Oxford: Clarendon, 1987.

Cartwright, Richard. "On the Logical Problem of the Trinity." In Cartwright, *Philosophical Essays.* Cambridge, Mass.: MIT Press, 1987. 187-200.

Cerfaux, Lucien. *La théologie de l'Église suivant saint Paul.* 2nd edn. Paris: Cerf, 1948.

Chadwick, Owen. *From Bossuet to Newman.* 2nd edn. Cambridge, UK: Cambridge University Press, 1987.

Charfi, Abdelmajid. "Christianity in the Qur'an Commentary of Tabarī." *Islamochristiana* 6 (1980): 105-48.

The Church Teaches: Documents of the Church in English Translation. Trans. John F. Clarkson, John H. Edwards, William J. Kelly, and John J. Welch. Rockford, Ill.: Tan Books, 1973.

Clarke, Adam. *A Discourse on the Nature, Institution, and Design of the Holy Eucharist.* 2nd edn. London: printed for the author, 1814.

Coburn, Robert C. "Personal Identity Revisited." *Canadian Journal of Philosophy* 15 (1985): 379-403.

Cohen, L. Jonathan. *The Dialogue of Reason: An Analysis of Analytical Philosophy.* Oxford: Clarendon, 1986.

Cohn-Sherbok, Dan. "Between Christian and Jew." *Theology* 83 (1980): 91-97.

Concilium Tridentinum diariorum actorum epistularum tractatuum nova collectio. Ed. Görresgesellschaft. Vol. 7 (Part 4, vol. 1). Freiburg: Herder, 1961.

Congar, Yves. "*Lutherana*: Théologie de l'eucharistie et christologie chez Luther." *Revue des sciences philosophiques et théologiques* 66 (1982): 169-97.

Congar, Yves. *Diversity and Communion.* Trans. John Bowden. London: SCM, 1984.

Congregation for the Doctrine of the Faith. *Mysterium Ecclesiae. Acta Apostolicae Sedis* 65 (1973): 396-408.

Cooper, John W. *Body, Soul, and Life Everlasting: Biblical Anthropology and the Monism-Dualism Debate.* Grand Rapids, Mich.: Eerdmans, 1989.

Crabtree, Arthur B. "The Eucharist in Baptist Life and Thought." In Swidler, *The Eucharist in Ecumenical Dialogue*, 106-13.

Craig, Clarence T. "The Church of the New Testament." In *Man's Disorder and God's Design: The Amsterdam Assembly Series*, vol. 1. New York: Harper & Brothers, 1948. 31-42.

Cranmer, Thomas. *A Defence of the True and Catholic Doctrine of the Sacrament of the Body and Blood of Our Saviour Christ.* 1550. London: Chas. J. Thynne, 1907.

Creed, John Martin. "Recent Tendencies in English Christology." In *Mysterium Christi: Christological Studies by British and German Theologians.* Ed. G. K. A. Bell and D. Adolf Deissmann. London: Longmans, Green, 1930. 123-40.

Creed, John Martin. *The Divinity of Jesus Christ: A Study in the History of Christian Doctrine since Kant.* Cambridge, UK: Cambridge University Press, 1938.

Cullmann, Oscar. *The Christology of the New Testament.* Revised edn. Trans. Shirley C. Guthrie and Charles A. M. Hall. Philadelphia: Westminster, 1963.

Cunningham, David S. *These Three Are One: The Practice of Trinitarian Theology.* Oxford: Blackwell, 1998.

Cupitt, Don. "The Finality of Christ." *Theology* 78 (1975): 618-28.

Cupitt, Don. "Jesus and the Meaning of 'God.'" In Goulder, *Incarnation and Myth,* 31-40.

Davidson, Donald. *Essays on Actions and Events.* Oxford: Clarendon, 1980.

Davis, Charles. "Understanding the Real Presence." In *The Word in History: The St. Xavier Symposium.* Ed. T. Patrick Burke. New York: Sheed and Ward, 1966. 154-78.

Davis, Stephen T. *Logic and the Nature of God.* London: Macmillan, 1983.

Davis, Stephen T., Daniel Kendall, and Gerald O'Collins, eds. *The Trinity: An Interdisciplinary Symposium on the Trinity.* New York and Oxford: Oxford University Press, 1999.

Demarest, Bruce. *The Cross and Salvation.* Wheaton, Ill.: Crossway, 1997.

Denzinger, Henry. *The Sources of Catholic Dogma.* Trans. Roy J. Deferrari. St. Louis: B. Herder, 1957.

Dodd, C. H. *The Parables of the Kingdom.* Revised edn. New York: Charles Scribner's Sons, 1961.

Dodd, C. H. *The Interpretation of the Fourth Gospel.* Cambridge, UK: Cambridge University Press, 1968.

Donovan, Vincent J. *Christianity Rediscovered.* 2nd edn. Maryknoll, N.Y.: Orbis, 1982.

Dublanchy, E. "Église." DTC. Vol. 4/2, col. 2108-224.

Dulles, Avery. *The Survival of Dogma: Faith, Authority, and Dogma in a Changing World.* 2nd edn. New York: Crossroad, 1982.

Dulles, Avery. *Models of Revelation.* Garden City, N.Y.: Doubleday, 1983.

Dulles, Avery. *Models of the Church.* Garden City, N.Y.: Doubleday, 1987.

Dummett, Michael. "Frege, Gottlob." In *Encyclopedia of Philosophy.* Ed. Paul Edwards. Vol. 3. New York: Macmillan, 1967. 225-37.

Dunn, James D. G. *Christology in the Making: A New Testament Inquiry into the Origins of the Doctrine of the Incarnation.* 2nd edn. London: SCM, 1989.

Durrwell, F.-X. *L'Eucharistie, sacrement pascal.* Paris: Cerf, 1981.

Ebeling, Gerhard. *Introduction to a Theological Theory of Language.* Trans. R. A. Wilson. Philadelphia: Fortress, 1973.

Edwards, Denis. *What Are They Saying about Salvation?* New York: Paulist, 1986.

Egender, D. N. "Vers une doctrine eucharistique commune dans la théologie protestante d'Allemagne." *Irenikon* 32 (1959): 165-77.

Evans, C. Stephen. *The Historical Christ and the Jesus of Faith: The Incarnational Narrative as History.* Oxford: Clarendon, 1996.

Evans, Gareth. *The Varieties of Reference.* Ed. John McDowell. Oxford: Clarendon, 1982.

Falcon, Joseph. *La crédibilité du dogme catholique: apologétique scientifique.* 2nd edn. Lyons: Emmanuel Vitte, 1948.

Feenstra, Ronald J. "Reconsidering Kenotic Christology." In Feenstra and Plantinga, *Trinity, Incarnation, and Atonement,* 128-52.

Feenstra, Ronald J., and Cornelius Plantinga, Jr., eds. *Trinity, Incarnation, and Atonement: Philosophical Essays.* Notre Dame, Ind.: University of Notre Dame Press, 1989.

Feser, E. "Has Trinitarianism Been Shown to be Coherent?" *Faith and Philosophy* 14 (1997): 87-97.

Flew, Antony. "Immortality." In *Encyclopedia of Philosophy.* Ed. Paul Edwards. Vol. 4. New York: Macmillan, 1967. 139-50.

Flew, Antony. "'Personal Identity and Imagination': One Objection." *Philosophy* 60 (1985): 123-26.

Forrest, Peter. "Divine Fission: A New Way of Moderating Social Trinitarianism." *Religious Studies* 34 (1998): 281-97.

Foster, John. "The Token-Identity Thesis." In *The Mind-Body Problem: A Guide to the Current Debate*. Ed. Richard Warner and Tadeusz Szubka. Oxford: Blackwell, 1994. 299-310.

France, R. T. "The Worship of Jesus: A Neglected Factor in Christological Debate?" In Rowdon, *Christ the Lord*, 17-36.

Franklin, R. William, ed. *Anglican Orders: Essays on the Centenary of* Apostolicae Curae, *1896-1996*. London: Mowbray, 1996.

Franzelin, Johannes Baptist. *Tractatus de ss. eucharistiae sacramento et sacrificio*. 3rd edn. Rome: Propaganda Fide, 1878.

Fuller, Reginald H. and Pheme Perkins. *Who Is This Christ? Gospel Christology and Contem-porary Faith*. Philadelphia: Fortress, 1983.

Gale, Richard M. "Some Difficulties in Theistic Treatments of Evil." In *The Evidential Argument from Evil*. Ed. Daniel Howard-Snyder. Bloomington, Ind.: Indiana University Press, 1996. 206-18.

Galtier, Paul. *L'Unité du Christ: Être . . . Personne . . . Conscience*. Paris: Beauchesne, 1939.

Gardeil, A. *Le donné révélé et la théologie*. Paris: Gabalda, 1910.

Gaudoin-Parker, Michael L., ed. *The Real Presence through the Ages*. Staten Island, N.Y.: Alba House, 1993.

Geach, Peter. "Identity." *Review of Metaphysics* 21 (1967): 3-12.

Geach, Peter. *Logic Matters*. Berkeley and Los Angeles: University of California Press, 1972.

Geach, Peter, and G. E. M. Anscombe. *Three Philosophers*. Oxford: Basil Blackwell, 1963.

Geiselmann, Josef. *Die Eucharistielehre der Vorscholastik*. Paderborn: Ferdinand Schöningh, 1926.

Ghysens, G. "Présence réelle eucharistique et transsubstantiation dans les définitions de l'Église catholique." *Irenikon* 32 (1959): 420-35.

Godefroy, L. "Eucharistie d'après le Concile de Trente." DTC. Vol. 5/2, col. 1326-56.

Goergen, Donald J. *The Death and Resurrection of Jesus*. Wilmington, Del.: Michael Glazier, 1988.

Goergen, Donald J. *The Jesus of Christian History*. Collegeville, Minn.: Liturgical, 1992.

Goulder, Michael, ed. *Incarnation and Myth: The Debate Continued*. Grand Rapids, Mich.: Eerdmans, 1979.

Goulder, Michael. "Paradox and Mystification." In Goulder, *Incarnation and Myth*, 51-59.

Gregory of Nyssa. "An Address on Religious Instruction." In *Christology of the Later Fathers*. Ed. Edward R. Hardy. Philadelphia: Westminster, 1954. 268-325.

Grensted, L. W. *A Short History of the Doctrine of the Atonement*. Manchester: Manchester University Press, 1920.

Guitmond. *De corporis et sanguinis Christi veritate in eucharistia*. PL 149: 1427-94.

Hagner, Donald A. *Matthew 14-28*. Word Biblical Commentary, 33B. Dallas: Word Books, 1995.

Haight, Roger. *Jesus, Symbol of God*. Maryknoll, N.Y.: Orbis, 1999.

Hallett, Garth L. *Darkness and Light: The Analysis of Doctrinal Statements*. New York: Paulist, 1975.

Hallett, Garth L. *Christian Moral Reasoning: An Analytic Guide*. Notre Dame, Ind.: University of Notre Dame Press, 1983.

Hallett, Garth L. *Logic for the Labyrinth: A Guide to Critical Thinking*. Lanham, Md.: University Press of America, 1984.

Hallett, Garth L. *Language and Truth*. New Haven, Conn.: Yale University Press, 1988.

Hallett, Garth L. *Christian Neighbor-Love: An Assessment of Six Rival Versions*. Washington: Georgetown University Press, 1989.

Hallett, Garth L. *Essentialism: A Wittgensteinian Critique*. Albany, N.Y.: State University of New York Press, 1991.

Hallett, Garth L. *Greater Good: The Case for Proportionalism*. Washington, D.C.: Georgetown University Press, 1995.

Hallett, Garth L. *Priorities and Christian Ethics*. Cambridge, UK: Cambridge University Press, 1998.

Hallett, Garth L. *A Middle Way to God*. New York: Oxford University Press, 2000.

Hamell, P. J. "Modalism." In *New Catholic Encyclopedia*. Vol. 9. New York: McGraw-Hill, 1967. 988-89.

Hanson, Anthony Tyrrell. *Grace and Truth: A Study in the Doctrine of the Incarnation*. London: SPCK, 1975.

Hanson, R. P. C. *The Continuity of Christian Doctrine*. New York: Seabury, 1981.

Hanson, R. P. C. *The Search for the Christian Doctrine of God: The Arian Controversy, 318-381*. Edinburgh: T. & T. Clark, 1988.

Härle, Wilfrid. "Kirche VII: Dogmatisch." In *Theologische Realenzyklopädie*. Vol. 18. Berlin: Walter de Gruyter, 1988. 277-317.

Harris, Charles. *Creeds or No Creeds?: A Critical Examination of the Basis of Modernism*. New York: E. P. Dutton, 1922.

Harris, Henry, ed. *Identity: Essays Based on Herbert Spencer Lectures Given in the University of Oxford*. New York: Oxford University Press, 1995.

Harris, Murray J. *Jesus as God: The New Testament Use of Theos in Reference to Jesus*. Grand Rapids, Mich.: Baker, 1992.

Harvey, Anthony. "Christology and the Evidence of the New Testament." In *God Incarnate: Story and Belief*. Ed. A. E. Harvey. London: SPCK, 1981. 42-54.

Hasker, William. "Tri-Unity." *Journal of Religion* 50 (1970): 1-32.

Hay, David. *Religious Experience Today: Studying the Facts*. London: Mowbray, 1990.

Hebblethwaite, B. L. "Incarnation and Atonement: The Moral and Religious Value of the Incarnation." In Goulder, *Incarnation and Myth*, 87-100.

Hellwig, Monika K. *Jesus the Compassion of God: New Perspectives on the Tradition of Christianity*. Wilmington, Del.: Michael Glazier, 1983.

Helminiak, Daniel A. *The Same Jesus: A Contemporary Christology*. Chicago: Loyola University Press, 1986.

Henry, Carl F. H. *The Identity of Jesus of Nazareth*. Nashville, Tenn.: Broadman, 1992.

Herbert, R. T. *Paradox and Identity in Theology*. Ithaca, N.Y.: Cornell University Press, 1979.

Hick, John. *Death and Eternal Life*. New York: Harper & Row, 1976.

Hick, John., ed. *The Myth of God Incarnate*. London: SCM, 1977.

Hick, John. "Jesus and the World Religions." In Hick, *The Myth of God Incarnate*, 167-85.

Hick, John. "Incarnation and Atonement: Evil and Incarnation." In Goulder, *Incarnation and Myth*, 77-84.

Hick, John. "Islam and Christian Monotheism." In *Islam in a World of Diverse Faiths*. Ed. Dan Cohn-Sherbok. New York: St. Martin's, 1991. 1-17.

Hick, John. *The Metaphor of God Incarnate: Christology in a Pluralistic Age*. London: SCM, 1993.

Hick, John. *Disputed Questions in Theology and the Philosophy of Religion*. New Haven, Conn.: Yale University Press, 1993.

Higgins, A. J. B. *The Lord's Supper in the New Testament*. Chicago: Henry Regnery, 1952.

Hill, Brennan. *Jesus the Christ: Contemporary Perspectives*. Mystic, Conn.: Twenty-Third Publications, 1991.

Hill, William J. *The Three-Personed God: The Trinity as a Mystery of Salvation*. Washington, D.C.: The Catholic University of America Press, 1982.

Hodgson, Leonard. *The Doctrine of the Trinity*. London: Nisbet, 1943.

Hugh of Langres. *Tractatus de corpore et sanguine Christi*. PL 142, 1325-34.

Hünermann, Peter. *Jesus Christus, Gottes Wort in der Zeit: Eine systematische Christologie*. Münster: Aschendorff, 1994.

International Theological Commission. *Select Questions on Christology*. Washington, D.C.: United States Catholic Conference, 1980.

Inwagen, Peter van. "And Yet They Are Not Three Gods but One God." In *Philosophy and the Christian Faith*. Ed. Thomas V. Morris. Notre Dame, Ind.: University of Notre Dame Press, 1988. 241-78.

Inwagen, Peter van. *God, Knowledge, and Mystery: Essays in Philosophical Theology*. Ithaca, N.Y.: Cornell University Press, 1995.

Jedin, Hubert. *A History of the Council of Trent*. Trans. Ernest Graf. Vol. 2. London: Nelson, 1961.

Jeremias, Joachim. *The Parables of Jesus*. 2nd revised edn. New York: Charles Scribner's Sons, 1972.

Jeremias, Joachim. *The Eucharistic Words of Jesus*. Trans. Norman Perrin. Philadelphia: Fortress, 1977.

Jomier, Jacques. "Unité de Dieu, Chrétiens et Coran selon Fahr Al-Dīn Al-Rāzī." *Islamochristiana* 6 (1980): 149-77.

Jones, Paul H. *Christ's Eucharistic Presence: A History of the Doctrine*. New York: Peter Lang, 1994.

Jorissen, Hans. *Die Entfaltung der Transsubstantiationslehre bis zum Beginn der Hochscholastik*. Münster: Aschendorff, 1965.

Journet, Charles. *Esquisse du développement du dogme marial*. Paris: Alsatia, 1954.

Journet, Charles. *The Church of the Word Incarnate: An Essay in Speculative Theology*. Trans. A. H. C. Downes. Vol. 1: *The Apostolic Hierarchy*. London: Sheed & Ward, 1955.

Joyce, G. H. "Church, The." In *The Catholic Encyclopedia*. Vol. 3. New York: Robert Appleton, 1908. 744-61.

Kasper, Walter. *Jesus the Christ*. Trans. V. Green. New York: Paulist; London: Burns & Oates, 1977.

Kehl, Medard, "Ekklesiologische und christologische Überlegungen zur Theologie Küngs." In *Zur Sache: Theologische Streitfragen im "Fall Küng."* Ed. Ludwig Bertsch and Medard Kehl. Würzburg: Echter, 1980. 119-53.

Kelly, David. Review of *Looking for Mary*, by Beverly Donofrio. *New York Times Book Review*, August 13, 2000, 9.

Kelly, J. N. D. *Early Christian Doctrines*. 5th edn. San Francisco: Harper, 1978.

Kenny, Anthony. *Reason and Religion: Essays in Philosophical Theology*. Oxford: Basil Blackwell, 1987.

Kierkegaard, Søren. *Concluding Unscientific Postscript*. Trans. David F. Swenson and Walter Lowrie. Princteon, N.J.: Princeton University Press, 1968.

Kilmartin, Edward J. *The Eucharist in the West: History and Theology.* Ed. Robert J. Daly. Collegeville, Minn.: Liturgical Press, 1998.

Kim, Jaegwon. *Mind in a Physical World: An Essay on the Mind-Body Problem and Mental Causation.* Cambridge, Mass.: MIT Press, 1998.

Kirvan, John J., ed. *The Infallibility Debate.* New York: Paulist, 1971.

Klinger, Elmar. "Modalism." In *Sacramentum Mundi: An Encyclopedia of Theology.* Ed. Karl Rahner and others. New York: Herder & Herder, 1968-1970. Vol. 4, 88-90.

Knox, John. *The Humanity and Divinity of Christ.* Cambridge, UK: Cambridge University Press, 1967.

Küng, Hans. *The Church.* Trans. Ray and Rosaleen Ockenden. New York: Sheed and Ward, 1967.

Küng, Hans. *The Church—Maintained in Truth: A Theological Meditation.* Trans. Edward Quinn. New York: Crossroad, 1980.

Küng, Hans. *Does God Exist? An Answer for Today.* Trans. Edward Quinn. Garden City, N.Y.: Doubleday, 1980.

Küng, Hans. *Eternal Life? Life After Death as a Medical, Philosophical and Theological Problem.* Trans. Edward Quinn. Garden City, N.Y.: Doubleday, 1984.

Kuschel, Karl-Josef. *Born Before All Time? The Dispute over Christ's Origin.* Trans. John Bowden. New York: Crossroad, 1992.

Kysar, Robert. *The Fourth Evangelist and His Gospel: An Examination of Contemporary Scholarship.* Minneapolis: Augsburg, 1975.

LaCugna, Catherine Mowry. "Philosophers and Theologians on the Trinity." *Modern Theology* 2 (1985-86): 169-81.

LaCugna, Catherine Mowry. *God For Us: The Trinity and Christian Life.* San Francisco: Harper, 1991.

Lanfranc. *De corpore et sanguine Domini.* PL 150: 407-42.

Lash, Nicholas. "Dogmas and Doctrinal Progress." In *Doctrinal Development and Christian Unity.* Ed. Nicholas Lash. London: Sheed and Ward, 1967. 3-33.

Lash, Nicholas. *Change in Focus: A Study of Doctrinal Change and Continuity.* London: Sheed and Ward, 1973.

Layman, C. Stephen. "Tritheism and the Trinity." *Faith and Philosophy* 5 (1988): 291-98.

Lebreton, Jules. *The Encyclical and Modernist Theology.* Trans. Alban Goodier. London: Catholic Truth Society, 1908.

Leenhardt, F.-J. *Ceci est mon corps: Explication de ces paroles de Jésus Christ.* Neuchatel: Delachaux & Niestlé, 1955.

Leenhardt, F.-J. "This Is My Body." In Oscar Cullmann and F. J. Leenhardt, *Essays on the Lord's Supper.* Trans. J. G. Davies. Richmond, Va.: John Knox, 1958. 24-85.

Leftow, Brian. "Anti Social Trinitarianism." In Davis, Kendall, and O'Collins, *The Trinity,* 203-49.

Leo the Great, Saint. *Select Sermons of S. Leo the Great on the Incarnation.* Trans. William Bright. London: J. Masters, 1886.

Lewis, David. "Survival and Identity." In Lewis, *Philosophical Papers.* vol. 1. New York: Oxford University Press, 1983. 55-72.

Lewis, David. *On the Plurality of Worlds.* Oxford: Basil Blackwell, 1986.

Liddon, H. P. *The Divinity of Our Lord and Saviour Jesus Christ.* 11th edn. London: Rivingtons, 1885.

Liébaert, Jacques. *La doctrine christologique de Saint Cyrille d'Alexandrie avant la querelle nestorienne.* Lille: Facultés catholiques, 1951.

Lindbeck, George. "Reform and Infallibility." *Cross Currents* 11 (1961): 345-56.

Lonergan, Bernard J. F. *Method in Theology*. New York: Herder & Herder, 1972.

Longenecker, Richard N. *The Christology of Early Jewish Christianity*. Naperville, Ill.: Alec R. Allenson, 1970.

Loughlin, Gerard. "Persons and Replicas." *Modern Theology* 1(1984-85): 303-19.

Lowe, E. J. *Kinds of Being: A Study of Individuation, Identity and the Logic of Sortal Terms*. Oxford: Blackwell, 1989.

Lubac, Henri de. *The Christian Faith: An Essay on the Structure of the Apostles' Creed*. Trans. Richard Arnandez. San Francisco: Ignatius, 1986.

Luther, Martin. *The Babylonian Captivity of the Church*. In *Luther's Works*, vol. 36: *Word and Sacrament II*. Ed. Abdel Ross Wentz and Helmut T. Lehmann. Philadelphia: Muhlenberg, 1959. 11-126.

Luther, Martin. *Against Hanswurst*. In *Luther's Works*, vol. 41: *Church and Ministry III*. Ed. Eric W. Gritsch. Philadelphia: Fortress, 1966. 185-256.

Luther, Martin. *On the Councils and the Church*. In *Luther's Works*, vol. 41: *Church and Ministry III*. Ed. Eric W. Gritsch. Philadelphia: Fortress, 1966. 3-178.

McBrien, Richard P. Untitled contribution in Kirvan, *The Infallibility Debate*, 35-65.

McBrien, Richard P. *Catholicism*. Vol. 2. Minneapolis, Minn.: Winston, 1980.

McDermott, Brian O. "Roman Catholic Christology: Two Recurring Themes." *Theological Studies* 41 (1980): 339-67.

McDermott, Brian O. *Word Become Flesh: Dimensions of Christology*. Collegeville, Minn.: Liturgical Press, 1993.

MacDonald, A. J. *Berengar and the Reform of Sacramental Doctrine*. London and New York: Longmans, Green, 1930.

McDonough, William K. *The Divine Family: The Trinity and Our Life in God*. New York: Macmillan; London: Collier-Macmillan, 1963.

McGrath, Alister. *Understanding Jesus: Who Jesus Christ Is and Why He Matters*. Grand Rapids, Mich.: Zondervan, 1987.

McGuckin, John A. *St. Cyril of Alexandria, the Christological Controversy: Its History, Theology, and Texts*. Leiden: E. J. Brill, 1994.

McIntyre, John. *The Shape of Soteriology: Studies in the Doctrine of the Death of Christ*. Edinburgh: T. & T. Clark, 1992.

McKenna, John H. "Eucharistic Presence: An Invitation to Dialogue," *Theological Studies* 60 (1999): 294-317.

Mackenzie, Ross. "Reformed and Roman Catholic Understandings of the Eucharist." In Swidler, *The Eucharist in Ecumenical Dialogue*, 70-76.

Macnamara, John, Marie La Palme Reyes and Gonzalo E. Reyes. "Logic and the Trinity." *Faith and Philosophy* 11 (1994): 3-18.

Macquarrie, John. "Kenoticism Reconsidered." *Theology* 77 (1974): 115-24.

Macquarrie, John. *Jesus Christ in Modern Thought*. Philadelphia: Trinity Press International; London: SCM, 1990.

McSorley, Harry J. Untitled contribution in Kirvan, *The Infallibility Debate*, 67-106.

Madell, Geoffrey. "Personal Identity and the Mind-Body Problem." In Smythies and Beloff, *The Case for Dualism*, 25-41.

Malcolm, Norman. "Scientific Materialism and the Identity Theory." In *The Mind-Brain Identity Theory*. Ed. C. V. Borst. New York: St. Martin's, 1970. 171-80.

Marchi, Sergio De. *La cristologia in Italia (1930-1990)*. Casale Monferrato (AL): Piemme, 1994.

Margerie, Bertrand de. *The Christian Trinity in History*. Trans. Edmund J. Fortman. Still River, Mass.: St. Bede's Publications, 1982.

Margolis, Joseph. "Difficulties for Mind-Body Identity Theories." In *Identity and Individuation*. Ed. Milton K. Munitz. New York: New York University Press, 1971. 213-31.

Marín-Sola, Francisco. *La evolución homogénea del dogma católico.* 1923. Madrid: Biblioteca de Autores Cristianos, 1952.

Marsh, Thomas. *The Triune God: A Biblical, Historical, and Theological Study.* Mystic, Conn.: Twenty-Third Publications, 1994.

Martinich, A. P. "Identity and Trinity." *Journal of Religion* 58 (1978): 169-81.

Martinich, A. P. "God, Emperor, and Relative Identity." *Franciscan Studies* 39 (1979): 180-91.

Marxsen, Willi. *The Resurrection of Jesus of Nazareth.* Trans. Margaret Kohl. Philadelphia: Fortress, 1970.

Mascall, E. L. "Egner on the Eucharistic Presence." *New Blackfriars* 53 (1972): 539-46.

Masi, Roberto. "La conversione eucaristica nella teologia odierna: transustanziazione e transignificazione." *Divinitas* 10 (1966): 272-315.

Mavrodes, George I. "The Life Everlasting and the Bodily Criterion of Identity." *Nous* 11 (1977): 27-39.

Meredith, Anthony. *The Cappadocians.* Crestwood, N.Y.: St. Vladimir's Seminary Press, 1995.

Mersch, Emile. *The Whole Christ: The Historical Development of the Doctrine of the Mystical Body in Scripture and Tradition.* Trans. John R. Kelly. Milwaukee: Bruce, 1938.

Mersch, Emile. *The Theology of the Mystical Body.* Trans. Cyril Vollert. St. Louis and London: B. Herder, 1951.

Mitchell, Nathan. *Cult and Controversy: The Worship of the Eucharist Outside Mass.* New York: Pueblo, 1982.

Moingt, Joseph. *L'homme qui venait de Dieu.* 2nd edn. Paris: Cerf, 1994.

Moingt, Joseph. "The Christology of the Primitive Church: The Cost of a Cultural Mediation." Trans. John Bowden. In *Who Do You Say That I Am?* Ed. Werner Jeanrond and Christoph Theobald. Maryknoll, N.Y.: Orbis; London: SCM, 1997. 61-68.

Moloney, Raymond. *The Eucharist.* London: Geoffrey Chapman, 1995.

Moltmann, Jürgen. *The Trinity and the Kingdom: The Doctrine of God.* Trans. Margaret Kohl. San Francisco: Harper & Row, 1981.

Mondin, Battista. *La Trinità mistero d'amore: Trattato di teologia trinitaria.* Bologna: Edizioni Studio Domenicano, 1993.

Montclos, Jean de. *Lanfranc et Bérenger: La controverse eucharistique du XIe siècle.* Louvain: Spicilegium Sacrum Lovaniense, 1971.

Moore, George Edward. *Commonplace Book 1919-1953.* Ed. C. Lewy. London: Allen & Unwin; New York: Macmillan, 1962.

Morel, Georges. *Questions d'homme.* Vol. 3: *Jésus dans la théorie chrétienne.* Paris: Aubier Montaigne, 1977.

Morris, Thomas V. *Understanding Identity Statements.* Aberdeen: Aberdeen University Press, 1984.

Morris, Thomas V. *The Logic of God Incarnate.* Ithaca, N.Y.: Cornell University Press, 1986.

Moule, C. F. D. "The Manhood of Jesus in the New Testament." In *Christ, Faith and History: Cambridge Studies in Christology.* Ed. S. W. Sykes and J. P. Clayton. Cambridge, UK: Cambridge University Press, 1972. 95-110.

Moule, C. F. D. *The Origin of Christology.* Cambridge, UK: Cambridge University Press, 1977.

Moule, C. F. D. "A Comment." In Goulder, *Incarnation and Myth*, 147-50.

Mozley, John Kenneth. "Christology and Soteriology." In *Mysterium Christi: Christological Studies by British and German Theologians*. Ed. G. K. A. Bell and D. Adolf Deissmann. London: Longmans Green, 1930. 167-90.

Murray, John Courtney. *The Problem of God: Yesterday and Today*. New Haven: Yale University Press, 1964.

Myers, David G. *The Human Puzzle: Psychological Research and Christian Belief*. San Francisco: Harper & Row, 1978.

Myers, Frederic W. H. *St Paul*. London: Macmillan, 1902.

Nagel, Thomas. "Physicalism." *Philosophical Review* 74 (1965): 339-56.

Nagel, Thomas. "What Is It Like to Be a Bat?" *Philosophical Review* 83 (1974): 435-50. Reprinted in Nagel, *Mortal Questions*. Cambridge, UK: Cambridge University Press, 1979. 165-80.

Nagel, Thomas. *The View from Nowhere*. New York: Oxford University Press, 1986.

Need, Stephen W. *Human Language and Knowledge in the Light of Chalcedon*. New York: Peter Lang, 1996.

Neuner, J., and J. Dupuis, eds. *The Christian Faith in the Doctrinal Documents of the Catholic Church*. Bangalore, India: Theological Publications in India, 1973.

A New Catechism: Catholic Faith for Adults. Trans. Kevin Smyth. New York: Herder & Herder, 1967.

The New Delhi Report: The Third Assembly of the World Council of Churches 1961. London: SCM, 1961.

Newman, John Henry. *An Essay on the Development of Christian Doctrine*. 9th edn. London: Longmans, Green, 1894.

Newman, John Henry. *Certain Difficulties Felt by Anglicans in Catholic Teaching*. Vol. 1. London: Longmans, Green, 1901.

Nichols, Aidan. *From Newman to Congar*. Edinburgh: T. & T. Clark, 1990.

Nichols, Aidan. *The Holy Eucharist: From the New Testament to Pope John Paul II*. Dublin: Veritas, 1991.

Noonan, Harold W. "Substance, Identity and Time." *Proceedings of the Aristotelian Society*, suppl. Vol. 62 (1988): 79-100.

Noonan, Harold W. *Personal Identity*. New York and London: Routledge, 1989.

Norris, Richard A., Jr., ed. *The Christological Controversy*. Philadelphia: Fortress, 1980.

Nozick, Robert. *Philosophical Explanations*. Cambridge, Mass.: Harvard University Press, 1981.

O'Collins, Gerald. *The Resurrection of Jesus Christ*. Valley Forge, Pa.: Judson, 1973.

O'Collins, Gerald. *What Are They Saying about the Resurrection?* New York: Paulist, 1978.

O'Collins, Gerald. *Fundamental Theology*. New York: Paulist, 1981.

O'Collins, Gerald. *Interpreting Jesus*. Ramsey, N.J.: Paulist; London: Chapman, 1983.

O'Collins, Gerald. *Jesus Risen: An Historical, Fundamental and Systematic Examination of Christ's Resurrection*. New York: Paulist, 1987.

O'Collins, Gerald. *Christology: A Biblical, Historical, and Systematic Study of Jesus Christ*. Oxford: Oxford University Press, 1995.

O'Collins, Gerald. "The Holy Trinity: The State of the Questions." In Davis, Kendall, and O'Collins, *The Trinity*, 1-25.

O'Collins, Gerald. *The Tripersonal God: Understanding and Interpreting the Trinity*. New York: Paulist, 1999.

Oderberg, David S. "Reply to Sprigge on Personal and Impersonal Identity." *Mind* 98 (1989): 129-33.

O'Donnell, John J. *The Mystery of the Triune God.* New York: Paulist, 1989.

O'Leary-Hawthorne, John and J. A. Cover. "Framing the Thisness Issue." *Australasian Journal of Philosophy* 75 (1997): 102-8.

Olson, Eric. "Is Psychology Relevant to Personal Identity?" *Australasian Journal of Philosophy* 72 (1994): 173-86.

O'Neill, Colman. *New Approaches to the Eucharist.* New York: Alba, 1967.

Pannenberg, Wolfhart. *Jesus—God and Man.* 2nd edn. Trans. Lewis L. Wilkins and Duane A. Priebe. Philadelphia: Westminster, 1977.

Parfit, Derek. *Reasons and Persons.* Oxford: Clarendon, 1984.

Parfit, Derek. "The Unimportance of Identity." In *Identity: Essays Based on Herbert Spencer Lectures Given in the University of Oxford.* Ed. Henry Harris. New York: Oxford University Press, 1995. 13-45.

Paul VI, Pope. *Mysterium Fidei.* Washington, D.C.: National Catholic Welfare Conference, 1965.

Pawlikowski, John. *Christ in the Light of the Christian-Jewish Dialogue.* New York: Paulist, 1982.

Pelikan, Jaroslav. *Development of Christian Doctrine: Some Historical Prolegomena.* New Haven: Yale University Press, 1969.

Pelikan, Jaroslav. *The Christian Tradition: A History of the Development of Doctrine.* Vol. 1: *The Emergence of the Catholic Tradition.* Chicago: University of Chicago Press, 1971.

Penelhum, Terence. *Survival and Disembodied Existence.* New York: Humanities, 1970.

Perkins, Pheme. *Peter: Apostle for the Whole Church.* Columbia, S.C.: University of South Carolina Press, 1994.

Perrone, Giovanni. *Praelectiones theologicae.* Vol. 2. Paris: Migne, 1842.

Perry, John. "The Same *F.*" *The Philosophical Review* 79 (1970): 181-200.

Perry, John. "A Dialogue on Personal Identity and Immortality." In *Reason and Responsibility: Readings in Some Basic Problems of Philosophy.* Ed. Joel Feinberg. 6th edn. Belmont, Calif.: Wadsworth, 1985. 320-37.

Perry, Paul. "Brushes with Death." *Psychology Today* 22 (September 1988): 14, 17.

Peters, Ted. *GOD as Trinity: Relationality and Temporality in Divine Life.* Louisville, Ky.: Westminster/John Knox, 1993.

Piolanti, Antonio. "La transustanziazione." In *Eucaristia: Il mistero dell'altare nel pensiero e nella vita della chiesa.* Ed. Antonio Piolanti. Rome: Desclée, 1957. 221-62.

Pitcher, George, ed. *Truth.* Englewood Cliffs, N.J.: Prentice-Hall, 1964.

Pius IX, Pope. "Inter gravissimas." *Pii IX Pontificis Maximi Acta,* 1/5. Graz, Austria: Akademische Druck- und Verlagsanstalt, 1971. 257-62.

Pollard, T. E. *Johannine Christology and the Early Church.* Cambridge, UK: Cambridge University Press, 1970.

Pourrat, P. "Le développement historique des dogmes eucharistiques du IXe siècle au Concile de Trente." In *Eucharistia: Encyclopédie populaire sur l'eucharistie.* Ed. Maurice Brillant. Paris: Bloud et Gay, 1934. 79-122.

Pousset, Édouard. "L'Eucharistie: Présence réelle et transsubstantiation." *Recherches de Science Religieuse* 54 (1966): 177-212.

Powers, Joseph M. "Mysterium Fidei and the Theology of the Eucharist." *Worship* 40 (1966): 17-35.

Powers, Joseph M. *Eucharistic Theology.* New York: Herder & Herder, 1967.

Prestige, G. L. *God in Patristic Thought*. London: SPCK., 1964.

Prince, Morton. *The Dissociation of a Personality: A Biographical Study in Abnormal Psychology*. London: Longmans, Green, 1905. Reprinted New York: Johnson Reprint Corporation, 1968.

Pusey, E. B. *The Doctrine of the Real Presence*. 1855. London: Walter Smith, 1883.

Rahner, Karl. "The Development of Dogma." In Rahner, *Theological Investigations* 1. Trans. Cornelius Ernst. Baltimore: Helicon; London: Darton, Longman & Todd, 1961. 39-77.

Rahner, Karl. *Theological Investigations* 4. Trans. Kevin Smith. Baltimore: Helicon; London: Darton, Longman & Todd, 1966.

Rahner, Karl. "The Concept of Mystery in Catholic Theology." In Rahner, *Theological Inves-tigations* 4, 36-73.

Rahner, Karl. "Considerations on the Development of Dogma." In Rahner, *Theological Inves-tigations* 4, 3-35.

Rahner, Karl. "The Presence of Christ in the Sacrament of the Lord's Supper." In Rahner, *Theological Investigations* 4, 287-311.

Rahner, Karl. "The Historical Dimension in Theology." *Theology Digest* 16, Sesquicentennial Issue (1968): 30-42.

Rahner, Karl. "Trinity, Divine." In *Sacramentum Mundi: An Encyclopedia of Theology*. New York: Herder & Herder, 1968-70. Vol. 6. 295-303.

Rahner, Karl. *Foundations of Christian Faith: An Introduction to the Idea of Christianity*. Trans. William V. Dych. New York: Seabury, 1978.

Rahner, Karl. *The Trinity*. Trans. Joseph Donceel. New York: Crossroad, 1997.

Rahner, Karl, and Herbert Vorgrimler. *Theological Dictionary*. Ed. Cornelius Ernst. Trans. Richard Strachan. New York: Herder & Herder, 1965.

Ratramnus. *De corpore et sanguine Domini*. PL 121: 103-70.

Redmond, R. P. "The Real Presence in the Early Middle Ages." *The Clergy Review* 8 (1934): 442-60.

Relton, Herbert M. *A Study in Christology: The Problem of the Relation of the Two Natures in the Person of Christ*. London: SPCK., 1922.

Richard, Lucien. *What Are They Saying about Christ and World Religions?* New York: Paulist, 1981.

Richardson, Cyril C. *Zwingli and Cranmer on the Eucharist (Cranmer dixit et contradixit)*. Evanston, Ill.: Seabury-Western Theological Seminary, 1949.

Rickaby, Joseph. *The Divinity of Christ*. St. Louis: B. Herder; London and Edinburgh: Sands, 1906.

Robinson, John A. T. *The Human Face of God*. Philadelphia: Westminster, 1973.

Rondet, Henri. *Do Dogmas Change?* Trans. Mark Pontifex. New York: Hawthorn, 1961.

Rowdon, Harold H., ed. *Christ the Lord: Studies in Christology Presented to Donald Guthrie*. Downers Grove, Ill.: Inter-Varsity, 1982.

Ruben, David-Hillel. *Explaining Explanation*. London and New York: Routledge, 1990.

Rupp, Gordon, *Patterns of Reformation*. Philadelphia: Fortress, 1969.

Russell, Bertrand. *The Analysis of Mind*. 3rd edn. London: Allen & Unwin, 1954.

Russell, Bertrand. *Why I Am Not a Christian and Other Essays on Religion and Related Subjects*. Ed. Paul Edwards. New York: Simon and Schuster, 1957.

Russell, Bertrand. *The Problems of Philosophy*. 1912. New York: Galaxy-Oxford University Press, 1959.

Sabom, Michael B. *Recollections of Death: A Medical Investigation*. New York: Harper & Row, 1982.

San, Ludovicus de. *Tractatus de ecclesia et Romano pontifice*. Bruges: Beyaert, 1906.

Savellos, Elias E. "How To Be a Consistent Identity-Relativist." *Philosophical Studies* 52 (1987): 239-59.

Sayes, José Antonio. *El misterio eucarístico*. Madrid: Biblioteca de Autores Cristianos, 1986.

Sayes, José Antonio. *La presencia real de Cristo en la Eucaristía*. Madrid: Biblioteca de Autores Cristianos, 1976.

Schaff, Philip. *The Creeds of Christendom*. Vol. 2. New York: Harper, 1890.

Schillebeeckx, Edward. *Revelation and Theology*. Vol. 1. Trans. N. D. Smith. New York: Sheed & Ward, 1967.

Schillebeeckx, Edward. *The Eucharist*. Trans. N. D. Smith. New York: Sheed and Ward, 1968.

Schillebeeckx, Edward. *Jesus: An Experiment in Christology*. Trans. Hubert Hoskins. New York: Seabury, 1979.

Schlink, Edmund. *The Coming Christ and the Coming Church*. Translator not named. Edinburgh: Oliver & Boyd, 1967.

Schnackenburg, Rudolf. *Jesus in the Gospels: A Biblical Christology*. Trans. O. C. Dean, Jr. Louisville, Ky: Westminster John Knox, 1995.

Schoonenberg, Piet. *The Christ: A Study of the God-Man Relationship in the Whole of Creation and in Jesus Christ*. Trans. Della Couling. New York: Herder & Herder, 1971.

Schoonenberg, Piet. "Transubstantiation: How Far Is This Doctrine Historically Determined?" Trans. Theodore L. Westow. In *The Sacraments: An Ecumenical Dilemma. Concilium* 24. Ed. Hans Küng. New York: Paulist, 1967. 78-91.

Schultes, Reginald-Maria. *De ecclesia catholica praelectiones apologeticae*. Paris: P. Lethiel-leux, 1925.

Scruton, Roger. *Modern Philosophy: An Introduction and Survey*. New York: Allen Lane, 1995.

Senor, Thomas D. "God, Supernatural Kinds, and the Incarnation." *Religious Studies* 27 (1991): 353-70.

Serenthà, Mario. *Gesù Cristo ieri, oggi e sempre: Saggio di cristologia*. 3rd edn. Turin: Elle Di Ci, 1988.

Sertillanges, A. D. *The Church*. Trans. A. G. McDougall. New York: Benziger, 1923.

Sesboüé, Bernard. *Jésus-Christ dans la tradition de l'Église: pour une actualisation de la christologie de Chalcédoine*. Paris: Desclée, 1982.

Sesboüé, Bernard. *Jésus-Christ l'unique médiateur: Essai sur la rédemption et la salut*. Vol. 1: *Problématique et relecture doctrinale*. Paris: Desclée, 1988.

Sheedy, Charles E. *The Eucharistic Controversy of the Eleventh Century against the Background of Pre-Scholastic Theology*. Washington, D.C.: Catholic University of America Press, 1947.

Shoemaker, Sydney S. "Self-Reference and Self-Awareness." *Journal of Philosophy* 65 (1968): 555-67.

Shoemaker, Sydney S., and Richard Swinburne. *Personal Identity*. Oxford: Blackwell, 1984.

Simcox, Carroll E. *The First Gospel: Its Meaning and Message*. Greenwich, Conn.: Seabury, 1963.

Skarsaune, Oskar. *Incarnation: Myth or Fact?* Trans. Trygve Skarsten. St. Louis: Concordia, 1991.

Smedes, Lewis B. *The Incarnation: Trends in Modern Anglican Thought*. Kampen: J. H. Kok, 1953.

Smedes, Lewis B. *All Things Made New: A Theology of Man's Union with Christ*. Grand Rapids, Mich.: Eerdmans, 1970.

Smythies, John R. and John Beloff, eds. *The Case for Dualism*. Charlottesville, Va.: University Press of Virginia, 1989.

Sobrino, Jon. "Sobre la discusion moderna acerca de la presencia real y la transustanciacion." *Ecclesiastica Xaveriana* 20:2 (1970): 3-87.

Sobrino, Jon. *Christology at the Crossroads: A Latin American Approach*. Trans. John Drury. Maryknoll, N.Y.: Orbis, 1978.

Sokolowski, Robert. *Eucharistic Presence: A Study in the Theology of Disclosure*. Washing-ton, D.C.: The Catholic University of America Press, 1994.

Staehelin, Ernst. *Das theologische Lebenswerk Johannes Oekolampads*. Leipzig: M. Heinsius Nachfolger, 1939.

Stephens, W. P. *The Theology of Huldrych Zwingli*. Oxford: Clarendon, 1986.

Stevens, George Barker, *The Christian Doctrine of Salvation*. Edinburgh: T. & T. Clark, 1909.

Stone, Darwell. *A History of the Doctrine of the Holy Eucharist*. 2 vols. London: Longmans, Green, 1909.

Stroll, Avrum. "Identity." *Encyclopedia of Philosophy*. Ed. Paul Edwards. Vol. 4. New York: Macmillan, 1967. 121-24.

Stump, Eleonore. Review of *The Logic of God Incarnate*, by Thomas V. Morris. *Faith and Philosophy* 6 (1989): 218-23.

Sturch, Richard L. "The Metaphysics of the Incarnation." *Vox Evangelica* 10 (1977): 65-76.

Sturch, Richard L. "Can One Say 'Jesus Is God'?" in Rowdon, *Christ the Lord*, 326-40.

Sturch, Richard L. *The Word and the Christ: An Essay in Analytic Christology*. Oxford: Clarendon, 1991.

Suárez, Francisco. *De incarnatione. Opera omnia*, vol. 17. Paris: Vivès, 1856.

Suárez, Francisco. *De eucharistia. Opera omnia*, vols. 20 (700-832) and 21. Paris: Vivès, 1856.

Sullivan, Francis A. *Magisterium: Teaching Authority in the Catholic Church*. New York: Paulist, 1983.

Sullivan, Francis A. *The Church We Believe In: One, Holy, Catholic and Apostolic*. New York: Paulist, 1988.

Sullivan, Francis A. *Salvation Outside the Church?: Tracing the History of the Catholic Response*. New York: Paulist, 1992.

Sullivan, Francis A. *Creative Fidelity: Weighing and Interpreting Documents of the Magisterium*. New York: Paulist, 1996.

Swidler, Leonard, ed. *The Eucharist in Ecumenical Dialogue*. New York: Paulist, 1976.

Swinburne, Richard. "Personal Identity." *Proceedings of the Aristotelian Society* 74 (1973-74): 231-47.

Swinburne, Richard. "Persons and Personal Identity." In *Contemporary British Philosophy: Personal Statements*. Ed. H. D. Lewis. London: Allen & Unwin, 1976. 221-38.

Swinburne, Richard. *The Evolution of the Soul*. Oxford: Clarendon, 1986.

Swinburne, Richard. *Responsibility and Atonement*. Oxford: Clarendon, 1989.

Swinburne, Richard. *Revelation: From Metaphor to Analogy*. New York: Oxford University Press; Oxford: Clarendon, 1992.

Swinburne, Richard. *The Christian God*. Oxford: Clarendon, 1994.

Swinburne, Richard. "Thisness." *Australasian Journal of Philosophy* 73 (1995): 389-400.

Sykes, S. W. "The Strange Persistence of Kenotic Christology." In *Being and Truth: Essays in Honour of John Macquarrie*. Ed. Alistair Kee and Eugene T. Long. London: SCM, 1986. 349-75.

Taliaferro, Charles. *Consciousness and the Mind of God*. Cambridge, UK: Cambridge University Press, 1994.

Tapia, Ralph J. *The Theology of Christ: Commentary*. New York: Bruce, 1971.

Taylor, Vincent. *The Names of Jesus*. London: Macmillan, 1953.

Taylor, Vincent. *The Person of Christ in New Testament Teaching*. London: Macmillan, 1963.

Temple, William. "The Divinity of Christ." In *Foundations: A Statement of Christian Belief in Terms of Modern Thought*. Ed. B. H. Streeter. London: Macmillan, 1912. 211-63.

Temple, William. *Christus Veritas*. London: Macmillan, 1924.

Teresa of Avila, Saint. *Interior Castle*. Trans. and Ed. E. Allison Peers. Garden City, N.Y.: Doubleday, 1961.

Toland, John. *Christianity Not Mysterious*. 1696. New York: Garland, 1978.

Torrance, Alan J. *Persons in Communion: An Essay on Trinitarian Description and Human Participation*. Edinburgh: T. & T. Clark, 1996.

Unger, Peter. *Identity, Consciousness and Value*. New York: Oxford University Press, 1990.

United States Catholic Conference. *The Küng Dialogue*. Washington, D.C.: Publications Office, 1980.

Vardy, Peter. "A Christian Approach to Eternal Life." In *Beyond Death: Theological and Philosophical Reflections on Life after Death*. Ed. Dan Cohn-Sherbok and Christopher Lewis. New York: St. Martin's, 1995. 13-26.

Vernet, F. "Bérenger de Tours." DTC. Vol. 2/1, col. 722-42.

Vernet, F. "Eucharistie du IXe a la fin du Xe siècle." DTC. Vol. 5/2, col. 1209-32.

Vincent of Lérins. "The Commonitory." Trans. C. A. Heurtley. In *A Select Library of the Nicene and Post-Nicene Fathers*. 2nd series. Ed. Philip Schaff and Henry Wace. Vol. 11. 1894. New York: Hendrickson, 1994. 123-56.

Vollert, Cyril. "The Eucharist: Controversy on Transubstantiation." *Theological Studies* 22 (1961): 391-425.

Waismann, Friedrich. "Über den Begriff der Identität." *Erkenntnis* 6 (1936): 56-64.

Walgrave, Jan Hendrik. *Unfolding Revelation: The Nature of Doctrinal Development*. Phila-delphia: Westminster; London: Hutchinson, 1972.

Weinandy, Thomas. Review of *The Logic of God Incarnate*, by Thomas V. Morris. *Thomist* 51 (1987): 367-72.

Welch, Claude. *In This Name: The Doctrine of the Trinity in Contemporary Theology*. New York: Charles Scribner's Sons, 1952.

Welch, Claude, ed. and trans. *God and Incarnation in Mid-Nineteenth Century German Theo-logy: G. Thomasius, I. A. Dorner, A. E. Biedermann*. New York: Oxford University Press, 1965.

Whalen, Teresa. *The Authentic Doctrine of the Eucharist*. Kansas City, Mo.: Sheed & Ward, 1993.

Wiggins, David. *Sameness and Substance*. Cambridge, Mass.: Harvard University Press, 1980.

Wiles, Maurice. *The Making of Christian Doctrine: A Study in the Principles of Early Doctrinal Development*. Cambridge, UK: Cambridge University Press, 1967.

Wiles, Maurice, and Herbert McCabe. "The Incarnation: An Exchange." *New Blackfriars* 58 (1977): 542-53.

Wilkes, Kathleen V. *Real People: Personal Identity without Thought Experiments*. Oxford: Clarendon, 1988.

Williams, C. J. F. "A Programme for Christology." *Religious Studies* 3 (1968): 513-24.

Williams, C. J. F. *What Is Identity?* Oxford: Clarendon, 1989.

Williams, H. A. "Incarnation: Model and Symbol." *Theology* 79 (1976): 6-18.

Williams, Rowan. "*Trinitate, De*." In *Augustine through the Ages: An Encyclopedia*. Ed.. Allan D. Fitzgerald. Grand Rapids, Mich.: William B. Eerdmans, 1999. 845-51.

Wilson, Ian. *The After Death Experience*. London: Sidgwick & Jackson, 1987.

Wiseman, Nicholas. *The Real Presence of the Body and Blood of Our Lord Jesus Christ in the Blessed Eucharist*. 1836. Ed. John M. T. Barton. London: Burns Oates & Washbourne, 1942.

Wittgenstein, Ludwig. *The Blue and Brown Books*. Ed. Rush Rhees. Oxford: Basil Blackwell, 1960.

Wittgenstein, Ludwig. *Notebooks 1914-1916*. Ed. G. H. von Wright and G. E. M. Anscombe. Trans. G. E. M. Anscombe. Oxford: Basil Blackwell, 1961.

Wittgenstein, Ludwig. *Philosophical Investigations*. Trans. G. E. M. Anscombe. 2d edn. Oxford: Basil Blackwell, 1967.

Wittgenstein, Ludwig. *Zettel*. Ed. G. E. M. Anscombe and G. H. von Wright. Trans. G. E. M. Anscombe. Oxford: Basil Blackwell, 1967.

Wohlmuth, Josef. *Realpräsenz und Transsubstantiation im Konzil von Trent: Eine historisch-kritische Analyse der Canones 1-4 der Sessio XIII*. 2 vols. Bern: Herbert Lang; Frankfurt am Main: Peter Lang, 1975.

Wolfson, Harry Austryn. *The Philosophy of the Church Fathers*. Vol. 1: *Faith, Trinity, Incarnation*. Cambridge, Mass.: Harvard University Press, 1964.

Yandell, Keith E. "The Most Brutal and Inexcusable Error in Counting?: Trinity and Consistency." *Religious Studies* 30 (1994): 201-17.

Young, Frances. "Incarnation and Atonement: God Suffered and Died." In Goulder, *Incarnation and Myth*, 101-3.

Zaleski, Carol. *The Life of the World to Come: Near-Death Experience and Christian Hope*. New York: Oxford University Press, 1996.

Zapelena, Timotheus. *De ecclesia Christi: pars apologetica*. 5th edn. Rome: Gregorian University Press, 1950.

Zwingli, Ulrich. "On the Lord's Supper." In *Zwingli and Bullinger*. Library of Christian Classics, 24. Trans. G. W. Bromiley. Philadelphia: Westminster, 1953. 185-238.

Zwingli, Ulrich. *On Providence and Other Essays*. Translated from the German. Durham, N.C.: Labyrinth, 1983.

Index